A Mediterranean Harvest

Paola Scaravelli
and Jon Cohen

ILLUSTRATIONS BY SUSAN GABER

A Mediterranean Harvest

E. P. DUTTON   NEW YORK

Published in the United States by E. P. Dutton,
a division of New American Library, 2 Park Avenue, New York, N.Y. 10016.

Library of Congress Cataloging-in-Publication Data

Scaravelli, Paola.
    A Mediterranean harvest.

    Includes index.
    1. Cookery, Mediterranean. I. Cohen, Jon S.
II. Title.
TX725.M35S28   1986   641.59′1182′2   86–4419

ISBN: 0–525–24438–7

Published simultaneously in Canada by Fitzhenry & Whiteside Limited,
Toronto

W

DESIGNED BY EARL TIDWELL

10 9 8 7 6 5 4 3 2 1

First Edition

To Vanda, Ethel, and Harry

[T]he Mediterranean is older than history and stronger than religion; one of the reasons why we love it so much is this unfailing sense of continuity with which it invests the present.

[V]ines, olives, cypresses; one comes to believe that they are Platonic abstractions rooted in the imagination of man. Symbols of the Mediterranean, they are always [t]here to welcome one.

The whole Mediterranean—the sculptures, the palms, the gold beads, the bearded heroes, the wine, the ideas, the ships, the moonlight, the winged gorgons, the bronze men, the philosophers —all of it seems to rise in the sour, pungent taste of these black olives between the teeth. A taste older than meat, older than wine. A taste as old as cold water.

[N]othing Mediterranean can change for it is landscape-dominated; its people are simply landscape-wishes of the earth, sharing their particularities with the wine and the food, the sunlight and the sea.

—LAWRENCE DURRELL

Contents

Preface

We've lived and traveled around the Mediterranean for many years and currently divide our time between our farm outside of Florence and our home in Toronto. Wherever we've gone, whether on the coast or into the mountains, in cities, villages, or rural hamlets, we have been struck by a similarity of spirit among the people that overwhelms superficial differences in customs, religion, or language. The Greek writer Nikos Kazantzakis, who lived for a while in Antibes, on the French Riviera, was well aware of this similarity. On a small plaque tucked away in the old part of the city, he thanks the townfolk for their hospitality and notes how delighted he was to discover a strong resemblance between his adopted home and his real one.

The parallel may be a consequence of geography and climate, of the physical presence of the sea itself. The weather is similar throughout the region—mild and wet in winter, hot and dry in summer. The olive is ubiquitous, and so, by and large, is the vine, the cypress, and the *Macchia mediterranea*—the low bush that decorates and perfumes the shores and hills that border the sea. The winds, similar throughout the area, are as much a part of the Mediterranean as the sun. The Italian poet Montale wrote about the *scirocco, tramontana,* and *maestrale,* while the French poet Mistral took the name of the cold Provençal wind as his own.

Sailors have traversed the Mediterranean since at least the

third millennium B.C. in search of markets, minerals, precious metals, and food supplies. Beginning with the Cretans and Mycenaean Greeks, if not earlier, those powerful enough to do so have set up and maintained offshore colonies to safeguard existing trade and, where possible, to expand it. Six great civilizations, the Phoenicians and Carthaginians, Greeks, Romans, Arabs, and Christians have, at one time or another, dominated the Mediterranean and exerted a unifying force on the philosophy, politics, architecture, technology, and food of the region. A strong Greek influence, for example, can be seen in the architecture of Etruscan cemeteries, the Romans brought bread and circuses, coliseums, and theaters to the entire Mare Nostrum, while the Arabs introduced astronomy, sophisticated navigation, mathematics, and the works of Plato and Aristotle to medieval Europe.

Even small, relatively insignificant archaeological sites occasionally reveal this unifying influence. A few years ago we stumbled across the remains of a small Roman settlement on the Mediterranean coast near Tangier. One of the more unusual features of the ruins was the huge, stone-lined rooms cut deep into the ground. We learned from the custodian that these were tanks where *garum* (fish sauce) was prepared before it was shipped to Rome and other places in the empire.

In all likelihood, natural and human forces combined to create this striking unity of spirit. And Mediterranean cuisine—joyous, inviting, unadorned—is a perfect metaphor to express it.

We make no pretense of being experts on the cuisine of every country in the area nor do we seek a perfect balance between them. The book is dominated by recipes from Italy, France, and Morocco, with representations from Spain, Greece, Turkey, and a few from Yugoslavia and the Middle East. The mix reflects our biases and expertise.

Morocco is a special case and deserves special attention. We've been there several times for extended visits and, aside from a total fascination with the country, adore the food. It's brilliantly spiced, subtle, and healthful. Paula Wolfert, in *Couscous and Other Good Food from Morocco,* noted that Moroccan food, one of the world's great cuisines, is hardly known outside the country. That, unfortunately, is still true twelve years later. Once you've tried a few of the Moroccan recipes in this book, we are certain you will become as enchanted with the food as we are.

All cookbooks, even those billed as comprehensive, are shaped by the tastes and preferences of the authors. We like food that is flavorful, straightforward, and sophisticated. We also have a pronounced bias in favor of meatless cuisine and, therefore, we feature fish and vegetable dishes in this book. Since our bias is very much in keeping with traditional fare of the Mediterranean, we have been able to draw on a vast treasure trove of meatless recipes. For those happy with such a diet, the book needs no elaboration. For those who eat meat, the book can be viewed as a rich source of fish and vegetable dishes with which to supplement the normal regimes.

Our objective is to capture the flavor of Mediterranean cuisine as it is prepared and eaten today. Cuisine, like everything else, evolves. It mirrors new trends in diet and life-style and good chefs are quick to take advantage of new ingredients. This is certainly the case in the Mediterranean. In France, Italy, and Spain, in particular, exciting new dishes mingle happily with traditional ones on restaurant menus and family tables. We have tried to blend, in the same way, the old and the new in the book; we include, for example, a modern Risotto with Pomegranate and a traditional Squash Risotto, a "nouvelle" warm salad of *chèvre,* and *Socca,* an ancient Provençal dish.

We have organized the recipes to suit North American dining habits, beginning with appetizers and salads and ending with desserts. Not all dishes fit naturally into these groupings. Our customs are not, after all, universal, and what is a main dish in one country is served as an appetizer elsewhere. All categories are, in any case, arbitrary, so feel free to reorganize to suit your taste, time, and needs.

A book of this sort is, in many respects, a joint venture. We collected the recipes, organized and tested them, and finally wrote them down. But it would have been impossible without the help of friends, relatives, family cooks, professional chefs, and the path-breaking work of other writers such as Elizabeth David, Paula Wolfert, Alan Davidson, Claudia Roden, and Penelope Casas. We can't thank everyone who helped but would like to mention Mimi

Serani, Paola Boni, Alberto Scaravelli, Francesco Colacicchi, Patrick Lucas, Guy Sagmoellen, Yvonne Horwitz, Toni Maraini, Abdillah, Kinzah, and Dries Melehi, Fatima Mohajer, Voula and Gianoula Vasilopoulos, Nicole Rouel, Elizabeth and Gerald Donaldson, and Mengü Büyükdavras of the Turkish embassy in Ottawa. A special thanks to our editor, Jennifer Josephy, for her guidance, patience, and encouragement.

Toronto, 1986

Introduction

Ingredients

In compiling the recipes for this book, we have tried to rely on ingredients that are reasonably familiar and widely available to most North American cooks. We do have a few tips about the handling of some of them. If they are difficult to find, we try to give substitutes.

Olives and Olive Oil

Cultivation of the olive, indigenous to Iran and Syria, goes back to the dawn of history. Records indicate that the Egyptians raised olives in 1700 B.C., as did the Minoans a few centuries later. The olive was introduced into Italy by the ancient Greeks and made its appearance in Spain around the same time. Olive trees, gnarled and twisted even when relatively young, live a very long time. Some trees on our farm are four hundred years old, and these are youngsters compared with the ancient giants of the south.

In Italy, olive oil is graded by acidity, from a minimum of 1 percent (extra virgin) to 4 percent (virgin). All virgin oils are from the first pressing of the olives; second, third, and subsequent pressings are just plain olive oil. Southern oils, and this includes oil from Spain, Portugal, Provence, Greece, and southern Italy, are greenish gold in color with a pleasantly acrid bouquet and a light, fruity taste. In these areas, the olives ripen on the trees and are collected after they fall.

In Tuscany, at the northern edge of olive cultivation, oil is made each year and the olives are picked, barely ripe, before they shrivel and fall. The oil is a deep, rich green with a mild, delicate bouquet and a robust, full flavor. Tuscans take their oil very seriously. When we make oil from the trees on our farm, a number of our customers show up at the press, taste the fresh oil as it oozes from the huge mats, and, if it's up to grade, buy it on the spot.

You should keep some of both oils in your larder, the Tuscan for salads and other dishes where you want a full flavor, the southern for Greek, Turkish, Moroccan, and Spanish dishes where a lighter oil is often desirable. There are, of course, no hard and fast rules, but Tuscan oil is used mostly in central and northern Italian dishes, the southern oils elsewhere.

Olives for cooking and eating vary enormously from country to country in terms of method of preparation, size, and degree of maturity when picked. We distinguish in the recipes between black and green olives and occasionally by country or region of origin. For the most part, Italian olives are acceptable for all recipes.

Other Oils

When we call for light seed oil in the recipes, we mean sunflower, corn, or peanut oil. Sunflowers are grown in great quantities in the Mediterranean; most of the seeds go into the production of oil. Sunflower oil is light, low in saturated fats, and thus ideal for frying. Corn and peanut oil, both light and low in saturated fats, are also excellent for frying. Peanut oil is used extensively in Moroccan cooking, both on its own and in combination with olive oil; it should be kept on hand along with another light seed oil and the olive oils. This variety may seem excessive, but each oil is distinctive and each has its particular use.

Rice

Rube Marcus, a retail grain merchant in Toronto, sells about twenty-five varieties of rice including two or three short-grain types from Italy, three basmatis from India, sticky rice from Japan, purple rice from Thailand, and a host of whole grain, parboiled, and flavored rice from the Carolinas and Louisiana. And this selection, Rube says, hardly does justice to the full range of rice produced in the world.

Rice made its way from Persia into the Middle East and from there into Europe with the Arabs. It is now cultivated intensively in at least four Mediterranean countries—Italy, Spain, France, and Turkey—and each has its own characteristic shape and flavor. For Italian rice dishes we recommend that you use an Italian rice (Arborio is the best). Italian rices are all short-grained, starchy, and excellent for risottos and most puddings. For Spanish dishes use rice from Valencia but, if unavailable, use Italian rice. Italian rice is also suitable for French dishes, although if you can obtain rice from the Camargue, use it. Unfortunately, output is small and most of it is consumed locally. Turkish rice dishes are best made with basmati, Carolina long-grain, or parboiled rice. For Greek rice pudding use Carolina short-grain or Italian rice, and for other dishes use parboiled or Carolina long-grain rice. You can, in some dishes, substitute brown rice for white but do not do so in risottos. Never use instant (precooked) rice—you make an enormous sacrifice in quality just to save a little time.

Vinegar

Any liquid that will ferment can be turned into vinegar but some, of course, are better than others. You can easily make first-rate vinegar from leftover wine. Cover it loosely and set aside for a month or so. At some point a thin weblike substance will begin to form in the wine. This is the active agent, the mother or starter, which, placed in other wine, quickly produces more vinegar. If you seem to have trouble getting vinegar from wine, add a little grain alcohol to the wine. This boosts the alcoholic percentage of the wine and facilitates the transformation. The better the wine, the more flavorful the vinegar.

Balsamic vinegar from Italy is very expensive but also very intensely flavored so that a little goes a long way. We recommend it for certain dishes in the book but, of course, any good wine vinegar will do. The operative word is *good.* Taste your vinegar and make sure that you like it—if you don't, change brands. The flavor of your vinegar, especially in salads, is critical.

Cheese

Most cheeses used in the book are easy to find in North America and, where we anticipate problems, we suggest substitutes. *Ricotta,* an Italian version of cottage cheese, is widely available and can be used instead of the French *fromage blanc,* which is almost identical. *Feta,* a fresh cheese preserved in brine, used in Greek and Turkish dishes, is sold in all Greek food shops. We usually rinse it before using to remove some of the salt.

Parmesan is used throughout the Mediterranean and you should keep a supply on hand. Buy the best, *Parmigiano Reggiano,* which comes from the area around Reggio nell' Emilia, in the region of Emilia-Romagna. The cheese can be made only from high-quality milk and must be aged at least two years. At its best, Parmesan is straw colored and slightly moist. It tends to dry out and lose its color and flavor over time, so wrap it tightly in a double layer of aluminum foil or seal it in a Ziploc bag and store in the refrigerator. Buy only as much as you will use in a couple of weeks. Always grate your own when you need it.

The best *mozzarella* comes from an area south of Naples and is made with milk from the European water buffalo. It is still produced, for the most part, in small workshops by skilled craftsmen. The cheese, when very fresh, is exquisite, with a clean, faintly sour taste and soft, silken texture. One can usually find buffalo milk mozzarella in the north but most Italians make do with mozzarella made from cow's milk. In North America, naturally, all mozzarella is made with cow's milk. It is sometimes possible to find fresh, soft mozzarella in Italian cheese shops. If you do, use it. You can improve the texture of hard mozzarella by soaking it in milk to cover for an hour or so.

Varieties of French *chèvre* or goat cheese are legion. Our cheese vendor in Antibes sold twenty kinds and he admitted that his selection was limited. For the recipes in this book, use the ones that taste good to you. We are particularly fond of well-aged *crottin* and fresh *cendre.* Most of the quality goat cheeses are still made, like Parmesan, at certain times of the year, so you may not always find your favorite.

Mascarpone, a soft Italian cheese from the north, resembles in texture North American cream cheese but has a milder flavor. You should be able to find it in shops that have a good selection of Italian cheeses. There is no perfect substitute for Mascarpone.

Crème fraîche is similar in texture to a very thick sour cream, with a taste that falls somewhere between sour and regular cream. It is now sold in some specialty cheese shops in North America but, with the recipe we give, you can also make a perfect facsimile with almost no effort.

Mushrooms

Until a few years ago, only one kind of mushroom, *Agaricus bisporus,* or, as a friend calls it, the supermarket champignon, was cultivated and sold commercially in most of North America. Today, mushroom fanciers can find, in well-stocked grocery stores, cultivated shiitake, oyster mushrooms, and chanterelles. This is still a far cry from the remarkable array of wild mushrooms in the markets of Italy and France in the fall, but it is progress. If you have a supply of these more exotic mushrooms, by all means use them. They have a better texture and much more flavor than the supermarket champignon. But, remember, the stem of these and other wild mushrooms is usually tougher than the cap and should be cooked longer. We often use the stems, especially those of fresh porcini, in pasta sauce and reserve the caps for grilling or baking.

The best dried wild mushrooms are porcini or cèpes *(Boletus edulis),* with morels running a close second. When using dried mushrooms, soak them in warm water for about 30 minutes to reconstitute, remove from the water, taking care not to stir up grit and sand that may have fallen to the bottom, and strain the water through a piece of cotton placed in the neck of a funnel. You can also pour the liquid through a coffee filter. Use the mushrooms and soaking liquid as directed. If you don't need the liquid, reserve it for use in soups and stews.

Fish

The fish population of the Mediterranean, while diminished, is still abundant, and most markets offer a large and varied selection of fresh fish. Mediterranean species are not in all cases identical to those found in North America, but we have tried to select dishes for which adequate substitutes are available here. For more information on Mediterranean fish and their non-Mediterranean counterparts, we highly recommend *Mediterranean Seafood* by Alan Davidson.

After much trial and error, we have found that the best way to make sure that the fish you buy is fresh is to do business with a good fishmonger. Try to purchase the fish the day you plan to use it, but, if that is impossible, keep it loosely wrapped in the coolest part of the refrigerator. Do not keep it over 24 hours—if you must, then use frozen fish or try another recipe. Take note, however, that frozen fish is much drier than fresh and is recommended only in emergencies. On the other hand, frozen shrimp, squid, octopus, cuttlefish, and scallops are fine.

Tagine

Tagine, like *paella,* refers to both a type of cuisine and the pot in which it is cooked. *Tagine* is a Moroccan stew as well as a shallow, bowl-shaped, unglazed earthenware pot with a tall conical cover. In Morocco, all stews are cooked in these pots and most families have at least two, one for fish and one for meat.

Buying and preparing a *tagine* requires almost as much skill as using it. Just outside Tangier there is a huge open-air market that specializes in earthenware cooking utensils, including *tagines.* Our friend Toni inspected several, tapping the bottom of each and listening to its ring, before she found one that sounded right.

When we returned to Tangier, Toni's cook, Fatima, went to work. First, she oiled and salted the inside of the pot, then inverted it over a gas flame on the stove to char it. She then placed the *tagine* in a hot oven for about 3 hours. The pot was ready, she said, but we still had to use it two or three times before it would achieve its full potential.

A *tagine* is normally cooked over hot coals but, with a heat diffuser, it can be done over a gas flame or electric burner. The pot can also be used in the oven. We always use our *tagine* to cook Moroccan stews, but any heavy, low-sided earthenware, enamel, or stainless steel saucepan will do. The key to cooking a *tagine* is to cook it very slowly for a long time. It must not be stirred, otherwise the ingredients will disintegrate.

Herbs and Spices

Herbs and spices are to Mediterranean cuisine what color is to a Matisse painting, its source of energy and individuality. Many herbs, such as rosemary, mint, oregano, and thyme, grow wild. A walk in the hills of Provence, Tuscany, or Corfu is as much an olfactory as a visual experience, each footfall stirring up the sweet aroma of the herbs that grow in low clusters on the slopes. Others, such as parsley, basil, and coriander, are carefully cultivated in gardens or pots. Most can be used either dried or fresh, but basil and coriander must be fresh or properly preserved to retain their flavor.

Spices are essential in the food of most Mediterranean countries but none use them as extensively and with such sophistication as the North Africans, particularly the Moroccans. Spice displays in most *souks* (markets) are dazzling, brilliantly colored pyramids of turmeric, sweet and hot paprika, ground cumin, cinnamon, and ginger. Once ground, spices must be stored in well-sealed containers in a dry, preferably cool, place. After one year, they should be replaced.

Herbs

Basil: A sweet, strongly aromatic herb, basil is used extensively in Italian and Provençal cooking. It is easy to cultivate in the summer in the garden or in pots set on the windowsill. In Greece, many families keep large pots of small-leaf basil on doorsteps and windowsills to keep out mosquitoes and other insects. The difficulty starts when days grow short. We have managed to keep basil reasonably healthy indoors through November, but the plant is, alas, a goner by January. We have experimented with a number of preserving techniques, in salt, in oil, and in the freezer, and none are entirely satisfactory. The best to date is the method described by Paula Wolfert to preserve coriander. The technique is given in the coriander section.

Coriander leaves: Known also as cilantro in North America, coriander leaves are the visible part of the coriander plant, the seeds of which are sweet and aromatic and used extensively in Indian and Mexican cooking. The leaves have a mildly metallic, very distinctive taste, completely different in flavor from the seeds. The herb is essential in Moroccan cooking, roughly the equivalent of tomatoes in Italian cuisine. If unavailable in your local grocery store, try an Indian or Chinese one. To preserve, try the following technique, which we learned from Paula Wolfert's excellent book, *Couscous and Other Good Food from Morocco.*

Rinse well and cut off the tough stems of the coriander. Place 3 cups of tightly packed leaves with 2 cups of cold water in a food processor or blender and mix until finely chopped. Place in ice cube containers and freeze. When frozen, remove from the containers and store in plastic bags in the freezer. One cube equals 2 tablespoons of chopped coriander leaves. The same process can be used to preserve basil.

Chervil: Used extensively in Provence both raw in salads and cooked in sauces, chervil looks like a cross between curly parsley and carrot tops. It has a mild flavor, faintly reminiscent of celery. Although it can be found in specialty stores in North America, it's easy to raise in a garden or in pots on a windowsill and worth the trouble. It can also be used to flavor vinegar.

Mint: A hardy perennial, which, once established in a garden, is practically impossible to eliminate. Use whatever variety you can obtain, fresh if possible, dried if necessary. Dried mint can be quite strong, so use with care.

Oregano: Another perennial that grows wild throughout much of the Mediterranean, both fresh and dried appear in the cooking of Greece and southern Italy. Greek oregano, sold dried in branches, is strongly flavored, aromatic, and the best one to use.

Parsley: A biennial in the garden, it is easily cultivated indoors. Parsley comes in two varieties, one with small curly leaves, the other with relatively large flat ones. The latter is much more fragrant and flavorful and we recommend you use it. Parsley is rich in vitamin C and minerals, so use it with abandon. If you munch on parsley leaves after eating raw garlic, friends and neighbors will find your breath somewhat less offensive.

Rosemary: Strongly aromatic, rosemary flourishes in warm arid areas where night dew is heavy, that is, along the shores of the Mediterranean. In fact, with the olive and cypress, it is, for us, one of the defining elements of the area. It is used extensively by Provençal and Italian cooks to flavor soups, stews, sauces, and even a few desserts. Rosemary, unlike many other herbs, must be cooked. Dried rosemary is stronger than fresh so adjust proportions accordingly. Rosemary thrives indoors if kept in a sunny, humid location. Frequent misting of the leaves in winter is recommended.

Sage: Known in the past as much for its medicinal properties as for its gustatory qualities, sage, a hardy perennial with a fresh, slightly bitter taste, is a main ingredient in a Provençal soup, *Aigo Boulido,* and an Italian vegetable dish, *Foglie di Salvia Fritte.* It is also employed to flavor many other soups, stews, and especially bean and lentil dishes. Sage can be used fresh or dried.

Thyme: A perennial that grows wild in much of the area, thyme, like rosemary and sage (all of the same family), is strongly aromatic with a slightly bitter flavor. No bouquet garni is complete without a sprig of thyme and, in Provence, it seems to turn up in nearly every dish. It is milder fresh than dried, but powerful in either guise, so use with discretion.

Bay leaf: The leaf of the evergreen bay laurel tree is used fresh, not dried, in Mediterranean cooking for the simple reason that the fresh leaf is available year round. It differs from the American laurel which is, in fact, an evergreen cherry. It is a mainstay of bouquet garni and figures in many soups and stews. To keep mealy bugs and moths out of your grains, flours, and dried beans, add a bay leaf to each container.

Bouquet Garni: Used extensively in Provençal cooking, bouquet garni is a mixture of herbs usually made with sprigs of thyme and rosemary and one or two bay leaves. In Provence, cooks prefer fresh herbs and we recommend them if available. Dried herbs are fine but tend to be stronger and more sharply flavored. If using a bouquet garni made with fresh herbs, tie together with string, use as directed in the recipe, then remove and discard before serving. If using dried herbs, wrap in cheesecloth and use as directed. Remove and discard before serving.

Spices

Cinnamon: There are two types of cinnamon, one from China, known and used in the West for thousands of years, and the other from Sri Lanka and southern India, introduced into Europe in the sixteenth century. The latter, more delicate and fragrant, is cultivated in the West Indies and is now the standard cinnamon. It is used in sweets and in Morocco in a number of savory dishes as well.

Cloves: The dried flowers in bud of a species of myrtle, cloves probably originated in China and were spread by the Dutch and others to the Moluccas, Mauritius, and the West Indies. They are used in this book primarily in desserts.

Cumin: A powerful spice, cumin, originally from the East, is essential in Moroccan cuisine. You can buy whole seeds and grind them as required in a mortar or buy cumin already ground. The latter is easier, the former preferable if you use it infrequently.

Ginger: Native to India, ginger made its way to southern Europe from the East just prior to the Romans and slowly spread north and west. It is a root and available fresh or dried. Dried ground ginger is used in a number of Moroccan tagines.

Orange blossom water: Not strictly speaking a spice, orange blossom water is, nevertheless, used in Moroccan and Provençal cooking for essentially the same purpose—to flavor food, especially desserts. The blossoms come from the bitter orange, an inedible species that is found, among other places, lining and perfuming the streets of Marrakech.

Paprika: The ground powder of the fruit of the pepper plant, paprika can be bought sweet, medium, or hot. The best comes from Hungary and we recommend that you use it. If unavailable, Spanish paprika is acceptable. Paprika is not just for color—when good and fresh, it has a distinct, pungent flavor, much like concentrated peppers.

Saffron: The dried stamen of a species of crocus, saffron has a distinct flavor and aroma and does wonders for rice dishes, soups, and stews. The best saffron we ever had was from Iran, but Spanish saffron is excellent, certainly the best available in North America. It is very expensive, in the same league as some drugs, but when one considers that 200 pounds of crocus flowers yield about 3 ounces of dried saffron, the cost is understandable. Always buy saffron unground. That way, at least you know exactly what you're getting. If very fresh, dry it for a couple of minutes on top of a warm stove, crush in a mortar, dilute with liquid, and use as directed.

Turmeric: A powder made from the ground root of a tropical plant of the ginger family, turmeric, a brilliant yellow spice, has an astringent taste, essential for some Moroccan soups and tagines.

Cooking Techniques

Toasting Nuts

The flavor of nuts is enhanced if they are lightly toasted. The technique is simple. Preheat the oven to 350°F., place the nuts on a cookie sheet or the equivalent, and bake for 5 minutes until lightly browned. Let cool and use as directed.

Peeling Bell Peppers and Handling Hot Peppers

Pepper peels are hard to digest and add an acrid taste to food, so for many recipes, especially Spanish ones, peppers should be peeled. It takes time but is well worth the effort.

Preheat the oven to 400°F. Wash and dry the peppers, place on a cookie sheet or the equivalent, and bake for 40 minutes, turning occasionally, until the skin begins to shrivel and char. As an alternative, spear with a long-handled fork and char the skin over a gas flame. Remove from the oven, place in a plastic or paper bag, and set aside until cooled. Peel with a sharp knife. Remove and discard core and seeds. Reserve as much of the pepper liquid as you can. Peeled peppers will keep a week in the refrigerator and can be frozen.

Fresh hot peppers come in many sizes and degrees of hotness, from very small, blisteringly hot red ones to large, relatively mild green and yellow ones. Seeds are always hotter than the flesh and should be retained or discarded according to taste. After handling hot peppers, wash hands thoroughly and brush fingernails. Do not touch eyes.

Dried Peppers

Dried peppers are used extensively in Spanish cooking and add a smoky, sweet flavor difficult to obtain with any other ingredient. It is, however, relatively easy to produce a facsimile of the dried Spanish pepper in your own kitchen.

Choose firm, fresh, ripe red bell peppers. Wash and pat dry with a clean dish towel. Cut in half, core, remove the seeds and white membranes, place on cookie sheets or the equivalent, and put in a warm oven (about 120°F.) for 2 days, until the peppers are perfectly dry and the flesh translucent. Store in paper bags in a cool, dry place. They are essential for *Romesco*.

Dried hot peppers have many of the same features as fresh ones. In most cases, they are crushed, then added to the dish. To eliminate seeds, break peppers in half and shake them loose. Again, wash hands and fingernails, and do not touch your eyes.

Peeling Tomatoes

Bring to a boil in a saucepan enough water to cover the tomatoes, add tomatoes, and blanch 15 seconds. Remove with a slotted spoon and, when cool enough to handle, prick the skin with a sharp knife and peel.

If tomatoes lack flavor, add a little tomato paste to the dish.

Sun-Dried Plum Tomatoes

It's time to shed some light on sun-dried tomatoes. The process is simple, inexpensive, and feasible for anyone with access to sunshine or an oven.

Wash whatever quantity of ripe plum tomatoes you wish to dehydrate, pat dry with a clean dish towel, cut in half, and scoop out the seeds and juice with your fingers. At this point you have a choice. If the sunlight where you live is very strong, place the tomatoes, skin side down, on straw baskets that allow air to circulate and put them in the sun until they are dried and shriveled like dried apricots. It will take about 2 days. Wind speeds up the drying process.

If you live, as we do, in the north, the sun is unlikely to do the trick. But an oven will. Preheat the oven to warm (about 120°F.), place the tomato halves on cookie sheets or the equivalent, and leave in the oven for 2 days. We've dried them both ways and find the results indistinguishable. When ready, the tomatoes should be faintly moist, soft, and pliable. Place in sterilized glass jars and cover with olive oil. You can, if you wish, add a few leaves of washed basil and a pinch of cayenne pepper. They will keep indefinitely.

Use a couple of these tomatoes, chopped up, to intensify the flavor of fresh tomatoes in sauces.

We also like to add them to salads or eat them on top of a slice of good crusty bread, together with capers and anchovies.

Preserved Lemons

Preserved lemons *(Hamed M'raked)* are one of the visual delights in *souks* (markets), huge glowing pyramids of sunshine. They stand in roughly the same relationship to fresh lemons as sauerkraut does to fresh cabbage, which means that fresh lemons are not a substitute for preserved lemons in recipes that call for the latter. In Morocco, they are used in cooking and as a condiment with olives or vegetables. You can also include the pulp in a vinaigrette to make a superb salad dressing.

Moroccan lemons tend to be smaller, juicier, and thinner skinned than those available in North America, but, if you choose carefully, you can approximate Moroccan ones. On the advice of our friend Toni Maraini, we tried limes and were delighted with the results. We now use them instead of lemons for our Moroccan dishes.   MAKES 1 QUART

5 or 6 small, whole thin-skinned   *⅓ cup salt*
lemons, or 6 or 7 limes, well   *Juice of 2 lemons*
washed

Cut the lemons or limes into quarters, leaving the quarters attached at the stem end. Sprinkle each lemon with 1 tablespoon of salt and fit together again. Place in a sterilized 1-quart Mason jar, squeezing them snugly to fit. Add the remaining salt, lemon juice, and enough warm water to cover the lemons or limes. Close the jar and shake to dissolve the salt. They are ready to use after 1 month. Rinse under running water to remove some of the salt and any film that may have formed. Traditionally, only the skin is used, but we find the pulp equally delicious. They can be kept up to one year.

Preparing Mesclun

The word *mesclun* derives from the Provençal word for "mixed" and is used to describe mixed salad sold in markets throughout Provence. A good *mesclun* may include a bit of conventional lettuce but will be heavily laced with arugula, wild chicory, purslane, and other wild grasses and herbs, as well as cultivated greens such as radicchio, endive, and escarole. It is always flavorful and slightly bitter. To make it at home, combine leaves of arugula, red or green radicchio, curly endive, and escarole. You can toss in fresh herbs and wild grasses, such as chicory, dandelion, purslane, and lamb's quarters, if you wish. Use as directed.

Cleaning and Butterflying Sardines

Sardines, abundant and inexpensive, are enormously popular among Mediterranean folk. They are usually sold whole and un-cleaned and, unless you have a very cooperative fishmonger, you will have to prepare them for cooking yourself. If you have trouble finding them, try an Italian or Portuguese fish market.

If you have a choice, select small ones, about 5 to 6 inches in length. With the dull part of a knife, scale, holding the fish by the tail and running the knife from the tail to the head. Rinse.

Break the head off and discard. Slit open the stomach and discard the insides. Rinse.

To butterfly, open the underneath (stomach side) of the fish completely with a sharp knife. Then, from the belly side, loosen the backbone from the flesh with a sharp knife, beginning at the head and going to the tail. Break off and discard the backbone, leaving the tail intact. The 2 halves of the fish should remain together. If bony, trim the top fin with sharp scissors. Flatten, pat dry, and use as directed.

Cleaning Squid

Don't let the unappetizing appearance of squid fool you, they figure in many glorious Mediterranean dishes. If you are unable to find squid at your local fish store, try an Italian, Greek, Portuguese, or Chinese market. They are sure to have them.

To clean, pull the tentacles away from the sac and set the former aside. Remove the translucent "bone" or shell from the sac as well as the thick gelatinous substance that surrounds it. Rinse well under running water. Make sure nothing remains in the sac. It is now ready to be stuffed or cut into pieces.

To clean the tentacles, cut off and discard the hard part at the top where the tentacles join—this removes the eyes and beak. Rinse and use as directed.

Cleaning Cuttlefish

Cuttlefish are stouter than squid, have a large white "bone" in the center instead of a thin translucent one, and contain a large amount of ink while the squid has very little. The ink was once used as a dye (sepia) and is often employed to flavor dishes.

Pull off the tentacles and set aside. Remove the bone and discard. With a sharp knife, cut the body of the cuttlefish vertically on the thin side. Open and peel off the rough inner and smooth outer membranes. Rinse under cold water, pat dry, and set aside.

The ink sac is light silver in color and is wedged beneath the tentacles. If you are planning to use it, remove and place in a small mixing bowl. If you are not, discard. Cut away the eyes at the top of the tentacles and discard. The tentacles should remain intact. Use as directed.

Cleaning Octopus

The true octopus has eight tentacles and two rows of suckers on each tentacle. It has a voracious appetite, hunts primarily at night, and lives on shellfish. In the Mediterranean, at least, in the summer, octopuses are fished close to shore, usually at night, with large lights. We have also seen Greek fishermen going after them with a white handkerchief tied to a stick. The white, apparently, lures them out into the open where they can be hooked. Once caught, they are quickly dispatched, then beaten against rocks or a boat dock until tender. Unless they are large, we find that long cooking is an effective way to tenderize octopus.

If you cannot persuade your fishmonger to clean it for you, here are instructions: Place the octopus flat on a cutting board and slit open the bulbous part from the tentacles to the top; cut out and discard the eyes, the inner organs, and the beak, which is lodged between the tentacles just below the eyes; rinse under cold water, pat dry, and use as directed.

Basics and Sauces

We include a relatively modest collection of sauces and a few basic recipes in this chapter. Some, such as Béchamel, Mayonnaise, and Tomato Sauce, are indispensable for Mediterranean cuisine, while others, such as *Romesco* and *Rouille,* are regional specialties that we like. We also give recipes for vegetable broth, fish stock, and savory pastry dough. A number of sauces, especially those served with pasta, appear elsewhere in the book.

‖ *PÂTE BRISÉE*   *France*
‖ Pastry Dough

This is the dough we normally use to make savory tarts and is perfect for all the recipes in this book.

MAKES ONE 10-INCH TART SHELL

2 cups unbleached all-purpose
    flour
Pinch of salt
¼ pound chilled unsalted butter,
    cut into small pieces

2 extra-large eggs
1 tablespoon lemon juice

Place the flour in a large mixing bowl with the salt, add the butter, and mix with your fingers or a pastry knife until the butter is the size of small peas. Add the remaining ingredients and mix well.

Turn the dough onto a lightly floured board or marble slab, knead briefly with the heel of your hand until the butter blends with the flour, shape into a ball, cover completely with wax paper, and place in the refrigerator for 1 hour.

If using for a flan, the dough should be prebaked. Preheat the oven to 400°F. and butter a 10-inch flan pan well. Roll out the dough on a lightly floured board or marble slab until large enough to cover the bottom and sides of the pan. It will be between ⅛ and ¼ inch thick. Allow extra dough to drape over the edge. Fit snugly into the pan and prick the bottom with the tines of a fork.

To trim the edges, roll a rolling pin across the rim and remove excess dough. There is some danger when preparing a pre-baked shell that the dough will shrink as it cooks. To avoid this, try leaving a ¼-inch overlap, then roll the overlap back on itself to form a lip. Score with a sharp knife or the tines of a fork.

Butter a piece of aluminum foil and fit it into the pan, over the dough. Put dried beans or pastry weights on the foil and bake the shell for 10 to 12 minutes, until the dough is set and lightly browned. Remove the weights and foil, and return to the oven for another 5 to 7 minutes. The shell is now suitable for a flan. It can be baked up to a day in advance and kept in the refrigerator.

FUMET DE POISSON   *France*
Fish Stock

Fish stock is easy to make and distinctive in flavor. It is the base for most fish soups and, with the addition of pieces of fish, makes an excellent hearty soup on its own. We recommend that you make extra and keep a batch frozen.   MAKES ABOUT 2 QUARTS

1 large onion, thinly sliced   *One 2-inch piece orange peel*
1 small celery stalk   *1 cup dry white wine*
1 bay leaf   *Salt to taste*
2 sprigs fresh parsley   *2 pounds fish heads, tails, and*
10 black peppercorns   *trimmings*
1 slice lemon

Place the ingredients in a heavy enamel or stainless steel stockpot. Add 2 quarts of cold water, bring slowly to a boil, cover, and simmer for 25 minutes. Strain through a fine sieve. Use as required.

Fish stock will keep a few days in the refrigerator and can also be frozen.

BRODO DI VERDURA
Vegetable Broth

Italy

Use on its own as a soup or in recipes that call for vegetable broth. Ingredients and quantities can be varied according to taste. High-quality powdered vegetable broth is often sold in health food stores and makes a good substitute.   MAKES ABOUT 10 CUPS

4 tablespoons olive oil
3 onions, chopped
3 celery stalks with leaves,
    chopped
3 carrots, peeled and chopped
4 garlic cloves, chopped
3 cups chopped Swiss chard
½ cup lentils or split peas
2 large ripe tomatoes, peeled,
    seeded, and chopped, or 1
    cup canned Italian plum
    tomatoes, with juice

½ cup fresh chopped parsley
½ cup fresh chopped basil
8 whole peppercorns
Pinch of oregano
2 bay leaves
½ teaspoon salt

Heat the oil in a large stockpot, add the onions, celery, carrots, and garlic, and sauté for 5 minutes. Add 3 quarts water and all the remaining ingredients. Bring to a boil, reduce heat to low, and simmer, covered, for 2 hours. Strain before using.

The broth will keep for a week in the refrigerator and can also be frozen.

VARIATION To make a cream soup, purée the vegetables with the broth, combine with 1 cup whipping cream, and heat before serving.

CRÈME FRAÎCHE   *France*

This cream can be bought in France in any grocery or cheese shop, but it is still difficult to find in North America. Fortunately, it is easy to make with ingredients available in supermarkets.

MAKES ABOUT 1½ CUPS

¾ *cup sour cream*   2 *teaspoons lemon juice*
1½ *cups whipping cream*

Mix together the sour cream and the whipping cream in a bowl. Allow to sit at room temperature for 6 to 8 hours. Place a coffee filter in a funnel, or something equivalent, add the mixture when ready and set aside to drain for 2 to 3 hours, until thick. Mix with the lemon juice and use as directed.

Store in the refrigerator. It will keep for at least 1 week.

SALSA DI POMODORO   *Italy*
Tomato Sauce

A good tomato sauce is essential in Mediterranean cooking. We usually devote one or two days in late summer to making tomato sauce, which we then can or freeze and use throughout the winter. If you don't have the time for such an undertaking, you can freeze plum tomatoes whole and use them to make your sauce in winter. You can also use sun-dried tomatoes (p. 14). If all else fails, use canned Italian plum tomatoes (they're the best on the market) to make the sauce when fresh tomatoes are out of season. Do not use fresh tomatoes in midwinter.

The whole object of making tomato sauce is to boil away the water and retain the richly flavored essence of tomato. To facilitate the process, use a wide, shallow saucepan that exposes as much surface area as possible to the heat and thus speeds up evaporation.   MAKES 1½ TO 2 CUPS

⅓ cup olive oil
1 large onion, finely chopped
3 pounds ripe plum tomatoes,
    halved and seeded, or 3 cups
    drained canned Italian plum
    tomatoes

1 teaspoon sugar
1 teaspoon salt
4 large basil leaves, roughly torn
Freshly ground pepper to taste

Heat 2 tablespoons olive oil in a large, heavy, wide-mouthed saucepan, add the onion, and sauté over medium-low heat until transparent, about 7 to 10 minutes. The onion should not brown. Add the tomatoes, sugar, and salt, and simmer, stirring occasionally with a wooden spoon, until the sauce thickens, about 20 to 25 minutes.

Pass the sauce through a food mill to purée and to eliminate seeds and skins, then return to the saucepan. Do not use a blender or food processor. The seeds contain a bitter oil that is released when ground. As an alternative, use the tomato squeezer available in well-stocked kitchen supply stores or hardware stores in Italian or Greek neighborhoods. This highly specialized gadget separates seeds and skins from the sauce with much less effort than a food mill.

Continue cooking until the desired consistency is obtained. The sauce can be thinned by adding water or thickened by longer cooking.

Remove from the heat, add basil, pepper, and the remaining olive oil. Use as required.

Tomato sauce keeps about 1 week in the refrigerator and for months in the freezer.

COULIS DE TOMATE   *France*
Provençal Tomato Sauce

This sauce, cooked with garlic and bouquet garni, is slightly more flavorful than the Italian tomato sauce. It can also be made in big batches and canned or frozen. Use as you would any tomato sauce. It is not uncommon to spice it up with some cayenne pepper.

MAKES ABOUT 1½ TO 2 CUPS

⅓ cup olive oil
1 pound onions, chopped
2 garlic cloves, chopped
Bouquet garni made with thyme,
*   rosemary, bay leaf, tied*
*   together (p. 11)*

3 pounds ripe tomatoes, chopped
1 teaspoon sugar
½ teaspoon salt
Freshly ground pepper to taste

Heat the oil in a wide, shallow saucepan, add the onions and garlic, and sauté until soft, about 5 minutes. Do not brown. Add the bouquet garni, tomatoes, sugar, salt, and pepper, and simmer uncovered, stirring occasionally, until the sauce thickens, about 20 to 25 minutes. Pass through a food mill or tomato squeezer to purée and remove seeds and skins. Do not use a blender or food processor.

Return to the saucepan and cook until desired consistency is obtained. The sauce is thinned by the addition of water and thickened by longer cooking. Use as directed.

Provençal tomato sauce keeps about 1 week in the refrigerator and for months in the freezer. Since garlic gains strength over time, if unfrozen, you may wish to adjust quantities if you intend to keep the sauce for a while.

‖ MAYONNAISE   *France*

Homemade mayonnaise is so far superior to any commercial brand that the two are essentially different products. In the old days before blenders and food processors there was perhaps some excuse for buying mayonnaise ready-made, but that excuse no longer exists.

Mayonnaise is an emulsion in which the oil is suspended in eggs or egg yolks. The trick is to make sure that the suspension holds. If you follow the recipe given below you will have no difficulty. It is best to work with all the ingredients at room temperature.

MAKES 1¾ CUPS

1 extra-large egg
1¼ cups olive oil, or mixture of
light seed oil and olive oil

Juice of ½ to 1 lemon, according
to taste
Salt and freshly ground pepper to
taste

Place the egg in a blender or food processor with the metal blade in place, and process 10 seconds. With the machine running, add the oil through the feed tube in a thin stream until all is used. Again with the machine running, add half the lemon juice and salt and pepper. Taste and adjust for seasoning. Pulse and set aside.

If, for some reason, the emulsion breaks down, remove the egg-and-oil mixture from the blender or food processor, add another whole egg, then, with the machine running, add the original mixture gradually.

Homemade mayonnaise will keep about 1 week in the refrigerator. Make sure you do not leave it out of the refrigerator for an extended period—mayonnaise builds up dangerous bacteria quickly.

AÏOLI   *France*
Garlic Mayonnaise

This is the queen of garlic sauces—regal, smooth, and pungent. It is served in Provence with *bourride,* vegetable soups, steamed or boiled vegetables, poached fish, and hard-boiled eggs. The Spanish have an identical sauce *(alioli)* and use it as the French do. The traditional way to make the sauce is to crush the garlic cloves in a mortar, combine with egg yolks, and beat with a whisk while olive oil is dribbled in a little at a time. Some argue that this method produces the smoothest, lightest *aïoli,* but we are perfectly happy with that made in a blender or food processor. We give a recipe for the machine-made version below. To make by hand, use 2 egg yolks, not whole eggs.   MAKES 1¼ CUPS

4 to 6 garlic cloves, crushed
1 extra-large egg
1 cup olive oil

Salt and freshly ground white
pepper to taste
2 tablespoons lemon juice
(optional)

Place the garlic in the work bowl of a blender or food processor, add the egg, and pulse. With the machine running, add the olive oil in a thin stream until all is used. Blend in the salt and pepper and, if desired, the lemon juice. *Aïoli* will keep at least 1 week in the refrigerator.

ANCHOÏADE   *France*
Anchovy Sauce

Use as a dip with raw celery, carrots, broccoli, and cauliflower and as a sauce with boiled artichokes and potatoes, steamed vegetables, and poached fish.   MAKES 1 CUP

¾ cup olive oil
10 anchovy fillets, cut in pieces
5 garlic cloves, crushed in a
   mortar
2 shallots, finely chopped
¼ teaspoon finely ground black
   pepper

¼ cup finely chopped fresh
   parsley
¼ teaspoon dried thyme, or 1
   tablespoon fresh basil
2 to 3 tablespoons good wine
   vinegar
1 egg yolk, beaten

Place the oil in a small skillet, add the anchovies, and cook over low heat, crushing the anchovies with a wooden spoon until they dissolve. Add the rest of the ingredients, except the egg yolk. Warm through and add the egg yolk, a little at a time, while stirring to prevent coagulation. The egg binds the sauce. Remove from heat as soon as it has thickened slightly, about 1 minute.

The sauce will keep a couple of days in the refrigerator.

BÉCHAMEL *Italy*
Béchamel Sauce

There is some dispute over the origin of béchamel sauce. The name in English derives from Louis de Bechamiel, *maître de chef* of Louis XIV, but there are thirteenth-century Italian recipes that feature a sauce virtually identical to béchamel. Like so many other "French" dishes, this may have come to France with Marie de Médicis early in the seventeenth century, to be popularized by Louis's man later. Whatever its origin, the sauce is indispensable in Mediterranean cuisine.   MAKES ABOUT 1 CUP

1 cup of milk
2 tablespoons unsalted butter
2 tablespoons unbleached
    all-purpose flour

⅛ teaspoon salt
Pinch of freshly ground white
    pepper

Heat the milk in a small saucepan, taking care that it does not scorch or boil.

Heat the butter in a heavy saucepan, add the flour, and cook over medium-low heat, stirring constantly for 1 minute. Add the hot milk a little at a time, stirring constantly, until all the milk is used. Season with salt and pepper and continue cooking, stirring until thick. Remove from heat.

This recipe makes a medium-thick sauce. To make it thicker, add less milk; to make thinner, add more.

If not using immediately, coat surface of the sauce with a thin film of butter and cover. As an alternative, seal tightly with plastic wrap. It is best to make the sauce just before using, but it can be kept for a day or two in the refrigerator. To reheat, add 2 tablespoons of milk and warm over low heat, stirring frequently, until the sauce is hot, creamy, and smooth.

To make a richer sauce, use half milk and half cream. You can also add an egg yolk to the sauce once it cools slightly. For more flavor, add 2 tablespoons minced onion to the butter and sauté before adding the flour.

ROMESCO   *Spain*
Hot Pepper and Nut Sauce

As Elaine Comelade says in her cookbook *La Cuisine Catalone*, *romesco* is a way of preparing food, a very ancient one at that, and not simply a sauce. Be that as it may, *romesco* makes a delicious accompaniment for grilled or sautéed fish and crustaceans, and can also be served to good effect with boiled potatoes and hard-boiled eggs.   MAKES ABOUT 1¼ CUPS

½ cup olive oil   *1 medium ripe tomato, peeled and*
2 dried bell peppers (p. 13)   *roughly chopped*
1 dried hot pepper   *24 blanched almonds, lightly*
4 garlic cloves   *toasted*
1 thick slice French or Italian   *⅓ cup dry white wine*
*   bread, crust removed*   *Salt to taste*

Heat ¼ cup of oil in a skillet, add the dried bell and hot peppers, fry lightly, and remove. Do not overcook—the peppers burn easily. Add the whole garlic cloves and bread, and fry until browned. Remove. Add the tomato and sauté 2 to 3 minutes, until soft and saturated with oil.

Place the peppers, garlic cloves, bread, tomato, and almonds in a blender or food processor equipped with the metal blade and process until a medium-coarse paste is obtained. Add the frying oil and the remaining ¼ cup of oil and pulse to combine. Add the wine and salt and blend. Serve at room temperature.

The sauce will keep at least 1 week in the refrigerator.

VARIATION Dilute the sauce with ¾ cup of water and use as broth in which to simmer fillets of fish such as halibut, monkfish, grouper, or snapper. Add cooked clams, mussels, shrimp, and lobster before serving. The sauce is adequate for about 2 pounds of fish.

TARATOR
Turkey
Pine Nut Sauce

Tarator, a delicious blend of pine nuts, oil, and vinegar, is usually eaten with poached or baked fish or, as in Turkey, with fried mussels. Recipes differ from region to region—the one included here is our favorite.   MAKES ABOUT ¾ CUP

*2 slices good white bread, crusts
    removed
½ cup pine nuts
3 tablespoons olive oil*

*3 tablespoons white wine vinegar
2 tablespoons Fish Stock (see p.
    22) or bottled clam juice
1 garlic clove, crushed*

Soak the bread in water to cover for a few minutes, then squeeze out excess water. Place pine nuts in blender or food processor, pulverize until finely ground, add the bread, and pulse a few times to combine. Add the remaining ingredients one at a time, pulsing to combine thoroughly. The sauce should be smooth and thick. Use as required.

The sauce will keep about 1 week in the refrigerator. Do not freeze.

HARISSA
Morocco
Hot Pepper Sauce

Used extensively in Morocco to spice up bland dishes, *harissa* is very easy to prepare at home. Vary the proportions according to taste.   MAKES ABOUT ¾ CUP

*3 dried hot peppers with seeds,
    crushed
1 teaspoon caraway seeds
5 or 6 garlic cloves*

*½ red bell pepper, peeled and
    seeded
½ teaspoon salt
½ cup olive oil*

Pulverize hot peppers in a mortar together with the caraway seeds. Add the garlic cloves, bell pepper, and salt, and mash until smooth. Place in a jar with a lid, add olive oil to cover, and store.

If you are using a blender or a food processor, first pulverize the peppers and the caraway seeds in a mortar, then place all the ingredients in the bowl of the blender or food processor and blend until smooth.

The sauce will keep about 3 weeks stored in the refrigerator.

ROUILLE   *France*
Red Pepper Sauce

Rouille is a fiery sauce used in Provence to flavor fish soups. Of the two versions we know, one from around Marseilles, the other from Nice, we prefer the latter. Although not the traditional method, we peel the pepper. *Rouille* can also be served with steamed vegetables or hard-boiled eggs.   MAKES 1¼ CUPS

1 red bell pepper, peeled, seeded,   *1 extra-large egg*
     and cut into small pieces   *1 cup olive oil*
¼ teaspoon cayenne pepper   *Salt and freshly ground pepper to*
2 garlic cloves   *taste*

Place the bell pepper, cayenne pepper, and garlic cloves in a blender or food processor equipped with the metal blade. Blend until smooth. Add the egg and blend another 10 seconds. With the machine running, pour in the oil in a thin stream until all is used. Season with salt and pepper and use as desired.

VARIATION For the Marseilles version, simply mash together in a mortar 1 red bell pepper, seeded and chopped; 1 slice of French bread with crust removed, soaked in water and squeezed dry; and 1 garlic clove. Add ¼ teaspoon cayenne pepper and 2 tablespoons each olive oil and fish stock to make a smooth, creamy sauce.

TAPENADE   *France*
Olive, Caper, and Garlic Sauce

This is the quintessential Provençal sauce, a pungent confection of olives, capers, garlic, anchovies, and olive oil. Serve on toast as an appetizer, use to liven up deviled eggs, as a stuffing for raw tomatoes, or with omelets. If you are unable to find Niçoise olives, use Italian olives but rinse in cold water to remove excess salt. Marc, a brandy-like liqueur, will add a distinctive Provençal flavor.

MAKES APPROXIMATELY 1 CUP

1 cup pitted black Niçoise olives
3 tablespoons capers
1 garlic clove, peeled
4 anchovy fillets, packed in oil,
    drained
½ teaspoon crushed peppercorns

¼ teaspoon fresh or dried thyme
5 leaves fresh basil
1 teaspoon Marc de Provence,
    light rum, or 1 tablespoon
    lemon juice
3 tablespoons olive oil

Place all ingredients except olive oil in the work bowl of a blender or food processor and mix until very finely chopped. Do not purée. Add the olive oil in a thin stream with the machine running. Transfer to a small bowl and set aside until ready to use.

Tapenade will keep in the refrigerator for 3 weeks.

SKORDALIA   *Greece*
Potato-Garlic Sauce

Some consider this a Greek version of *aïoli* but it may be more correct to view *aïoli* as a refined *skordalia*. Whatever the case, *skordalia*, like *aïoli*, is a pungent garlic sauce, perfect with steamed vegetables, poached fish, and especially beet salad.

MAKES ABOUT 1½ CUPS

1 pound potatoes, unpeeled
5 or more garlic cloves
Yolk of 1 extra-large egg

½ cup olive oil
Juice of 1½ to 2 lemons
Salt to taste

Place the potatoes in a saucepan, add water to cover, bring to a boil, lower heat, and cook, covered, until the potatoes are tender, about 20 minutes. Drain and set aside to cool. When ready, peel, cut into small cubes, and set aside.

While the potatoes cook, crush the garlic in a mortar. Add the potatoes and egg yolk, and mash to a fine, smooth pulp. Add the olive oil to the mortar in a fine stream, mixing and mashing constantly with the pestle until the oil is entirely absorbed. Blend in the juice of 1½ lemons, taste, and add more if necessary. Correct for salt.

Skordalia made in this way is best because it is light and granular. It can also be made in a blender or food processor but be careful not to overprocess the potatoes. To use a blender or food processor, cook and peel the potatoes, process briefly in the machine, add the egg yolk and garlic, and pulse again to blend. Add the oil in a thin stream, pulsing to combine. Blend in the lemon juice and correct for salt.

The sauce will keep about 1 week in the refrigerator. Take note that the garlic flavor will intensify over time, so adjust accordingly.

CHARMOULA   *Morocco*
Fish Marinade

In Morocco, fish is often marinated in this or a similar spicy marinade before being cooked. Vary the quantity of cayenne pepper to suit your taste and tolerance. This recipe makes enough marinade for a 2-pound fish.   MAKES ABOUT ½ CUP

*½ cup finely chopped fresh
     coriander leaves*
5 garlic cloves
1 tablespoon sweet paprika
¼ teaspoon cayenne pepper
2 teaspoons ground cumin

3 tablespoons peanut oil
Juice of 1 lemon
¼ teaspoon salt
*¼ teaspoon freshly ground black
     pepper*

Place all ingredients in a blender or food processor and run until a smooth paste is obtained. As an alternative, grind to a smooth paste in a mortar. Use as directed.

The sauce will keep for about 2 weeks, but the garlic will become stronger.

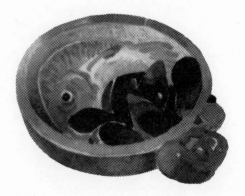

Appetizers and Salads

We divide the chapter into three sections, Raw Appetizers and Salads, Cooked Appetizers and Salads, and Fish and Seafood Appetizers and Salads. We have chosen dishes from the vast array of Mediterranean appetizers, variously called *mezze, tapas,* antipasti, and hors d'oeuvres, that are served prior to the meal as well as from salads, which, at least in Italy and France, come at the end not the beginning. A number of the dishes are nourishing enough to act as the main dish for a luncheon. Use them as your needs and tastes dictate, but remember that if served before the meal, they should stimulate the appetite not satiate it, so serve modest amounts.

One of the most delightful ways to begin a meal is with a selection of mixed appetizers. It requires more work on the part of the cook, but most can be prepared in advance and almost all are very easy to make. We urge you to combine across countries, trying to create a spread that contrasts flavors, textures, and ingredients. For example, Scallion Salad with Tomatoes and Raisins, Zucchini Yogurt Salad, Lemon Salad with Olives, Grated Carrots with Orange Juice, and Chilled Squid Salad with Peppers, garnished with olives, tomato wedges, and radishes, make a sensational mixed appetizer. Or try Fatima's Mussels served with small slivers of Swiss Chard Tart, Beet Salad with Garlic Sauce, and Endive Salad with Fresh Coriander. You can also stick just to seafood salads or even mussels. These are just ideas—the only risk you run is undue caution.

Raw Appetizers and Salads

POIVRONS FARCIS AU FROMAGE DE CHÈVRE   *France*
Peppers Stuffed with Goat Cheese

Excellent with either a mature or a fresh goat cheese, this appetizer from western Provence can also be made with a mild blue cheese, such as a bleu de Bresse, or, in a pinch, with a Brillat-Savarin. In Greece, a virtually identical dish is made with feta. Try to find tender, juicy peppers—it's the astrigent flavor of the green pepper combined with the cheese-spice mixture that gives the dish its sparkle.   SERVES 4 TO 6

2 medium green bell peppers
2 tablespoons butter
1 cup finely chopped onions
½ pound goat cheese
4 tablespoons finely chopped fresh
     chives
2 teaspoons cumin seed

1 teaspoon sweet paprika
2 garlic cloves, crushed
Pinch cayenne pepper
Salt and freshly ground pepper to
     taste
Lettuce leaves for serving

Remove the stems, cores, and seeds from the peppers, taking care not to break the skins. Set aside.

Heat the butter in a skillet, add the onions, and sauté over low heat until translucent. Transfer to a mixing bowl, add the cheese, and blend thoroughly. Add the remaining ingredients, except for the lettuce leaves, and mix well.

Pack the peppers solidly with the cheese mixture. Place in the refrigerator for 2 hours.

When ready to serve, slice the peppers with a sharp knife into rounds about ¼ inch thick. Place on lettuce leaves and serve on individual plates or a serving platter.

SALADE DE MESCLUN AU CHÈVRE CHAUD France
Mixed Salad with Warm Goat Cheese

We regard this as a winter salad, perhaps because we first had it in Provence in January, but also because the sharp, fresh flavor of goat cheese is perfectly matched by the strong, slightly bitter taste of winter salad greens. The problem is, what kind of goat cheese? In a good French cheese shop, one can usually choose from twenty or more types—some aged, some fresh, some very goaty, some mild. We find a mature, sharp, but not goaty *cendre* works perfectly in this salad. Serve as a salad or as a main dish for a light supper or luncheon.   SERVES 4

4 tightly packed cups mesclun
    (p. 16)
4 tablespoons olive oil
2 tablespoons fruit vinegar
Salt and freshly ground pepper to
    taste

1 ounce goat cheese
8 thinly sliced pieces good French
    bread
1 or 2 garlic cloves, peeled

Wash and dry the *mesclun,* then tear into medium-size pieces. Place in a mixing bowl. In a separate small bowl, combine the oil, vinegar, salt, and pepper, pour over the salad, and mix well.

Preheat oven to 450°F.

Slice goat cheese into 8 pieces. Toast the bread lightly, rub with garlic, place in a baking dish in a single layer, distribute slices of goat cheese evenly over the bread, and bake until the cheese begins to melt, about 5 minutes.

While the cheese is baking, distribute the salad on four salad plates, leaving space in the middle of each for the cheese. When ready, put 2 pieces of bread and cheese on each plate and serve immediately.

RADICCHIO AL GORGONZOLA   *Italy*
Radicchio with Gorgonzola Vinaigrette

If not the original blue cheese dressing, certainly the best. The recipe calls for red radicchio but a mixture of escarole, endive, romaine, and arugula makes an excellent substitute.   SERVES 4

3 heads red radicchio   *3 tablespoons wine vinegar*
¼ pound mild Gorgonzola   *Salt and freshly ground pepper to*
5 tablespoons olive oil   *taste*

Cut the radicchio in wedges and place in a salad bowl. Mash the cheese with the tines of a fork, then combine with oil, vinegar, and salt to make a smooth paste. When ready to serve, pour over the radicchio, season with pepper, toss, and serve.

INSALATA DI CARCIOFI CRUDI   *Italy*
Raw Artichoke Salad with Sliced Parmesan

Do not let the simplicity of this dish mislead you. The combination of raw artichoke hearts and fresh Parmesan with a light lemon and oil dressing is truly inspired. Choose fresh, tender artichokes, preferably small, Italian violet ones if available.   SERVES 4

8 to 12 (depending on size)   *4 tablespoons extra-virgin olive*
   small, tender artichokes   *oil*
Juice of 1 lemon plus 2   *Salt and freshly ground pepper to*
   tablespoons   *taste*
¼ pound fresh Parmesan, sliced
   very thinly into squares
   about 1½ inches per side

Remove all but the most tender inner leaves from the artichokes, cut in half, remove chokes, if any, and place in water with the juice of 1 lemon until ready to use.

Remove the artichokes from the water, drain, and slice into very thin wedges with a sharp knife. Place in a serving bowl with the Parmesan slices, combine 2 tablespoons lemon juice, olive oil, and salt and pepper, blend with the artichokes and cheese, and serve.

PIPIRRANA   **Spain**
Pepper and Tomato Salad

We first had this dish near Jaen in Andalusia, the highlight of an otherwise ordinary meal. Versions of it are popular throughout Andalusia and Valencia.   SERVES 4 TO 6

1 cup peeled, seeded, and diced
   cucumber
½ cup diced Spanish onion
2 cups seeded and diced fresh
   tomatoes
½ cup peeled (p. 13) and diced
   green and red bell peppers

2 tablespoons chopped fresh
   parsley
3 tablespoons olive oil
2 tablespoons vinegar
Salt and freshly ground pepper to
   taste

Combine the vegetables and parsely in an attractive serving bowl. Mix the remaining ingredients in a small bowl, add to the vegetables, and toss. Chill for 1 or 2 hours before serving.

For an interesting variation, cut up 3 or 4 anchovy fillets and add them to the salad.

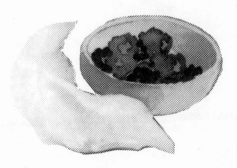

BIBER SALATASI   *Turkey*
Spicy Pepper Salad with Tomatoes and Pine Nuts

SERVES 4 TO 6

2 green bell peppers, cored,
    seeded, and diced
2 large ripe tomatoes, peeled,
    seeded, and diced
3 scallions, roughly chopped
¼ cup pine nuts
⅓ cup tomato paste

2 tablespoons lemon juice
¼ cup olive oil
1 teaspoon ground cumin
¼ teaspoon cayenne pepper
Salt and freshly ground pepper to
    taste

Place the peppers, tomatoes, scallions, and pine nuts in a serving bowl. Combine the remaining ingredients in a mixing bowl and pour over the vegetables. Mix well. Serve at room temperature.

SHALADA BEL HAMED AU ZITOUN   *Morocco*
Lemon Salad with Olives

This is an astounding salad in which raw lemon is the main ingredient. It does have punch but is wonderfully refreshing. If you are unable to find Moroccan olives, use those from Italy. The salad can be made up to a day in advance and kept in the refrigerator.

SERVES 4 TO 6

2 lemons
2 tablespoons salt
½ cup chopped parsley, tightly
    packed
2 tablespoons peanut oil
2 tablespoons olive oil
¼ teaspoon cayenne pepper
1 tablespoon sweet paprika

¼ teaspoon ground cumin
10 green olives, preferably
    Moroccan, rinsed well if
    salty, pitted, and cut in half
10 red or black olives, preferably
    Moroccan, rinsed well if
    salty, pitted, and cut in half

Remove the peel from the lemons, leaving the white membrane. The peel can be reserved for dishes that call for lemon zest. Cover the lemons with water, add the salt, and soak for 2 hours.

When ready, remove and rinse the lemons, cut in half, squeeze, and reserve the juice. Remove some of the internal filaments. Cut the lemons into ¼-inch to ½-inch cubes, place in a mixing bowl, and sprinkle with parsley. Combine the oils and spices in a small mixing bowl and pour over the lemons. Add the olives and toss. Just prior to serving, add 1 or 2 tablespoons of lemon juice. Serve at room temperature.

VARIATION A similar salad can be made with oranges. Peel and thinly slice 2 navel oranges. Cut the slices in half and place in a bowl with the olives. Combine the olive oil (omit the peanut oil) with the cayenne pepper, paprika, and cumin, mix well, combine with the oranges, and serve at room temperature.

SHALADA BE LICHIN OU L'KHOSS   *Morocco*
Shredded Lettuce and Orange Salad

The orange blossom water is not essential but it does add the particular perfumed aroma and flavor characteristic of this dish. You should be able to find it in specialty food shops or those that feature Middle Eastern or North African foods.   SERVES 4

2 large navel oranges, peeled,   *1 teaspoon sugar*
    seeded, and diced   *¼ teaspoon salt*
Juice of 1 orange   *1 teaspoon orange blossom water*
1 tablespoon lemon juice   *12 romaine lettuce leaves, finely*
2 tablespoons peanut oil   *sliced*

Place the oranges in a salad bowl. Mix together the juices, oil, sugar, salt, and orange blossom water in a small mixing bowl and pour over the oranges. Combine well. When ready to serve, add the lettuce leaves, toss, and serve at room temperature.

SHALADA "D'ENDIVES" BEL KASBOUR   *Morocco*
Endive Salad with Fresh Coriander

A simple salad given a certain distinction through the addition of coriander leaves and the pulp of preserved lemons.   SERVES 4

5 small Belgian endives, hard cores removed, cut into ¼-inch segments
4 tablespoons peanut oil
Juice of ½ lemon

Salt and freshly ground pepper to taste
¼ cup preserved lemon pulp (p. 15)
2 tablespoons chopped fresh coriander leaves

Put the endives in a salad bowl. Combine the oil, lemon juice, salt and pepper, and lemon pulp in a small mixing bowl. When ready to serve, pour the dressing over the endives, add the coriander, toss, and serve.

KHIZZO DE ASSER LICHIN   *Morocco*
Grated Carrots with Orange Juice

Orange juice and grated carrots are perfect complements and together make a bright and refreshing salad.   SERVES 6 TO 8

1½ pounds carrots, peeled and grated
Juice of 6 oranges
Juice of 1 lemon
2 tablespoons sugar

1 tablespoon orange blossom water
¼ teaspoon ground cumin
¼ teaspoon salt

Combine all the ingredients in a bowl. Stir well so that the sugar and salt dissolve. Allow to marinate in a cool place for a couple of hours before serving. Serve in small bowls with the juice.

CHOU CRU D'ANTIBES   *France*
Cole Slaw, Antibes Style

An open-air food market is a great source of information on local
dishes. Here's a terrific way to make cole slaw, a traditional recipe
passed on to us by Madame Riou, a vegetable vendor in the Antibes market. The cabbage should be young and tender. You may
need more or less dressing, depending on the size of your cabbage.
Keep the proportions the same.   SERVES 4 TO 6

1 small cabbage
1 garlic clove, crushed in a
   mortar
6 tablespoons olive oil
2½ tablespoons red or white wine
   vinegar

3 or 4 anchovy fillets, packed in
   oil, drained and minced
1 teaspoon Dijon mustard
Salt and freshly ground pepper to
   taste

   Wash the cabbage, remove tough outer leaves, cut in half and
remove core. Slice very thinly with a sharp knife or with the thin-
slicing disk of a food processor. Place in a salad bowl and set aside.
   Combine the remaining ingredients in a small bowl, mix well,
then blend with the cabbage. Allow to sit 10 minutes before serving.

INSALATA DI CAROTE E SEDANO DI VERONA
Carrot and Celery Root Salad   *Italy*

In this original and delicious salad from the Veneto in northeast-
ern Italy—one of the many recipes passed on to us by Paola Boni,
our cook in Fiesole—the two vegetables are grated and combined
with a rich tuna-flavored mayonnaise. The vegetables and the
dressing can be prepared ahead of time but it is best to mix them
within an hour of serving.   SERVES 6

2 cups grated carrots

2 cups grated celery root

Juice of 1 lemon

One 3½-ounce can Italian tuna
    fish, packed in oil, drained

1 cup Mayonnaise (see recipe)

3 anchovy fillets, packed in oil,
    drained and mashed with a
    fork

1 tablespoon chopped capers

1 small head curly endive

Combine the grated vegetables in a mixing bowl with the lemon juice. Keep chilled until ready to use.

Combine the tuna fish with the mayonnaise, and blend until smooth in a blender or food processor. Add the anchovy fillets and capers and mix thoroughly. Chill until ready to use.

When ready to serve, combine the vegetables with the dressing and serve on curly endive leaves on individual dishes or in a serving bowl garnished with curly endive leaves.

Cooked Appetizers and Salads

SHALADA DEL KHOBZ YABESS   Morocco
Stale Bread Salad

We were in Asilah, a small fishing village on Morocco's Atlantic coast, waiting in the street for friends to join us. We heard the sound of a flute from an adjacent road and peeked around the corner to find a large old man, barefoot, dressed in a dark brown, coarsely woven djellaba, a burlap sack in one hand, a small wooden flute in the other. He shouted some words we didn't understand, played a melody on his wooden flute, and shouted again. He rang a doorbell and waited. Our friends arrived and we asked what was going on. This man, it turns out, collects stale bread from relatively prosperous households and sells it to those less well off, who cannot afford fresh bread. We figured there had to be some good, simple recipes for stale bread and, after much cajoling, we finally persuaded Fatima, our friend's cook, who was reluctant to serve us food of the poor, to prepare a dish using stale bread. She came up with this salad, spruced up for our consumption, but nonetheless delicious.   SERVES 6

2 *tablespoons* Harissa *(see recipe)*
2 *tablespoons lemon juice*
4 *tablespoons olive oil*
¼ *cup water*
Salt to taste
6 *slices whole-wheat bread, stale or dried in the oven, cut into slices ½ inch thick*

3 *hard-boiled eggs, peeled and sliced*
24 *black Italian, Moroccan, or Niçoise olives, pitted*
1 *cup tuna fish, packed in oil, drained*

Combine the *harissa,* lemon juice, oil, water, and salt in a mixing bowl, add the bread, and soak until the bread is soft. Add more water if necessary.

Heat the oven to 350°F. Place the bread on a cookie sheet and bake for 10 minutes. Remove and transfer to a serving platter. Dress the bread slices with the eggs, olives, and tuna, and serve warm.

TOURTE DE BLETTES   *France*
Swiss Chard Pie

Every morning a fresh, still-warm Swiss chard pie decorated the window of the bakery we frequented in Antibes, and almost every morning we bought a slice and munched it as we walked to the market. We could also have bought it at the market and in every other bakery and pastry shop in town, or, for that matter, in any town along the coast. We sometimes wondered how so few people could consume so many pies but the answer was obvious—they make excellent snacks, perfect street food, and great appetizers.

The pie can also be served as the main course for a light luncheon. In France, a modified puff pastry is used, but we prefer a simple short dough.   SERVES 6 TO 8

Pâte Brisée *(see recipe)* made
   with:
   3 cups unbleached all-purpose
     flour
   Pinch of salt
   ½ pound chilled unsalted
     butter
   2 extra-large eggs
   1½ tablespoons lemon juice
   1¾ pounds Swiss chard, well
     washed, stalks removed
2 tablespoons butter
2 garlic cloves, chopped

Béchamel *(see recipe)* made
   with:
   1 cup milk
   2 tablespoons butter
   2 tablespoons flour
   3 tablespoons freshly grated
     Parmesan
   Salt and freshly ground pepper
     to taste
   2 extra-large eggs, beaten
     separately

Make the *pâte brisée* and place in the refrigerator to rest for 1 hour.

In the meantime, bring ½ cup of water to a boil in a large saucepan, add the chard, and simmer, covered, until tender, about 20 minutes. When the chard is cooked, drain, and squeeze out as much water as possible. To facilitate this, place the chard in a colander and press with a wooden spoon. Transfer to a cutting board, chop roughly, and set aside.

Heat the butter in a skillet, add the garlic, and sauté over medium heat for 1 minute. Add the chard and continue cooking, stirring constantly, for a few minutes, until the ingredients are thoroughly combined and the chard dry. Remove from the heat, transfer to a mixing bowl, and set aside.

Make the béchamel sauce, remove from the heat, and when cooled slightly, add one of the eggs. Blend the sauce into the chard, combine, and set aside.

Preheat the oven to 375°F. and butter well a 10-inch flan pan.

Divide the dough into 2 parts, one slightly larger than the other. Leave the smaller piece in the refrigerator. Roll out the larger piece ⅛ inch thick. Line the bottom and sides of the pan snugly with the dough, allowing excess to drape over the edge of the pan. Spread the chard and béchamel mixture evenly over the surface of the dough and set aside.

Roll out the remaining dough ⅛ inch thick and place over the pan. Trim off excess pastry and join the top to the sides well, using water as a sealer and pinching the dough with your fingers. Press firmly all around the edge with the tines of a fork.

Lightly whisk the remaining egg, brush on top, and bake 40 to 45 minutes, until the crust is crisp and golden. Remove from the oven and allow to cool at least 15 minutes before eating. Serve warm or at room temperature.

CROSTINI AI FUNGHI PORCINI *Italy*
Wild Mushrooms on Toast

These are usually made with fresh porcini but are almost as good made with reconstituted dried ones. If you are fortunate enough to obtain fresh porcini *(Boletus edilus),* by all means use them.

SERVES 6

2 ounces dried porcini mushrooms, or ½ pound fresh porcini mushrooms, chopped	1 tablespoon plus 1 teaspoon lemon juice
1 tablespoon olive oil	Salt and freshly ground pepper to taste
1 garlic clove, peeled and crushed	1 tablespoon whipping cream
1 egg yolk	Six 4-inch-square slices Italian bread, toasted

Soak the dried mushrooms for 30 minutes in 2 cups of warm water. Remove the mushrooms carefully from the soaking liquid, taking care not to stir up the grit and sand deposited at the bottom of the container. Chop finely and set aside. You should have about ¾ cup of mushrooms. Strain ¾ cup of the soaking liquid through a wad of cotton placed in the neck of a funnel. Reserve the liquid.

Heat the oil in a skillet, add the mushrooms and garlic, and sauté over medium-high heat for 2 minutes. Add the ¾ cup of soaking liquid, cover, and simmer over low heat for 15 minutes. Remove the cover and cook over medium heat for 5 minutes, stirring frequently, until the liquid evaporates. If using fresh mushrooms, sauté them with the garlic and proceed with the recipe.

Combine the egg yolk and lemon juice in a small mixing bowl, then blend into the mushrooms. Return to the heat to warm through, season with salt and pepper, add cream, and stir until warm. Remove from heat. Let cool slightly, spread on the bread slices, and serve.

PEPERONI ARROSTITI ALLA RUSTICA   *Italy*
Roasted Peppers on Toast

This recipe is an adaptation of a Romagnolo peasant dish. It's perfect for buffets.   SERVES 6

3 large yellow or red bell peppers,
   peeled (p. 13)
2 garlic cloves, peeled
3 anchovies, packed in oil,
   drained
4 tablespoons olive oil

6 slices Italian bread or
   whole-wheat toast,
   approximately 4 inches
   square
2 tablespoons chopped fresh
   parsley or basil
Abundant freshly ground pepper

Halve the peppers, discard seeds and cores, and set aside. When heating the peppers to facilitate peeling, a liquid is produced; try to reserve as much of this liquid as possible. Set aside.

Grind the garlic in a mortar, then add the anchovies and 2 tablespoons olive oil and grind until a smooth paste is obtained. Blend in the reserved pepper liquid. Spread this mixture over the toasted bread and place on a serving platter. Put ½ pepper on each bread slice, sprinkle with the remaining oil and parsley or basil, grind pepper over the top, and serve at room temperature.

CIBOULES À LA TOMATE   *France*
Scallion Salad with Tomatoes and Raisins

Since good-quality scallions are available all year round and canned tomatoes work as well as fresh ones, we often serve this salad in winter. Its marvelous sweet and spicy flavor can brighten the dullest day. It is best made a day ahead.   SERVES 4 TO 6

2 cups drained canned Italian plum tomatoes, or 2 cups peeled, seeded, and chopped fresh, ripe tomatoes
1 small dried hot pepper, crushed, or ¼ teaspoon cayenne pepper
4 tablespoons white wine vinegar

½ cup white raisins, soaked in warm water to cover for 15 minutes, drained
3 bunches scallions
Salt and freshly ground pepper to taste
Lettuce leaves for garnish

Place tomatoes in a skillet with the hot pepper or cayenne pepper and cook over medium heat, stirring frequently, until the sauce thickens, about 15 minutes. Blend the vinegar and raisins into tomatoes while still hot and set aside. Keep warm.

Wash and trim the scallions, retaining some of the green, cut into 2-inch segments, then into thin slivers. Place in a mixing bowl, add the tomato sauce, and combine well. Season with salt and pepper and refrigerate for at least 2 hours before serving. Even better, leave in the refrigerator overnight. Serve at room temperature on lettuce leaves.

YOGURTLU KABAK   *Turkey*
Zucchini-Yogurt Salad

This wonderfully refreshing salad is made with zucchini, yogurt, and garlic and is perfect on a hot summer's day. It can be made a day ahead.   SERVES 4 TO 6

6 medium zucchini

2 tablespoons olive oil

1 cup yogurt

2 garlic cloves, minced

½ teaspoon dried mint, or 2
    teaspoons finely chopped
    fresh mint

1 tablespoon lemon juice

Salt to taste

Lettuce leaves for garnish

Cut the zucchini into julienne strips and set aside. Heat 1 tablespoon of olive oil in a skillet, add the zucchini, and simmer over low heat for 10 to 15 minutes, until most of the water given off by the zucchini evaporates. Remove from the heat and cool.

Combine the remaining ingredients, including the remaining tablespoon of olive oil. Add the zucchini, mix well, and chill for at least 2 hours. Serve on lettuce leaves.

SHALADA DEL FELFLA MEKLIA BE SALSA   Morocco D'MATICHA
Salad of Fresh Peppers and Tomatoes

SERVES 4 TO 6

½ cup light seed oil for frying

1 pound Italian frying peppers,
    cut in half, stems and seeds
    removed

1 pound firm tomatoes, cut into
    ½-inch slices, seeds removed

2 tablespoons peanut oil

Juice of 1 lemon

2 tablespoons chopped fresh
    parsley or coriander leaves

1 teaspoon ground cumin

Heat the light seed oil in a skillet and when hot add the peppers, a few at a time, and fry on both sides until tender, about 5 minutes. Drain thoroughly on paper towels.

Fry the tomatoes in the same oil until tender, about 2 minutes, then drain on paper towels.

When cooled, peel the peppers and tomatoes, and place them in an alternating overlapping pattern on an attractive serving dish. Combine the remaining ingredients and pour over the peppers and tomatoes. Refrigerate for at least 1 hour before serving.

SHALADA D'MATICHA AU FELFLA   *Morocco*
Pepper Salad with Tomato Sauce and Fresh Coriander

This wonderful salad can be made a day ahead of time.

SERVES 6

3 pounds fresh tomatoes, peeled, seeded, and chopped
3 garlic cloves, minced
Rind of ½ preserved lemon (p. 15), cut into small squares (optional)
2 hot red peppers, finely chopped

4 green bell peppers, peeled (p. 13), seeded, and cut into 1-inch squares
3 tablespoons chopped fresh parsley
2 tablespoons olive oil
1 tablespoon finely chopped fresh coriander leaves
Lettuce leaves for garnish

Combine the tomatoes with the garlic in a saucepan and simmer until a thick paste is formed, about 20 minutes. Add the preserved lemon rind and hot peppers and simmer another 5 minutes. Stir in the green peppers, parsley, and olive oil and simmer for 5 minutes, stirring occasionally. The peppers should be firm.

Remove from the heat and transfer to a mixing bowl. When cooled, blend in the coriander leaves and chill for at least 2 hours. Serve cold on lettuce leaves.

SHALADA DEL REMOLACHA   *Morocco*
Beet Salad with Orange Blossom Water

This is one of many glorious salads that Fatima made for us during our most recent visit to Morocco. She uses more orange blossom water than we recommend. It's a matter of taste, of course, but a little seems to go a long way. Serve along with other salads as an appetizer.

SERVES 6

1 pound beets, scrubbed, leaves   ½ teaspoon ground cumin
    removed (leave 1-inch stalks)   Pinch of cinnamon
½ teaspoon sweet paprika   Juice of 1 lemon
1 tablespoon sugar   4 scallions, chopped
1 teaspoon orange blossom water   Salt to taste

Place the beets in a saucepan with 1 quart of water, bring to boil and simmer, covered, until tender, about 1 hour. The beets are cooked when they peel easily. Remove the beets from the water and set aside. Reserve 1 cup of cooking liquid.

While the beets cool, combine the remaining ingredients in a mixing bowl and add the reserved cooking liquid. Peel the beets, slice thinly, place in an attractive bowl, and pour the marinade over the beets. Combine thoroughly and allow to marinate in the refrigerator for at least 1 hour. Serve with the marinade in small bowls.

SALATA BADZARIA SKORDALIA   *Greece*
Beet Salad with Garlic Sauce

SERVES 4

1 pound beets, washed, leaves   2 tablespoons wine vinegar
    removed (leave 1-inch   Pinch of sugar
    stalks)   ½ small onion, thinly sliced
3 tablespoons Greek olive oil   1 cup Skordalia (see recipe)

Place the beets in a saucepan, cover with water, bring to a boil, lower heat, and simmer, covered, until the beets are tender, about 1 hour. Drain, reserving 2 tablespoons of the cooking liquid, and, when cool enough to handle, peel, slice thinly, place in an attractive serving bowl, and set aside.

Combine the oil, vinegar, the reserved cooking liquid, and the sugar. Pour over the beets, add the onion, and mix well. Chill for an hour. Serve with *skordalia*.

KOKE AU LICHIN
Morocco
Artichoke Hearts with Oranges

An improbable but delicious combination, this salad can, in a pinch, even be made with canned artichoke hearts. It's a great winter salad when all the ingredients are at their best. The recipe is adapted from Irene and Lucienne Karsenty's *Cuisine Pied-Noir.* The salad can be made a day in advance. **SERVES 4**

12 fresh, small artichokes, or one 14-ounce can artichoke hearts, drained and cut in half
Juice of 2 lemons
2 tablespoons olive oil
5 garlic cloves, crushed
Pinch of saffron, soaked in 3 tablespoons water
1 teaspoon sugar

Salt and freshly ground pepper to taste
¼ teaspoon cayenne pepper
1 lemon, peeled, white membrane removed
2 oranges, peeled, white membrane removed
1 tablespoon thinly sliced orange rind

If using fresh artichokes, remove all but the most tender inner leaves, trim the bottom to expose the tender white flesh, remove and discard the choke, if any, and place in a mixing bowl with the juice of 1 lemon and water to cover until ready to use.

Heat the oil in a low-sided saucepan, enamel or stainless steel, add the garlic, and sauté over medium heat for 1 minute. Add the juice of the second lemon, saffron with water, sugar, salt and pepper, and cayenne pepper. Add the artichoke hearts and 1 cup water, if using fresh artichokes, ¼ cup for canned. If using fresh, partly cover the pan and simmer, stirring occasionally, for about 20 minutes, until the artichokes are cooked but still firm. If using canned artichokes, cook, stirring gently, for 2 to 3 minutes to heat through.

Cut the lemon and oranges into thin disks, then quarter each disk. Add to the artichokes together with the orange rind, and simmer, stirring once or twice, for 5 minutes. Transfer to a serving platter, allow to cool, and serve at room temperature.

ALCACHOFAS EN ESCABECHE   *Spain*
Fried Artichokes Marinated in Garlic Vinaigrette

Escabeche comes from the Arabic word *cisbech,* which means acid food. The Spanish marinate both vegetables and fish in this fragrant variation of vinaigrette. We find the artichokes achieve a wonderful consistency in this pungent salad.   SERVES 4

12 medium artichokes
Juice of 1 lemon
½ cup dry white wine
4 tablespoons olive oil
½ cup flour
4 tablespoons white wine vinegar

2 to 4 garlic cloves, crushed in a
  mortar
Salt and freshly ground pepper to
  taste
⅛ teaspoon cayenne pepper
2 tablespoons minced fresh parsley

Remove all but the most tender inner leaves of the artichokes, quarter, remove the chokes, and place in a bowl with the lemon juice and water to cover until ready to cook.

Drain the artichokes, place in an enamel or stainless steel saucepan with 1 cup of water and ½ cup of wine, bring to a boil, lower the heat, and simmer, covered, until barely tender, about 15 minutes. Drain, pat dry with paper towels, and set aside.

Heat the oil in a skillet, dredge the artichokes very lightly with flour, place in the skillet, and fry until browned on all sides. Remove from the heat and place in a serving bowl. Pour any remaining cooking oil over the artichokes.

Combine the remaining ingredients except for the parsley, mix well, then spread over the artichokes. Add the parsley, blend thoroughly, and chill for a couple of hours before serving.

VARIATION Use 2 medium eggplants instead of artichokes. Peel, slice ⅜ inch thick, and sprinkle salt over eggplant. Let sit for 30 minutes. Rinse, pat dry, and dredge in flour. Fry in olive oil on both sides and proceed as above.

KHIZZO METAIEB BEL KAMOUN　　　*Morocco*
Cooked Carrots Marinated in Cumin and Vinegar

SERVES 4 TO 6

6 medium carrots, peeled, cut in
　　quarters lengthwise, then cut
　　into 2-inch segments
2 garlic cloves, roughly chopped
1 teaspoon sweet paprika
¼ teaspoon cayenne pepper

2 tablespoons peanut oil
2 tablespoons vinegar
½ teaspoon ground cumin
1 tablespoon chopped fresh
　　parsley

Place the carrots in a saucepan with 1 cup of water, garlic, paprika, cayenne pepper, and oil. Cook, covered, over medium heat for about 10 minutes, until the carrots are cooked but still firm. Uncover and continue to simmer until about ½ cup of liquid remains. Remove from the heat and set aside.

Combine the vinegar, cumin, and parsley in a small mixing bowl. Transfer the carrots and the cooking liquid to a small serving bowl, add the vinegar sauce, toss, then marinate at least 2 hours at room temperature before serving.

SHALADA DE DENJALE　　　*Morocco*
Eggplant Salad

Every Mediterranean country has its own eggplant salad, much as every region in Texas has its special chili recipe. We decided to include two, Melitzanes Salata from Greece and Shalada de Denjale from Morocco. The Moroccan variation is a spicy blend of eggplant, parsley, coriander leaves, turmeric, cumin, cayenne pepper, and paprika. Serve on lettuce leaves with hearty French or Moroccan bread. The salad can be made a day in advance and kept in the refrigerator.　　　SERVES 6

2 pounds eggplant, peeled if
    large, cut into large cubes
3 tablespoons olive oil
1 medium ripe tomato, peeled,
    seeded, and chopped
2 tablespoons tomato paste
4 garlic cloves, chopped
3 tablespoons chopped fresh
    parsley

3 tablespoons chopped fresh
    coriander leaves
1 teaspoon ground turmeric
½ teaspoon ground cumin
¼ teaspoon cayenne pepper
½ teaspoon sweet paprika
Salt to taste
Lettuce leaves for garnish

Steam the eggplant for 10 minutes, until tender. When cool enough to handle, squeeze the eggplant gently to remove bitter juice and set aside.

Heat the oil in a skillet, add the remaining ingredients, and sauté over medium heat, stirring frequently, for 5 minutes. Mash the eggplant with the tines of a fork or pound in a mortar—do not purée in a blender or food processor—then add to the skillet. Cook another 10 to 15 minutes, until most of the liquid evaporates. Set aside in a cool place for at least 2 hours before serving. Serve at room temperature on lettuce leaves.

VARIATION Cut the eggplant lengthwise in slices about ½ inch thick. Broil or fry in ½ cup of seed oil, then place them, slightly overlapping, in a large bowl. Make a marinade with the above ingredients, omitting the tomato, adding ¼ cup lemon juice and ½ cup olive oil. Pour over the eggplant slices and let sit for at least 2 hours.

MELITZÁNES SALATA   *Greece*
Eggplant Salad

This Greek version of eggplant salad, made with vinegar and cooked onions, is delicately flavored and particularly satisfying. It can also be made a day in advance and kept in the refrigerator.

SERVES 4

1 pound eggplant
2 tablespoons olive oil plus ¼
    cup
½ cup finely chopped onion
1 tablespoon vinegar
Pinch of oregano
1 garlic clove, finely chopped
1 tablespoon chopped fresh
    parsley

1 canned Italian plum tomato,
    drained
Salt and freshly ground pepper to
    taste
Lettuce, Greek olives, and sliced
    tomatoes for garnish

Place the whole eggplant under a hot broiler or over hot coals and cook, turning occasionally, until very tender, about 15 to 20 minutes. Remove and set aside until cool enough to handle.

Heat the 2 tablespoons of oil in a saucepan, add the onion, and cook over low heat, stirring frequently, until the onion is tender and transparent, about 5 minutes. It should not brown.

When the eggplant has cooled sufficiently, peel, squeeze out bitter juice, and remove as many of the seeds as possible. Place in a blender or food processor, add the onion, vinegar, oregano, garlic, parsley, tomato, salt, and pepper and process until smooth. Then, with the machine running, add the remaining oil and continue processing until the purée is light and smooth.

Serve chilled on a bed of lettuce garnished with olives and tomato slices.

VARIATIONS In Lebanon, the purée is made without onion, tomato, and oregano, lemon juice is substituted for vinegar, and 1 or 2 tablespoons of tahini are added to the purée.

In Provence, the purée is made with about 2 tablespoons finely chopped raw onion, 2 tablespoons chopped fresh parsley, juice of ½ lemon, 1 finely chopped garlic clove, and 4 tablespoons olive oil, all combined with the cooked eggplant. It is often served in the skin of a hollowed-out eggplant garnished with raw carrots and celery.

PURÉ DE VERDURAS   *Spain*
Purée of Roasted Vegetables

Eggplants, peppers, tomatoes, and onions are first baked, then combined with oil and vinegar in a rich, subtly flavored purée. It can be served as a dip with bread or crackers or eaten as a salad or appetizer. The dish can be prepared a day in advance; in fact, it improves with a little aging.   SERVES 6

1 pound eggplant
1 pound red and green bell
   peppers
1 pound ripe tomatoes
1 pound onions, preferably
   Spanish, peeled
4 large garlic cloves, unpeeled
½ pound new potatoes

6 tablespoons olive oil
4 tablespoons vinegar
¼ teaspoon cayenne pepper
Salt and freshly ground pepper to
   taste
¼ cup thin cucumber slices
2 tablespoons chopped fresh
   parsley or basil

· Preheat oven to 375°F.

Prick the eggplant with the tines of a fork.

Lightly oil a large baking pan, add the vegetables, and bake until tender. The vegetables cook at different speeds and should be removed when done. The tomatoes will take about 20 minutes; the peppers and garlic cloves about 30 minutes; the onions, potatoes, and eggplant about 50 minutes. When cool enough to handle, peel and seed the tomatoes, and squeeze out excess liquid. Peel the peppers, garlic cloves, potatoes, and eggplant. Cut the vegetables into 1- or 2-inch cubes, place them in the work bowl of a blender or food processor, add the oil, vinegar, cayenne pepper, and salt and pepper to taste, and process until smooth.

Place in a serving bowl, garnish with the cucumber slices, chopped parsley or basil, and chill for at least an hour before serving. You can also serve the purée on lettuce leaves on individual plates, with cucumber slices on the side.

PATATE CON CIPOLLE AGRO-DOLCE *Italy*
Potatoes with Onions in Sweet and Sour Sauce

In this delightful Sicilian salad, the potatoes and onions are cooked together with olives and capers, then dressed with a sweet-sour sauce. It takes no time to prepare and will keep for a few days in the refrigerator without loss of flavor.   SERVES 4

3 tablespoons olive oil
1 medium onion, thinly sliced
8 small new potatoes (about 1
    pound), peeled, cut into
    ½-inch cubes
2 tablespoons water

2 tablespoons capers
8 to 10 black or green Italian
    olives, rinsed well if salty,
    pitted, and cut into quarters
1½ tablespoons sugar
3 tablespoons red wine vinegar

Heat the oil in a saucepan, add the onion, and sauté for a few minutes. Add the potatoes and cook, stirring constantly, for 2 minutes to mix well and coat the potatoes with the oil. Add water, capers, and olives. Cover and cook, stirring occasionally, until the potatoes are cooked but firm, about 5 minutes. Remove the cover, raise heat to evaporate any water, and keep warm.

Dissolve the sugar in the vinegar, pour over the potatoes, blend thoroughly, then set aside to cool for at least 1 hour before serving.

RINRAN *Spain*
Potatoes with Puréed Pepper Dressing

Potatoes seasoned with a sauce of puréed peppers in this Andalusian dish make a novel and exceptionally good salad. If possible, use small new potatoes.   SERVES 4

1 pound new potatoes
1 pound red bell peppers, peeled
(p. 13), cored, seeded, and
cut into quarters
¼ teaspoon cayenne pepper
Pinch of sugar
4 anchovy fillets, packed in oil,
drained and minced

3 tablespoons olive oil
1 tablespoon wine vinegar
12 black olives, pitted, rinsed and
cut into quarters
Salt and freshly ground pepper to
taste
1 hard-boiled egg, sliced for
garnishing

Place the potatoes, unpeeled, in a saucepan, cover with water, bring to a boil, lower heat, and simmer, covered, until tender, about 20 minutes. When cooked, drain; when cool enough to handle, peel, and cut into 1-inch cubes. If small, leave whole or cut in half. Set aside.

Place the peppers, the cayenne pepper, sugar, and anchovy fillets in the work bowl of a food processor or blender, and process until puréed. With the machine running, add the oil and vinegar. Transfer to a mixing bowl, add the olives, and adjust for salt and pepper.

Distribute the purée on a serving platter or on individual dishes. Place the potatoes on top of the purée, garnish with slices of hard-boiled egg, and serve chilled.

POLENTA ALLA GRIGLIA CON FUNGHI   *Italy*
Grilled Polenta with Mushrooms

This traditional country dish from the Veneto can be served either as an appetizer or as a first course. The polenta is often fried but it is lighter and thus more to our taste if broiled. We recommend that you use freshly ground coarse cornmeal. All types of cornmeal will work, but the texture improves if the meal is coarse. Use fresh porcini, shiitake, chanterelles, or oyster mushrooms, if available.

SERVES 4 TO 6

4 cups water
½ teaspoon salt
Freshly ground pepper to taste
1 cup coarse cornmeal
¼ cup olive oil

1 pound mushrooms, washed,
    trimmed, thinly sliced
2 garlic cloves, chopped
1 tablespoon chopped fresh
    parsley

Place water in a large, heavy saucepan, add salt and pepper, bring to a boil, then add the cornmeal slowly in a thin stream, stirring constantly with a wooden spoon. Reduce heat to low and cook, stirring frequently, for 30 minutes. The polenta should be dense enough to support the wooden spoon upright when cooked.

Wet the surface of a large cutting board or marble slab, then spread the polenta evenly over the surface using a wet spatula or the blade of a large kitchen knife. The polenta should be approximately ½ inch thick. Set aside to cool.

While the polenta cools, heat the oil in a skillet, add the mushrooms and garlic, and sauté over high heat until wilted. Set aside and keep warm.

Cut the polenta into 2-inch-square pieces, place them on a lightly oiled cookie sheet, and broil on both sides until golden. Place the polenta squares on a serving dish, cover with the mushrooms, sprinkle with parsley, and serve warm.

VARIATION Instead of mushrooms, sauté 2 thinly sliced onions until golden and serve on top of the polenta.

SOCCA   *France*
Chick-pea Flour Crêpe

Socca, a flat bread made with chick-pea flour, is sold all over the old town of Nice, in the markets, on street corners, at roadside fast-food stands. It's oily, peppery, and delicious. There's real culinary lore attached to *socca.* For example, those in the know maintain that it should be cooked in special copper pans, almost impossible to find now, even in Nice, and it should be baked in a wood-fired oven. Fortunately for those of us who lack the pan and the oven, it is possible to turn out a very respectable *socca* with a normal pizza pan and an ordinary oven. Always serve the *socca* piping hot, preferably wrapped in a napkin or absorbent paper. We use it as a snack or serve it with cocktails before a meal.

SERVES 6

1¼ *cups chick-pea flour*   *Salt to taste*
1¼ *cups water*   *Abundant freshly ground pepper*
2 *tablespoons olive oil*

Place the chick-pea flour in a mixing bowl, add the water, a little at a time, beating with a wire whisk as the water is added. Add the olive oil and salt and pepper, combine well, and set aside for 30 or 40 minutes. You can also combine the ingredients using a food processor. Place the metal blade in the work bowl, add the flour, then, with the machine running, add first the water, then the oil, salt, and pepper. Set aside to rest for 30 to 40 minutes.

Meanwhile, preheat the oven to 425°F. and oil very well a 12-inch pizza pan or the equivalent.

When ready, add the chick-pea batter to the pan and bake until browned, about 10 minutes. The *socca* should be quite thin, no more than ⅛ inch thick. When half cooked, brush olive oil that accumulates on the side of the *socca* over the top and continue cooking until done. Remove, grind some more fresh pepper over the *socca,* and serve immediately.

VARIATIONS A very similar dish is prepared in Tangier, popularly known as *caliente,* with an egg added to the batter. As in Nice, *caliente* is street food, sold primarily in marketplaces. Our guess is that the name *caliente* is of Spanish origin—the uncommon Arabic name is *hummus mthoun.*

Along the Tuscan and Ligurian coast in Italy, the identical dish is called *cecina* and is often served as stuffing in a *schiacciata,* a flat bread similar to pizza but dressed with coarse salt and, occasionally, rosemary.

PANELLE   *Italy*
Fried Chick-pea Flour Patties

This dish comes from Palermo but clones can be found along the Ligurian coast *(panissa)* and in Provence *(panisse)*. It's not unlikely that the Romans had a similar dish. Fried polenta, in which corn-meal instead of chick-pea flour is used, is a more recent variation on this very ancient theme. Like all such fare, it was originally poor people's food—inexpensive, nourishing, and filling. In Italy and France it is eaten as a snack; we serve it with drinks before a meal.

SERVES 6

1½ *cups chick-pea flour*
3 *cups water*
Salt to taste

½ *cup light seed oil for deep*
frying

Combine the flour with the water and salt in a mixing bowl, beating with a wire whisk to eliminate lumps. Place in a heavy saucepan and cook over low heat, stirring constantly with a wooden spoon, until the mixture begins to pull away from the sides of the pan, about 5 to 7 minutes. Continue to stir off the heat for a minute to obtain a smooth, homogeneous mixture. Set aside.

Wet a marble or wooden work surface and spread the batter over the surface, about ⅛ inch thick. To facilitate this operation, wet the back of a spatula or the blade of a large knife and use it to spread the mixture. Allow to cool.

When ready to serve, heat the oil in a skillet suitable for deep frying. Cut the dough into circles or squares roughly 3 inches across, and fry until golden on both sides. Drain on paper towels, sprinkle with salt, and keep warm until all are cooked. Serve hot.

CECI CON SALSA D'ACCIUGHE   *Italy*
Chick-pea Salad in Anchovy Sauce

SERVES 4

¾ cup dried chick-peas
1 tablespoon flour
¼ cup olive oil
5 anchovy fillets, packed in oil,
*   drained*

3 tablespoons chopped fresh
*   parsley*
1 teaspoon black peppercorns,
*   crushed in a mortar*
1 small red onion, thinly sliced

Soak the chick-peas in 4 cups of water with 1 tablespoon flour for 8 hours or overnight. When ready, drain, rinse, and cook until tender, 30 minutes in a pressure cooker, 1½ hours otherwise. As an alternative, use 1½ cups canned chick-peas.

Heat the olive oil in a skillet over low heat, add the anchovy fillets, and cook, mixing constantly, until the anchovies dissolve. Remove from the heat, add the parsley and pepper, and combine thoroughly.

Place the chick-peas in a serving bowl, add the oil mixture, the onion, and blend well. Allow to marinate 2 hours. Serve chilled or at room temperature.

ENSALADA DE LENTIJAS   *Spain*
Lentil Salad with Herb Vinaigrette

Lentils eaten cold with a vinaigrette dressing are popular throughout the Mediterranean. We include a Spanish version of this classic salad—the combination of cooked lentils and blanched vegetables seems to bring out the best of both.   SERVES 6

1 cup dried lentils

3 medium carrots

1 small onion, cut in half

1 bay leaf

2 medium turnips

1 large leek, including some green

1 tablespoon chopped fresh basil

2 tablespoons chopped fresh parsley

1 tablespoon chopped fresh chives

4 tablespoons olive oil

2 tablespoons red wine vinegar

1½ teaspoons Dijon mustard

Pinch of sweet paprika

Salt and freshly ground pepper to taste

Lentils need not be soaked before cooking, especially if small and tender, although soaking for a few hours speeds up cooking.

Place lentils in a saucepan with 4 cups of water, add 1 carrot, cut in 4 pieces, the onion, and bay leaf, bring to a boil, lower heat and simmer until the lentils are cooked but still firm—about 20 minutes if previously soaked, about 30 minutes if not. Remove and discard the vegetables and bay leaf, drain the lentils (reserving the liquid for soup, if desired), transfer the lentils to a mixing bowl, and set aside.

Peel and julienne the remaining carrots and the turnips. Clean the leek, discard tough outer parts, and julienne. Blanch each of the vegetables separately for approximately 2 minutes, until just tender. Set aside.

Combine the herbs and set aside.

Make a vinaigrette with remaining ingredients. Combine three-quarters of the dressing with the lentils, mix well, and place on an attractive serving plate. Decorate the lentils with the julienned vegetables, sprinkle the remaining dressing over them. Chill in the refrigerator for a few hours but remove at least 30 minutes prior to serving.

FAVA SALATA ME YIAOURTI   *Greece*
Fava Bean Salad with Yogurt

This salad, a blend of beans, yogurt, garlic, and lemon juice, is usually made with fresh fava beans, but works almost as well with baby lima beans, a distinct advantage since the latter are much more accessible in North America than the former. It will keep for a few days in the refrigerator but beware—the garlic gains strength over time.　　　　　　　　　　　　　　　　　　SERVES 4

1 pound shelled fresh or frozen
　　tender fava beans or baby
　　lima beans
1 piece English (seedless)
　　cucumber, about 3 inches
　　long
1 garlic clove, minced

2 tablespoons olive oil
Juice of 1 lemon
1 tablespoon lemon zest
1 teaspoon chopped fresh mint, or
　　½ teaspoon dried mint
½ cup yogurt
Salt to taste

Cook the lima or fava beans in boiling salted water until tender, about 5 minutes for frozen beans, 20 minutes (depending on size) for fresh. Drain and set aside.

Meanwhile, peel the cucumber, cut in half lengthwise, sprinkle with salt, and set aside to drain for 20 minutes. When ready, rinse, pat dry, and dice into cubes roughly the size of the beans.

In a mixing bowl, combine the remaining ingredients. Add the beans, the cucumber, and blend thoroughly. Chill for at least 1 hour before serving.

SHALADA DEL FOULE BE ZITOUN　　　*Morocco*
Fava Bean Salad with Olives

If you are unable to find fresh, tender fava beans, use fresh or frozen baby lima beans. The mixture of preserved lemons and fresh coriander leaves gives this salad a unique and exciting flavor.

SERVES 4

2 cups shelled, tender, fresh or
    frozen fava beans or baby
    lima beans
2 tablespoons olive oil
1 garlic clove, crushed
12 black olives, preferably
    Moroccan, rinsed well if
    salty and pitted

1 tablespoon sweet paprika
¼ cup chopped fresh coriander
    leaves
Rind of ¼ preserved lemon (p.
    15), rinsed, thinly sliced
Salt to taste
Juice of ½ lemon

Combine the lima or fava beans with the oil, the garlic, and 1 cup of water in a saucepan. Cook until tender, about 5 minutes for frozen beans, 20 minutes for fresh. Add water as necessary as the beans cook. When done, about ¼ cup liquid should remain. Add the olives, paprika, coriander leaves, and lemon rind. Add salt if desired, but remember that the lemon rind and olives are both salty. Simmer together for 5 minutes. Remove from the heat, blend in the lemon juice, and let cool. Serve at room temperature.

Fish and Seafood
Appetizers and Salads

INSALATA DI RISO CON TONNO   *Italy*
Rice and Tuna Salad with Basil Vinaigrette

We often serve this salad as the main dish for a summer luncheon or light dinner. In smaller amounts, it makes a delightful appetizer for a more substantial repast. Italian pickled vegetables add zest to this salad. They are usually available in Italian food shops and go under the name *giardiniera.* If unavailable, dill pickles will make an acceptable substitute.   SERVES 8 TO 10

FOR THE SALAD:

1½ cups Italian or Carolina
    long-grain rice
Two 7-ounce cans Italian tuna,
    packed in oil, drained
1 cup thinly sliced carrots
1 cup sliced celery
2 medium firm tomatoes, cubed

FOR THE DRESSING:

5 anchovy fillets, packed in oil,
    drained, roughly chopped
    (optional)
½ cup olive oil
¼ cup wine vinegar

3 tablespoons capers
1 cup Italian pickled vegetables
    or dill pickles, cut into small
    pieces
½ cup black Italian olives, rinsed
    well if salty, pitted, cut in
    half

Salt to taste
¼ teaspoon freshly ground pepper
2 tablespoons chopped fresh basil
2 tablespoons chopped fresh
    parsley

Bring 4 cups salted water to a boil, add the rice, and cook until al dente. Drain, rinse with cold water, and set aside.

Combine the remaining salad ingredients in a large salad bowl. Blend the dressing ingredients in a small mixing bowl and pour over the rice. Add the rice to the salad bowl and combine thoroughly. Serve cool or at room temperature.

LOTTE EN BROCHETTE   *France*
Monkfish Grilled on Skewers

Monkfish, enormously popular along the shores of the Mediterranean and slowly gaining favor in North America, is a veritable gargoyle of the deep, but its taste is spectacular when it is cooked properly. Its firm, succulent flesh has a delicate flavor reminiscent of lobster. Marinated, then roasted over hot coals or grilled in a broiler, and served on a bed of salad lightly dressed with a mustard vinaigrette is one of the easiest and most satisfying ways to prepare it. Serve either as a substantial appetizer or a light main dish.

SERVES 4

FOR THE MARINADE:

3 tablespoons olive oil

1 tablespoon white wine vinegar

2 bay leaves

1 teaspoon each minced fresh thyme, parsley, and chervil, or 3 teaspoons minced fresh parsley

Salt and freshly ground pepper to taste

1 pound monkfish, cut into 1-inch cubes

8 pieces red or green bell pepper, cut into 1½-inch squares

4 cups tightly packed mesclun *(p. 16)*

FOR THE VINAIGRETTE:

4 tablespoons light olive oil

2 tablespoons lemon juice

½ teaspoon Dijon mustard

Salt and freshly ground pepper to taste

4 lemon wedges for garnish

Combine the ingredients for the marinade in a mixing bowl, add the monkfish pieces, coat with the marinade, and place in the refrigerator for at least 1 hour, turning occasionally.

Remove the pieces of monkfish from the marinade and distribute them evenly on 4 small metal or wooden skewers, placing a piece of pepper at either end. Set aside.

Distribute the *mesclun* attractively on four plates on which the monkfish will be served. Combine the ingredients for the vinaigrette in a small mixing bowl and distribute it evenly over the *mesclun.* Place a lemon wedge on each plate.

Broil the fish in the oven or grill over hot coals until done, about 1½ minutes per side. Monkfish is tender and cooks quickly.

Place a skewer on each plate and serve immediately.

SARDINAS EN ESCABECHE   *Spain*
Broiled Sardines in Spicy Vinaigrette

The Spanish technique of marinating cooked fish in a strong vine-gary sauce, a practice widespread in the cuisine of Latin American countries as well, is probably of Arabic origin. Whatever the source, the results are outstanding. This dish must marinate for a full day to achieve peak flavor—it's the perfect prepare-in-advance appetizer.   SERVES 4

1 pound fresh sardines, heads
    removed and boned, if large
    (p. 16)
4 tablespoons olive oil
5 tablespoons white wine vinegar
2 tablespoons chopped fresh basil
    and/or parsley
Sprig of fresh thyme, or ½
    teaspoon dried thyme

1 bay leaf
1 clove
Peel of ½ orange, finely chopped
¼ teaspoon cayenne pepper
¼ teaspoon sweet paprika
Salt and freshly ground pepper to
    taste
¼ cup thinly sliced onion

Prepare the sardines, drizzle with 2 tablespoons of olive oil, and broil close to the heat until browned on both sides, about 2 minutes per side. Do not overcook. Place on a serving platter and set aside.

Combine the remaining ingredients, except for the onion, in a mixing bowl. Distribute the onion slices over the fish, then add the marinade, cover, and place in the refrigerator for 24 hours. Serve at room temperature.

SARDELES TIYANITES ME SALTSA DOMATA
Fried Sardines in Pungent Tomato Sauce   *Greece*

A Greek variation of *escabeche,* the sardines are first fried, then marinated in a tart tomato sauce.   SERVES 4

1 pound fresh sardines, heads
   removed and boned, if large
   (p. 16)
2 tablespoons flour
¼ to ⅓ cup light seed oil for
   frying
3 tablespoons olive oil
2 garlic cloves, chopped

1¼ cups chopped canned Italian
   plum tomatoes, with juice, or
   1¼ cups peeled, seeded, and
   chopped ripe tomatoes
2 tablespoons wine vinegar
2 tablespoons chopped fresh
   parsley
Salt and freshly ground pepper to
   taste

Prepare the sardines and dredge lightly in flour. Heat the seed oil in a skillet, add the fish a few at a time, and fry until golden on both sides, about 2 minutes per side. Drain on paper towels and set aside.

Heat the olive oil in a saucepan, add the garlic, and sauté until it begins to color, about 2 minutes. Add the tomatoes, vinegar, parsley, and salt and pepper, and continue cooking, stirring frequently, for 10 to 15 minutes, until the sauce just begins to thicken. Remove from the heat.

Place the sardines on a serving platter, dress with the tomato sauce, and allow to marinate in the refrigerator for a few hours before serving. The fish should be served cool or at room temperature, not cold, so remove from the refrigerator about 30 minutes prior to serving.

ACCIUGHE MARINATE   *Italy*
Anchovies in Orange-Lemon Marinade

Although every serious connoisseur of seafood in Italy has his or her favorite marinade for raw anchovies, none that we know of compares to that of Carmelo's restaurant in Rome. The first time we tasted their marinated anchovies, we immediately ordered three more servings. You must use very fresh anchovies, preferably small, and, to achieve full flavor, allow them to marinate at least 36 hours. You should be able to find fresh anchovies in Italian or Portuguese fish stores. Anchovies can be cleaned and filleted the

same way as sardines. The dish is worth whatever trouble it entails
—it's fabulous.   SERVES 4 TO 6

1 pound small, fresh anchovies
   (about 5 inches long),
   cleaned, heads and
   backbones removed, filleted
   (p. 16)
Juice of 1 orange

Juice of 2 lemons
2 tablespoons dry white wine
1 tablespoon peppercorns
¼ teaspoon salt
1 or 2 dried hot peppers, crushed
1 teaspoon orange zest

Place the anchovy fillets in a small bowl. Combine the remaining ingredients and pour over the fish. Marinate, turning occasionally, for 36 hours in the refrigerator. Serve cool with a chilled dry white wine.

TARTARE DE SAUMON AUX QUATRE SAUCES   *France*
Salmon Tartare with Assorted Sauces

On our last trip to France, we got to know Patrick Lucas and Guy Sagmoellen, owners of an excellent, casually elegant little restaurant, La Mirabelle, in Cannes. This was one of their spring specialties, raw minced salmon served with assorted sauces, a wonderful and stylish appetizer. Serve with good French bread.

SERVES 6

1 pound very fresh salmon

1 cup Mayonnaise (see recipe)

3 tablespoons finely chopped fresh
chives

2 tablespoons finely chopped fresh
parsley

2 tablespoons finely chopped fresh
basil

1 tablespoon Dijon mustard

⅓ cup olive oil

2 tablespoons good herbed or
Balsamic vinegar

Salt and freshly ground pepper to
taste

½ cup Crème Fraîche (see
recipe)

½ cup peeled, seeded, and cubed
ripe tomatoes, or ½ cup
drained canned Italian plum
tomatoes

Boston or Bibb lettuce leaves for
garnish

⅓ cup small capers

Using a very sharp knife, chop the salmon finely, place in a bowl, and put in the refrigerator until ready to use.

To make the first sauce, combine ½ cup mayonnaise and the chives in a small bowl and set aside. To make the second, combine the remaining mayonnaise with the parsley and basil and set aside. For the third, mix the mustard, oil, vinegar, salt, and pepper, and set aside. For the fourth, blend the *crème fraîche* with the tomatoes and season with salt and pepper.

When ready to serve, place lettuce leaves and salmon on 6 individual plates. Put the sauces and capers in separate serving bowls and serve with the salmon. Each diner sauces the fish as he or she wishes.

BACALAO PICANTE   *Spain*
Salt Cod with Hot Peppers

In this dish, one we discovered in an unpretentious but excellent restaurant and *tapas* bar in Eljido, a village on the Mediterranean coast near Almería, garlic and hot peppers transform the relatively bland salt cod into a tasty appetizer. Use skinned and deboned salt cod if you can find it.

SERVES 6

1 pound salt cod, preferably
    deboned and skinned
2 tablespoons flour
4 tablespoons olive oil
4 garlic cloves, roughly chopped
2 dried hot peppers, seeded and
    crushed

2 tablespoons chopped fresh
    parsley
Salt and freshly ground pepper to
    taste

Soak the cod in cold water to cover for 24 to 36 hours, changing the water occasionally. If necessary, skin and debone.

Cut the cod into 1½-inch pieces, dredge in the flour, and set
aside. Heat the oil in a skillet, add the cod pieces, and sauté until
tender and golden on all sides, about 5 to 7 minutes. Drain on
paper towels and keep warm.

Add the garlic to the skillet and sauté for 1 minute. Add the
peppers and parsley, heat through, then pour over the cod. Season
with salt and pepper and serve warm.

INSALATA DI CALAMARI   *Italy*
Chilled Squid Salad with Peppers

Squid cooked briefly with peppers and garlic, seasoned with lemon
juice, and chilled before serving makes a delightful antipasto or a
main course for a light luncheon. The salad can be made a day
ahead.   SERVES 4

3 tablespoons olive oil
4 garlic cloves, thinly sliced
1 cup green or red bell peppers,
    cut into ½-inch squares
1 fresh or dried hot pepper,
    minced (p. 14)
1 pound small squid, cleaned (p.
    17), cut into thin disks,
    tentacles included

¼ cup lemon juice
3 tablespoons minced fresh parsley
Salt and freshly ground pepper to
    taste
Curly endive or romaine lettuce
    leaves for garnish

Heat the oil in a skillet and add the garlic and the bell and hot peppers. Sauté over medium heat, stirring, for 1 minute. Add the squid and continue cooking, stirring constantly, until the squid turns white and loses its translucency, about 3 to 5 minutes. Remove from the heat and transfer to a mixing bowl. Add the lemon juice, parsley, and salt and pepper, combine well, and chill for at least 2 hours. Serve cold on endive or lettuce leaves.

OKTAPODI PSITO   *Greece*
Grilled Octopus

Each day at sunset we made our way to the café overlooking the little fishing port in Náousa on the island of Paros where we would settle down with a glass of ouzo or retsina, perhaps some olives, feta, and tomatoes, and always, a few pieces of charcoal-grilled octopus. An octopus in Greece is tenderized before grilling in a simple, effective manner—it is held by the tentacles and smashed against a rock for an hour or so, a job usually assigned to a youngster. If you use relatively small ones and marinate them, you can skip the tenderizing step. In any case, ask your fishmonger for advice. The octopus is best if grilled over charcoal, but a conventional oven broiler does an acceptable job.   SERVES 4 TO 6

1 pound small octopuses, cleaned (p. 18), cut into 3-inch sections
3 tablespoons olive oil

Juice of 1 lemon
Salt and freshly ground pepper to taste

Marinate the octopus in the oil, lemon juice, and salt and pepper for 2 hours. Put on skewers and broil, turning occasionally and basting with the marinade, for about 20 minutes, until browned and tender. Serve warm.

VARIATION Italians and Spaniards like broiled squid. Clean small ones and marinate in the same marinade with the addition of chopped garlic. Stuff the tentacles into the sac and broil until browned and tender. Squid are more tender than octopus and take about 10 minutes to cook.

OKTAPODI TOURSI   *Greece*
Marinated Octopus

SERVES 4

1 pound octopus, cleaned (p. 18)   *4 tablespoons olive oil*
1 cup dry red wine   *4 tablespoons wine vinegar*
2 cloves   *1 garlic clove, minced*
1 bay leaf   *Salt to taste*

Place the octopus in a saucepan. Add the wine, cloves, and bay leaf, cover with water, bring to a boil, reduce heat, and simmer, covered, until tender, about 1 hour. Octopus is cooked when the tines of a fork pierce the flesh with ease. Drain and when cool enough to handle, remove the outer skin if it comes off easily, cut into ½-inch-square pieces, and place in a serving bowl.

Combine the remaining ingredients in a small mixing bowl, pour over the octopus, mix well, and chill for 1 hour before serving.

POLPI DEL DIAVOLO   *Italy*
Braised Spicy Octopus

This dish, in which octopus is simmered slowly in a richly flavored tomato-wine sauce, is immensely popular in Italy and, with variations, in other Mediterranean countries. It can also be served as the main course for an informal dinner.   SERVES 4 TO 6

6 tablespoons olive oil
3 garlic cloves, thinly sliced
4 tablespoons chopped fresh
    parsley
1 dried hot pepper, crushed or
    finely chopped
1½ pounds small octopuses,
    cleaned (p. 18), cut into
    3-inch sections

¼ teaspoon black peppercorns,
    crushed in a mortar
½ cup dry white wine
Salt to taste
2 large ripe tomatoes, peeled and
    minced, or 1 cup drained
    and chopped canned Italian
    plum tomatoes

Heat the olive oil in a saucepan, preferably earthenware, add the garlic, parsley, and hot red pepper, and sauté over medium heat for 2 minutes. Add the octopus and continue to cook for 2 minutes. Add the black pepper, wine, and salt, and cook, uncovered, for 10 minutes. Add the tomatoes, lower the heat, and simmer, covered, stirring occasionally, until the octopus is tender, about 1 hour. When done, the octopus should be in a dense, richly flavored sauce. Serve hot or at room temperature.

MIDYE TAVASI   **Turkey**
Batter-Fried Mussels on Skewers

This is an immensley popular appetizer in Turkey, and with reason. It's delicious and relatively easy to prepare. As with all fried foods, the mussels should be fried and served immediately. However, they can be steamed open and the batter prepared in advance. The mussels, sometimes coated with batter, sometimes just dipped in flour and beer, are usually fried individually and served on a toothpick. We prefer to place a few on small wooden skewers, dip them in batter, and fry them as a group. It works well and greatly facilitates preparation.   SERVES 4

½ cup flour
1 extra-large egg, separated
¼ to ½ cup beer
Pinch of salt

40 large mussels (about 3½
    pounds)
½ cup light seed oil for frying
1 cup Pine Nut Sauce (see recipe)

Place the flour in a mixing bowl, add the egg yolk, and combine with a fork. Add the beer slowly, beating constantly with a wire whisk, until a smooth batter similar in consistency to a thick pancake batter is formed. Season with salt and set aside to rest for 1 hour.

In the meantime, bring 1 cup of water to boil in a large saucepan, add the mussels, cover, and cook, shaking the pot frequently, until the mussels open, about 2 to 3 minutes. When cool enough to handle, remove the mussels from their shells, discard the shells, dry the mussels on paper towels, and set aside.

When ready to fry, beat the egg white until stiff and fold into the batter. Place 5 mussels on each of 8 small wooden skewers. Heat the oil to almost smoking in a skillet suitable for frying, dip the mussels in the batter, and fry until golden on both sides. Drain on paper towels, and serve immediately with pine nut sauce (*tarator*).

SALADE DE MOULES   *France*
Mussel Salad

This can be made up to a day in advance and kept in the refrigerator until ready to serve.   SERVES 4 TO 6

1 medium onion, quartered	1 teaspoon Dijon mustard
1 bay leaf	2 tablespoons finely chopped fresh
2 garlic cloves	parsley
½ cup dry white wine	2 scallions, thinly sliced
½ cup water	Salt and freshly ground pepper to
3 pounds mussels, scrubbed,	taste
beards removed	Boston or Bibb lettuce leaves and
½ cup Mayonnaise (see recipe)	arugula

Place the onion, bay leaf, garlic, wine, and water in a large saucepan. Bring to a boil, add the mussels, cover, and cook 3 minutes, shaking the pan occasionally to distribute the mussels. Remove the opened mussels with a slotted spoon, place in a large bowl, and let cool. When cool enough to handle, remove the mussels and discard the shells. Reduce the mussel liquid by half. To strain, place a wad of cotton in the neck of a funnel and pour the liquid through it. Reserve.

Combine the mayonnaise with the mustard, parsley, and scallions, then blend in the mussel liquid. Taste and adjust for seasoning. Pour over the mussels and allow to marinate for 1 hour before serving. Serve at room temperature surrounded by lettuce leaves and arugula.

MEJILLONES RELLENOS EN SU CONCHA　　Spain
Stuffed Mussels on the Half Shell

We had these delectable *tapas* with a chilled glass of *fino* (dry sherry) in a small, unpretentious bar in Seville. After much coaxing, we persuaded the chef to share the recipe with us. The mussels can be prepared ahead of time but should be broiled just before serving. We calculate 6 mussels per person.　　SERVES 4

¼ cup dry white wine
½ cup water
1 tender celery stalk with leaves
1 bay leaf
½ small onion
6 whole peppercorns
24 large mussels (about 2
　　pounds), scrubbed, beards
　　removed
1 tablespoon olive oil
1 tablespoon minced onion

1 drained and minced canned
　　Italian plum tomato
Béchamel (see recipe) made
　　with:
　1 tablespoon butter
　1 tablespoon flour
　½ cup milk
　Pinch of salt
2 tablespoons bread crumbs
1 tablespoon butter

Place the wine, water, celery, bay leaf, onion, and peppercorns in a large saucepan, bring to a boil, add the mussels, and steam, covered, shaking the pan frequently, until the mussels open, about 2 to 3 minutes. Remove from the pan and set aside until cooled. Reduce the cooking liquid to ½ cup. To strain the liquid, place a wad of cotton in the neck of a funnel and pour liquid through it. Reserve the liquid.

When cooled sufficiently to handle, remove mussels from their shells, discard one of the two halves, and retain the other. Chop the mussels roughly and set aside.

Heat the olive oil in a small skillet, add the onion, and sauté over medium heat until transparent. Add the tomato and cook until most of the water evaporates. The sauce should be smooth and fairly thick. Set aside.

Make a light béchamel sauce, using the reserved mussel liquid along with the milk. Add to the béchamel the tomato sauce and the chopped mussels, and combine well. Use the mixture to stuff the half shells. When ready to broil, sprinkle bread crumbs lightly over the mussel mixture, dot with butter, and broil until a golden crust forms. Serve hot.

MOULES AU PERSIL ET AIL   *France*
Mussels with Parsley and Garlic

These mussels, a specialty of the restaurant L'Oursin in Antibes, are similar to Escargots à la Bourguignon. They are simple to prepare and, we think, even better than snails. We calculate about 6 mussels per person when served as an appetizer.   SERVES 4

½ cup dry white wine	*3 shallots, finely chopped*
½ cup water	*½ cup finely chopped fresh*
½ medium onion	*parsley*
24 large mussels (about 2	*½ cup olive oil*
pounds), scrubbed, beards	*Salt to taste*
removed	*Abundant freshly ground pepper*
5 garlic cloves, finely chopped	*Lemon wedges for garnish*

Place the wine, water, and onion in a large saucepan, bring to a boil, add the mussels, and steam, shaking occasionally, until opened, about 3 minutes. When opened, remove the mussels with a slotted spoon and set aside. To strain the liquid, place a wad of cotton in the neck of a funnel and pour the liquid through it. Reserve 2 tablespoons of the liquid.

When the mussels have cooled, remove from each the top

shell, and place the bottom half, with the attached mussel, in a baking dish.

Combine the garlic, shallots, parsley, oil, salt, and the 2 tablespoons of the cooking liquid. Pour a teaspoon of the mixture on each mussel.

Preheat the oven to 450°F.

When ready to serve, bake for 5 minutes, until the oil is sizzling. Grind pepper over the mussels, and serve immediately garnished with the lemon wedges.

MOULES AU SAFRAN   *France*
Mussels with Saffron

All the elements of this dish can be prepared in advance but the sauce should be heated and poured over the mussels just before serving. We calculate 6 mussels per person as an appetizer.

SERVES 4

¾ cup dry white wine
½ cup water
½ medium onion
24 *large mussels (about 2*
    pounds), scrubbed, beards
    removed
4 cups mesclun *(p. 16)*
2 tablespoons butter
4 shallots, finely chopped
1 bay leaf

⅓ cup peeled, seeded, and
    roughly chopped tomatoes, or
    ⅓ cup drained and chopped
    canned Italian plum
    tomatoes
Pinch of saffron
Salt to taste
2 tablespoons finely chopped fresh
    parsley
Abundant freshly ground pepper

Combine ½ cup of wine with the water and onion in a large saucepan, bring to a boil, add the mussels, cover, and steam, shaking occasionally, until the mussels open, about 3 minutes. Remove the opened mussels with a slotted spoon and set aside. Reduce the cooking liquid to ½ cup. To strain the liquid, place a wad of cotton in the neck of a funnel and pour the liquid through it. Reserve the liquid.

Distribute the *mesclun* on 4 small salad plates. When cool

enough to handle, discard the top half of each mussel shell, and place 6 of the remaining half shells with mussels on the *mesclun* on each plate. Set aside.

In a small skillet, melt the butter and add the shallots. Sauté for a few minutes, until golden. Add the bay leaf, tomatoes, remaining wine, the mussel liquid, and the saffron. Simmer, stirring occasionally, for 10 minutes. Taste and adjust for salt.

When ready to serve, remove and discard the bay leaf, add the parsley to the sauce, mix well, then distribute 1 teaspoon of sauce over each mussel. Grind pepper over the mussels and serve immediately.

BOUZROUG DE FATIMA   *Morocco*
Fatima's Mussels

Fatima, our friend Toni Maraini's cook in Tangier, often served this marvelous mussel preparation once she discovered how much we liked it. We've since learned that the Algerians have a similar dish but, for us, it remains Fatima's mussels. We calculate 6 mussels per person when served as an appetizer. The dish can be prepared a few hours in advance. In fact, the mussels are tastier if they marinate for a while in the sauce.   SERVES 4

½ cup Fish Stock or Vegetable
    Broth (see recipes)
½ cup water
½ medium onion
24 large mussels (about 2
    pounds), scrubbed, beards
    removed
4 cups thinly sliced romaine
    lettuce, escarole, or curly
    endive

2 tablespoons olive oil
4 garlic cloves, finely chopped
1 teaspoon sweet paprika
¼ teaspoon cayenne pepper
1 teaspoon all-purpose flour
1 teaspoon ground cumin
3 tablespoons vinegar

Place the stock or broth in a large saucepan with the water and the onion, bring to a boil, add the mussels, cover, and steam until opened, about 3 minutes. Remove the mussels with a slotted spoon and set aside. To strain the liquid, place a wad of cotton in the neck of a funnel and pour the liquid through it. Reserve ½ cup.

Distribute the lettuce on 4 salad plates. When mussels have cooled, remove top shells and place 6 bottoms with the mussels on each of the plates.

Heat the oil in a skillet, add the garlic, and sauté until golden, about 2 minutes. Add the paprika and cayenne pepper, and cook another minute. Mix the flour with the mussel liquid and add to the pan. Simmer for 1 minute, stirring constantly. Add the cumin and vinegar, and simmer, stirring constantly, for 2 to 3 minutes. You should have a relatively thick sauce.

Spoon a teaspoon of the sauce on each mussel, then set aside to cool. Serve at room temperature.

CROSTINI DI VONGOLE   *Italy*
Baby Clams on Toast

In the past, when the sea was cleaner and sea life more abundant, at most beaches along Italy's Tyrrhenian coast, you could run your fingers through the sand, trap *vongole,* and eat them on the spot. You can't do that anymore but *vongole* are still readily available in markets and as popular as ever. We have been unable to find them fresh in North America, but there are a number of dishes, such as this one, in which canned baby clams from the Mediterranean are perfectly adequate substitutes for fresh ones.   SERVES 4 TO 6

4 tablespoons olive oil
2 garlic cloves, finely chopped
One 5-ounce can baby clams
   (vongole), drained, juice
   reserved, or 2 pounds fresh
   baby clams
2 tablespoons chopped fresh
   parsley

2 egg yolks
Juice of 1 lemon
Salt and freshly ground pepper to
   taste
Pinch of cayenne pepper
   (optional)
Twenty-four 2-inch-square slices
   Italian bread, toasted

Heat the oil in a skillet, add the garlic, and sauté until golden, about 2 minutes. Add the canned clams, parsley, and 3 tablespoons of reserved juice, and simmer, stirring frequently, for 5 minutes. Set aside.

If using fresh clams, place 1 cup of water in a large saucepan, bring to a boil, add the clams, and steam, covered, shaking the pan occasionally, until the clams open, about 4 minutes. Remove the flesh from the shells and discard the latter. To strain the liquid, place a wad of cotton in the neck of a funnel and pour the liquid through it. Reserve 5 tablespoons. From this point, proceed as above.

Combine the egg yolks with the lemon juice, salt and pepper, cayenne pepper, and 2 more tablespoons of the reserved juice. Bring the clams to a simmer, remove from the heat and pour the egg mixture over the clams in a steady stream, stirring constantly. Spread the mixture over the toast and serve warm.

TORTILLITAS DE CAMARÓNES   *Spain*
Shrimp Pancakes

These exquisite little appetizers, shrimps fried in a chick-pea flour batter, are a specialty of Cádiz, a little outside our jurisdiction perhaps, but too good to leave out. If you can find flavorful baby shrimp, use them whole instead of the chopped larger shrimp.

SERVES 6

1 cup unbleached all-purpose flour
1 cup chick-pea flour
Salt and freshly ground black pepper to taste
¾ cup minced onions
4 tablespoons minced fresh parsley
½ pound shrimp, shelled, deveined, and coarsely chopped
Approximately 1 cup cold water
½ cup light seed oil for frying

Combine all the dry ingredients with the onions, parsley, and shrimp in a large mixing bowl. Add the water and mix well. Add more water, a tablespoon at a time, until a lumpy batter with the consistency of oatmeal is obtained. Set aside in the refrigerator for 2 to 3 hours.

When ready to serve, heat the oil in a large skillet until almost smoking, spread ¼ cup of batter thinly in the hot oil, fry until golden on one side, flip and fry to golden on the other. Remove, drain on paper towels, and keep warm until all the batter is used. Serve hot.

MESCLUN AUX CREVETTES   *France*
Shrimp with Mixed Salad and Warm Vinaigrette

This is a marvelous salad, elegant, easy to prepare, and delicious. It is enormously popular in France, especially in winter, when escarole, curly endive, and radicchio are available. The dish depends very much on the quality of vinegar used in the vinaigrette. A good fruit vinegar, first-class wine vinegar from France, or Balsamic vinegar from Italy should be used if at all possible.

SERVES 6

24 large shrimp, shelled and
    deveined
4 cups mesclun (p. 16)
1 large ripe tomato, peeled,
    seeded, and chopped
1 avocado, peeled and cut
    lengthwise into 18 thin slices
3 large cultivated mushrooms,
    washed and thinly sliced

Hearts of 3 fresh artichokes,
    rubbed with lemon juice,
    very thinly sliced
6 tablespoons light olive oil or
    peanut oil
3 tablespoons high-quality,
    flavorful vinegar
2 tablespoons Dijon mustard
2 egg yolks
Salt to taste

Bring 3 cups of salted water to a boil, add the shrimp, and simmer until just tender, about 3 minutes. Drain and set aside. Keep warm.

Distribute the *mesclun* attractively on 6 individual plates. Do the same with the tomato, avocado, mushrooms, and artichokes. Place 4 shrimp on each plate, butterflied if very large.

To make the dressing, bring water to a boil in the lower half of a double boiler and place the remaining ingredients in the top half. Stir with a wire whisk for a few minutes, until the dressing begins to thicken. Pour the warm dressing over the shrimp and the salad and serve at once.

SALADE DE SAINT-JACQUES AVEC POIVRONS   *France*
Warm Scallop Salad with Peppers

This dish, which we first sampled at La Tamarissière, an excellent restaurant in Languedoc just at the mouth of the Hérault River, proves that in cooking often the sum is far greater than the parts. A few scallops, some peppers, a little salad, and caviar and you have the makings of a wonderful appetizer, easy to prepare, elegant, and delicious. If you use frozen scallops, thaw first and pat dry.   SERVES 6

4 tablespoons butter
2 red bell peppers, peeled, cored,
*   seeded, and sliced thinly*
*   lengthwise (p. 13)*
¼ teaspoon cayenne pepper
24 large sea scallops
1 Belgian endive

1 head red radicchio
6 tablespoons black caviar
1 tablespoon fresh chopped chives
18 carrot sticks or baby carrots,
*   2 inches long, parboiled*
*   (optional)*

Heat 2 tablespoons of butter in a skillet, add the peppers and cayenne pepper, and sauté over low heat, stirring frequently, for 3 minutes. Remove from the heat and set aside.

Heat the remaining butter in another skillet, add the scallops, and sauté over high heat until browned on both sides, about 2 to 3 minutes. Remove from the heat but keep warm.

Place a few leaves of endive and radicchio on 6 salad plates. Put the scallops on the salad leaves, 4 to a plate, and distribute the sliced peppers equally among the servings, placing them in the center of each plate. Put a teaspoon of caviar on each pepper serving, and sprinkle with chives. Decorate with the carrots and serve immediately.

INSALATA FRUTTI DI MARE   *Italy*
Cold Seafood Medley

Some version of this salad is found all over Italy and many other countries of the Mediterranean. It's relatively easy to prepare, will keep for a few days in the refrigerator, and makes a splendid appetizer for a buffet or an elegant dinner party.

SERVES 6 TO 8

4 tablespoons olive oil
½ cup dry white wine
½ small onion, chopped
3 garlic cloves, chopped
¼ teaspoon freshly ground pepper
Salt to taste
½ cup water
2 pounds small clams, scrubbed
2 pounds mussels, scrubbed,
    beards removed

1 pound small octopus or squid,
    or ½ pound each, cleaned
    (pp. 17–18), cut into
    1-inch pieces
1 pound small shrimp in shells
Juice of ½ lemon
1 tablespoon chopped fresh
    parsley
½ teaspoon dried oregano
Lettuce leaves and lemon wedges
    for garnish

Place 2 tablespoons oil, the wine, onion, 2 garlic cloves, pepper, salt, and water in a large saucepan, bring to a boil, add the clams, and steam, covered, shaking the pan occasionally, until the clams open, about 3 to 4 minutes. Remove with a slotted spoon and set aside. In the same saucepan, add the mussels, and steam, covered, shaking the pan occasionally, until the mussels open, about 3 minutes. Remove with a slotted spoon and set aside. Strain the liquid through a wad of cotton placed in the neck of a funnel and return the liquid to the pan.

Bring the liquid to a simmer, add the squid, and cook, covered, until tender, about 3 to 4 minutes. If using octopus, allow about 10 minutes. If using both, cook the octopus about 7 minutes before adding the squid, and continue cooking until the tines of a fork easily pierce the flesh. Remove with a slotted spoon and place in a serving bowl.

Add the shrimp to the saucepan and cook 3 minutes, until tender. Remove with a slotted spoon and when cool enough to handle, peel, place the shrimp in the serving bowl, and return the shells to the saucepan.

Reduce the liquid in the pan to 1 cup, strain through a fine sieve, discard the shells, and reserve the liquid.

Remove the clams and mussels from their shells, discard the shells, and place the flesh in the serving bowl.

Pour the cooking liquid over the seafood and add the remaining oil, garlic, lemon juice, parsley, and oregano. Mix well and chill a few hours before serving. Serve on lettuce leaves with lemon wedges.

First Courses

It was at one time believed that Marco Polo brought the art of pasta making to Italy from China but it has been pointed out that Italians were eating pasta long before Marco was born. On the other hand, the China connection did not originate with Marco Polo, so there still may be some basis to the argument that the Italians learned about pasta from the Chinese. Whatever the case, Italian cooks have been preparing pasta for at least a millennium and, not surprisingly, have managed to create in that time a veritable treasure trove of superb dishes. The pasta dishes that make up the first section of this chapter, with one exception, come entirely from Italy for the simple reason that Italians make the best pasta.

Rice is enormously popular in the Mediterranean and, in a number of countries—Italy, Turkey, and Spain in particular—the fine art of rice cookery rivals that of Iran, India, and the Far East. Rice differs among countries and so does the way it is cooked. Italian chefs are justly famous for their risottos, dishes in which rice is first sautéed in butter or oil, then cooked with hot broth that is added a little at a time. A good risotto is creamy and slightly moist with the rice grains cooked through but still firm.

Turks favor long-grain rice and tend to cook it like the Persians. The rice is always washed to remove excess starch and is then cooked with water or broth, herbs, spices, and vegetables. At the end, it is allowed to sit for a while, covered tightly, so that the steam evaporates and the rice becomes light and fluffy. Rice in Turkey is often served cold.

"Spanish rice" may be the most famous of all Mediterranean rice dishes although such a dish does not exist in Spain. Instead, Spain has a great variety of such dishes, any one of which qualifies as "Spanish rice." The most famous are *paellas,* or rice dishes cooked in a *paella,* a shallow metal pan that resembles a wok. The rice is first sautéed for a few minutes in oil. Herbs, spices, vegetables, and hot broth are then added. The rice simmers until almost cooked on top of the stove and is then placed in a medium oven until completely cooked and the liquid absorbed. Spanish rice dishes are served warm.

In most Mediterranean countries, dinners are usually small and very often include a soup. Soup has features that make it particularly appealing to Mediterranean folk. It is nourishing, filling, and inexpensive to prepare. In consequence, Mediterranean cooks have developed an assortment of soups that, in range and quality, are unmatched anywhere in the world.

The last section includes tarts, croquettes, and such delicacies as Peppers Stuffed with Fish from Spain, baked or fried cheese-filled dumplings from Turkey, and pizzas from France, Italy, Spain.

Pastas

PASTA FATTA IN CASA   *Italy*
Homemade Pasta

We give instructions for making pasta with a hand-cranked machine. The process is simple and relatively quick. If you use a good, hard wheat or all-purpose flour, preferably unbleached, fresh eggs, and good olive oil, the pasta will be first-rate.

To make the pasta, you will need a place to clamp the machine and two 3-foot spaces, one to roll out the dough, the other to lay out sheets of pasta before cutting. Prepare these before you begin.

We figure ½ pound of pasta serves 2 to 3 people and give the recipe for this amount. If you want to increase or decrease the amount, just remember to maintain the same proportion among ingredients, that is, 1 egg to 1 cup of flour to 1 teaspoon of oil.

A note of caution—fresh pasta cooks quickly so check often to avoid overcooking.   SERVES 2 TO 3

2 cups unbleached all-purpose
   flour
2 extra-large eggs

Pinch of salt
2 teaspoons olive oil
Water as necessary

Mound the flour on a board or marble slab, form a well in the center, add the eggs, salt, and oil, and drawing the flour from the inside wall of the well, combine with the liquid in the center. When all the flour is incorporated, knead for 5 minutes. The dough should be fairly stiff but tractable. If too stiff, add water, a little at a time, kneading thoroughly between each addition. If too soft, add flour. Divide the dough into 2 or 3 balls and cover with a clean dish towel.

Attach the machine to the work surface. Set the rollers at the widest setting, flatten 1 of the balls, and pass it through the rollers. Fold in 3, making the packet of dough the width of the machine, and pass it through the rollers again. Repeat about 8 times, until a smooth, homogeneous dough is obtained. If the dough is sticky, sprinkle flour on the surface before folding. Reduce the opening of the rollers by 1 notch, and pass the dough through. Do not fold. Reduce the opening again, and pass once more. Continue, reducing the opening 1 notch after each pass, until you achieve the desired thickness. We recommend the ultimate or penultimate setting. Place the pasta sheet on a dry, lightly floured dish towel and set aside. Repeat with the remaining balls. Allow the pasta to rest 10 minutes.

Meanwhile attach the cutter to the machine. When ready, cut the pasta into sheets about 18 to 20 inches long. To make the noodles, simply pass the pasta through the cutter, holding the sheet of dough with one hand, cranking the machine with the other. You can cook at once or set aside to dry. If using soon, dry over a towel or broomstick suspended between chairs. Otherwise, place on a dry, lightly floured dish towel, shape into circular nests, sprinkle with flour, and set aside. Store in a paper bag, or the equivalent, in a dry spot until ready to use.

VARIATIONS

1. To make lasagna, roll the dough to the penultimate setting, cut the sheets of pasta into sections roughly half the length of the dish in which the pasta will be baked. Set aside for 30 minutes on

a dry, floured dish towel. Cook according to instructions in the recipe.

2. To make green pasta, cook 5 to 6 ounces of spinach until tender, drain, squeeze dry, and chop finely with a sharp knife or in a food processor. Place the spinach in the well with the other ingredients and proceed as directed above.

3. To make red pasta, add 2 teaspoons of tomato paste to the liquid ingredients in the well and proceed as directed above.

4. You can incorporate other ingredients into the pasta dough. Try, for example, about 1 ounce finely minced reconstituted dried porcini, or fresh herbs such as minced basil or parsley.

5. You can use a food processor to help knead the dough but the proportions of ingredients must be altered. Place the metal blade in the work bowl, add 2¼ cups of flour and a pinch of salt. With the machine running, add 2 teaspoons of oil through the feed tube, then, one at a time, 3 extra-large eggs. Continue running the machine until the dough forms a ball and clears the sides of the bowl. Remove the dough, divide into 2 or 3 balls, and proceed as above. You should be able to cut the initial number of passes from 8 to 4. If you want a less rich pasta, substitute approximately 1 tablespoon water for the third egg.

PENNE ALLA FORTE DEI MARMI   *Italy*
Pasta with Cheeses and Cream

A creamy, rich sauce, ideal with short stout pasta, this is a specialty of the Versilia coast, where Paola spent many summers as a child. The recipe calls for grated Romano or sharp pecorino cheese, both made from ewe's milk and available in most Italian cheese shops. Pecorino is typical of central Italy, where pasture land is limited and of relatively poor quality, inadequate for cows but ideal for sheep. Even in the age of electronics, pecorino is usually made in small workshops by skilled cheesemakers and sold locally. If you have the opportunity to travel around Tuscany, sample the pecorinos in different villages—your palate will be thrilled by the diversity. The best sharp pecorino for grating and the most accessible outside of Italy is pecorino Sardo.   SERVES 4 TO 6

2 tablespoons butter
1 large onion, thinly sliced
½ cup water
½ cup drained canned Italian
    plum tomatoes, or ½ cup
    peeled, seeded, and finely
    chopped ripe tomatoes

1 cup whipping cream
1 pound penne or other short,
    stout pasta
1 cup grated Gruyère
½ cup freshly grated Romano or
    sharp pecorino
Freshly ground pepper to taste

Heat the butter in a saucepan, add the onion, and sauté over medium-low heat until golden, about 7 to 10 minutes. Add water, cover, and cook for 10 to 15 minutes, until the onion begins to disintegrate and the water has evaporated. Add the tomatoes and cream and simmer, uncovered, 5 minutes. Set aside.

Bring 4 quarts of salted water to a rapid boil in a large saucepan or stockpot, add the pasta, and cook until al dente, stirring occasionally with a wooden spoon. Drain and return the pasta to the pan. Place the pan over low heat, add the cream sauce and the grated cheeses, blend well with a wooden spoon, and cook 1 minute. Transfer to a serving bowl, grind pepper over the pasta, and serve immediately.

PÂTE FRAÎCHE AU CHÈVRE ET BASIL   *France*
Fresh Pasta with Goat Cheese and Basil

We have a bias in favor of Italian pasta dishes and, we think, with good reason. But this dish, which we had near Menton, in France, right on the Franco-Italian border, rivals the best in Italy, perhaps because it combines French sensitivity to ingredients with Italian know-how. Use either a mild or sharp fresh goat cheese; both are good in this dish.   SERVES 4 TO 6

2 large, ripe tomatoes, peeled,
     seeded, and chopped
¼ cup chopped fresh basil leaves
4 ounces goat cheese, cut into
     small pieces
2 garlic cloves, minced
3 tablespoons olive oil

2 tablespoons whipping cream
1 pound Homemade Pasta (see
     recipe), made as fettuccine
⅓ cup freshly grated Parmesan
½ teaspoon freshly ground black
     pepper

Place the tomatoes, basil, goat cheese, garlic, oil, and cream in a large serving bowl and combine. Set aside.

Bring 4 quarts of salted water to a rapid boil, add the pasta, and cook until al dente, stirring occasionally with a wooden spoon. Remember fresh pasta cooks very quickly. Drain, and transfer immediately to the serving bowl. Add the Parmesan and pepper, mix thoroughly to combine ingredients, and serve at once.

SPAGHETTI CON CACIO E PEPE   *Italy*
Spaghetti with Sharp Pecorino and Pepper

The sauce for this classic Roman pasta dish is nothing more than sharp pecorino and coarsely ground black pepper. And therein lies its greatness—simple ingredients, intelligently combined. Serve on any occasion.   SERVES 4 TO 6

1 pound spaghetti
1½ cups good, sharp pecorino or
     Romano, freshly grated

½ to 1 teaspoon black
     peppercorns, coarsely ground
     in a mortar

Bring 4 quarts of salted water to a rapid boil, add the pasta, and cook until al dente, stirring occasionally with a wooden spoon. Just before draining, remove and reserve 1 cup of water in which the pasta cooked. Drain, place in a large bowl, add the cup of reserved water, the cheese, and the pepper, mix well, and serve immediately.

FETTUCCINE AL PESTO BIANCO   *Italy*
Fettuccine with Walnuts and Ricotta

In this creamy, delicate sauce, a specialty of La Spezia, fresh ricotta
is combined with walnuts, garlic, and Parmesan.   SERVES 4 TO 6

1 cup shelled walnuts	*⅓ cup freshly grated Parmesan*
3 to 4 garlic cloves	*Salt to taste*
2½ ounces ricotta	*1 pound Homemade Pasta (see*
½ cup milk	*recipe), made as fettuccine*
2 tablespoons butter	*½ teaspoon freshly ground pepper*
2 tablespoons olive oil	

Place the walnuts, garlic, ricotta, milk, butter, oil, Parmesan,
and salt in a blender or food processor, and blend to a smooth
paste. Place 2 tablespoons in a large serving bowl and set the rest
aside.

Bring 4 quarts of salted water to a rapid boil, add the pasta,
and cook until al dente, stirring occasionally with a wooden spoon.
Drain, place in the serving bowl, cover with the remaining sauce,
add the pepper, mix well, and serve immediately.

PENNE CON PISELLI   *Italy*
Penne with Peas

A simple but delicious dish, it is equally suited to an elegant dinner
party or a family meal.   SERVES 4 TO 6

1 ounce dried porcini (Boletus *edulis) mushrooms*	*½ teaspoon sugar*
5 tablespoons olive oil	*Salt and freshly ground pepper to taste*
3 garlic cloves, finely chopped	*1 pound penne or other short, stout pasta*
3 tablespoons finely chopped fresh parsley	*1½ cups freshly grated Parmesan*
2 cups shelled peas, fresh or frozen	

Soak the mushrooms in 1 cup warm water until soft. Remove the mushrooms carefully from the soaking liquid, taking care not to stir up the grit and sand that will have fallen to the bottom of the bowl. Chop the mushrooms finely and set aside. To strain the soaking liquid, which will be used to cook the peas, place a wad of cotton in the neck of a funnel and pour the liquid through it. Reserve the liquid.

Heat the oil in a saucepan, add the garlic, and sauté over medium heat for 1 minute. Add the parsley, peas, sugar, salt and pepper, and the soaking liquid, and cook, covered, until the peas are tender, about 5 to 7 minutes for frozen peas, 15 to 20 minutes for fresh peas. Add water as necessary. Some broth should remain when the peas are cooked. Set aside, but keep warm.

Bring 4 quarts of salted water to a rapid boil, add the pasta, and cook until al dente, stirring occasionally with a wooden spoon. Drain in a colander, place in a large serving bowl, add 1 cup of Parmesan, mix, then add pea sauce and combine thoroughly. Serve immediately, passing the remaining Parmesan for those who wish to add it.

SPAGHETTI FINTA CARBONARA   *Italy*
Spaghetti with Egg Sauce

The first thing Paola's brother, Alberto, did when he received a copy of our previous book, which we dedicated to him, was to search the index for his favorite pasta recipe, Finta Carbonara. It wasn't there, much to his disappointment, so he wrote it out on an index card, and inserted it where he thought it belonged. It's every bit as good as Alberto maintains.   SERVES 4 TO 6

1 pound spaghetti or spaghettini   *1 cup freshly grated Parmesan*
2 extra-large eggs, beaten   *3 tablespoons olive oil*
1 teaspoon black peppercorns,   *4 garlic cloves, roughly chopped*
   crushed in a mortar

Bring 4 quarts of salted water to a rapid boil, add the pasta, and cook until al dente, stirring occasionally with a wooden spoon.

While the pasta cooks, combine the eggs, pepper, and Parmesan in a serving bowl. Heat the oil in a small saucepan, add the garlic, and sauté over medium heat until the garlic begins to brown.

When the pasta is cooked, drain immediately, reserving 1 cup of the cooking water. Transfer the pasta to the serving bowl, add the reserved water, mix well, then add the oil and garlic, combine, and serve at once.

PASTA INTEGRALE CON CIPOLLE   *Italy*
Whole-Wheat Pasta with Onion Sauce

Once we finally found decent whole-wheat pasta (both de Cecco and Barilla now make it), we needed the right kind of sauce. Paola Boni came up with a rich, spicy, onion sauce that brings out the robustness of whole-wheat pasta while moderating its strong flavor. It works equally well with spaghetti or short, stout pasta.

SERVES 4 TO 6

5 tablespoons olive oil
2 pounds onions, thinly sliced
1 or 2 dried hot peppers, crushed
¼ teaspoon salt
½ teaspoon peppercorns, crushed
*   in a mortar*

1 tablespoon chopped fresh
*   parsley*
1 pound whole-wheat pasta
½ cup freshly grated Parmesan

To prepare the sauce, heat 3 tablespoons of oil in a skillet, add the onions and hot pepper, cover, and cook over low heat, stirring occasionally, for 15 minutes. Remove the cover, raise the heat to medium, and cook until the onions brown, about 10 minutes. Add salt, pepper, parsley, and the remaining oil. Set aside.

Bring 4 quarts of salted water to a rapid boil, add the pasta, and cook until al dente, stirring occasionally with a wooden spoon.

When ready, drain the pasta, place in a warm serving bowl, add the sauce, mix well, and serve immediately. Pass Parmesan for those who want to add it.

CONCHIGLIE CON PEPERONI   *Italy*
Shells with Bell Pepper Sauce

The sauce for this pasta dish is nothing more than bell peppers flavored with herbs and spices—but it is absolutely delicious.

SERVES 4 TO 6

*3 large red bell peppers, seeds
    removed, cut into ½-inch
    squares
1 fresh or dried hot pepper,
    chopped
1 cup water
3 tablespoons olive oil
4 garlic cloves, finely chopped*

*2 tablespoons chopped fresh basil
    or parsley
Salt and freshly ground pepper to
    taste
1 pound shell-shaped pasta or
    rigatoni
⅔ cup freshly grated Parmesan*

Place both kinds of peppers in a saucepan, add water, cover, and simmer until the peppers are cooked but still crisp, about 10 minutes. Drain, reserve the water, and set aside the saucepan with the peppers.

Heat the olive oil in a small skillet, add the garlic, and sauté 1 minute. Add the water in which the peppers were simmered and simmer until the liquid is reduced by half. Return the liquid with the garlic to the saucepan that contains the peppers. Add parsley or basil and salt, and set aside. Keep warm.

Bring 4 quarts of salted water to a rapid boil, add the pasta, and cook, stirring occasionally with a wooden spoon until al dente. Drain, transfer to a serving bowl, blend in the Parmesan, add the pepper sauce, mix thoroughly, and serve immediately.

SPAGHETTI CON ORIGANO   *Italy*
Spaghetti with Oregano

We sometimes wonder how Mimi Serani, a friend and excellent cook, ever manages to please simultaneously the palates of her husband, her two daughters, and herself. They all have strong likes and dislikes, with almost no areas of agreement. She swears by this dish, a simple combination of pasta baked with tomatoes, olives, oil, and oregano. Everyone in her family loves it and so do we.

SERVES 4 TO 6

2 pounds ripe tomatoes, peeled,
seeded, and chopped, or 2½
cups drained and chopped
canned Italian plum
tomatoes
3 tablespoons capers
2 tablespoons chopped fresh
parsley

½ cup black olives, pitted, rinsed,
and chopped
1 teaspoon dried oregano
½ cup extra-virgin olive oil,
preferably from Tuscany
1 pound spaghetti

In a mixing bowl, combine all the ingredients except the spaghetti. Set aside.

Preheat oven to 400°F. Oil very lightly an 8-inch-square attractive baking dish or the equivalent.

Cook spaghetti in 4 quarts of boiling salted water, stirring occasionally with a wooden spoon, until *very* al dente—better underdone than overdone for this recipe. Drain and combine well with the tomato mixture.

Place in the baking dish and bake until the pasta begins to brown, about 20 minutes. Serve hot or cold.

FUSILLI CON CARCIOFI   *Italy*
Fusilli with Artichokes

This Sardinian artichoke and pasta dish is a favorite of our friend Sandra. It is a delectable combination of artichokes, mint, cream, and Parmesan baked together with pasta, ideal for a buffet or elegant dinner party.

SERVES 6

Juice of 1 lemon
8 medium artichokes
4 tablespoons olive oil
1 medium onion, finely chopped
1 garlic clove, finely chopped
Salt and freshly ground pepper to
   taste

4 tablespoons whipping cream
½ teaspoon crushed, dried mint,
   or 1 teaspoon finely chopped
   fresh mint
1 pound fusilli
1 cup freshly grated Parmesan

Combine the lemon juice with about 6 cups cold water in a large mixing bowl. Trim the artichokes, remove all but the most tender outer leaves, cut in half, remove the chokes, and place in the mixing bowl with the acidulated water. Set aside.

Heat the oil in a saucepan, add the onion and garlic, and sauté over medium heat for about 5 minutes, until they just begin to color. While the onion and garlic cook, cut the artichokes into very thin wedges, about 6 per half. Add to the onion and garlic, along with salt and pepper. Cover and simmer, stirring occasionally, for 15 minutes. Add water only if necessary, a little at a time. The artichokes should be dry when cooked. Add the cream and mint, cover, and simmer another 5 minutes, until the artichokes are just tender. Set aside.

Preheat the oven to 375°F. and butter well a 12-by-8-inch baking dish.

Bring 4 quarts of salted water to a rapid boil, add the fusilli, and cook until just al dente, stirring occasionally with a wooden spoon. Drain and set aside.

Distribute half the pasta in the bottom of the baking dish. Cover with half the artichoke mixture, then half the Parmesan. Repeat, ending with the Parmesan. Bake until lightly brown, about 10 to 15 minutes. Remove and let stand 5 minutes. Serve hot directly from the baking dish.

SPAGHETTINI CON VONGOLE   *Italy*
Spaghettini with Baby Clams

Vongole, a Mediterranean specialty, are very small, delicious clams that cluster along sandy beaches. When Paola was a child, the

Italian Mediterranean was still rich in marine life and even in a popular resort like Forte dei Marmi, fishermen were able to dredge enough *vongole* to keep them and their summer customers happy. Her mother bought directly from the fishermen who, after dragging the shoreline with their specially designed rakes, wandered the beaches selling their catch from huge dripping burlap sacks. The *vongole,* of course, were still alive and the family rushed home to put them in seawater for a day or two to disgorge sand. The children, equipped with little buckets, were given the delightful task of bringing clean water from the sea. Those *vongole* made the best pasta sauce imaginable. SERVES 4 TO 6

One 5-ounce can baby clams
   (vongole), *or 2 pounds*
   fresh baby clams
4 tablespoons butter
3 garlic cloves, finely chopped
⅓ cup finely chopped onion
2 tablespoons flour

1 cup dry white wine
Salt and freshly ground pepper to
   taste
1 pound spaghettini
3 tablespoons finely chopped fresh
   parsley

If using fresh baby clams, place 1 cup of water in a large saucepan, bring to a boil, add the clams and steam, covered, shaking the pan occasionally, until the clams open, about 4 minutes. Strain ½ cup of the cooking liquid through a wad of cotton placed in the neck of a funnel and use instead of the clam juice or fish stock. When cool enough to handle, remove the flesh and discard the shells. If using canned clams, drain, reserving ½ cup of the clam juice.

Heat the butter in a small saucepan, add the garlic and onion, and sauté over medium heat until transparent, about 5 minutes. Stir in the flour and cook another minute. Add the clam juice, fish stock, or cooking liquid, then the wine, a little at a time, stirring constantly. Cook 3 minutes—add the clams and salt and pepper and heat through. Set aside but keep warm.

Cook the pasta in 4 quarts of rapidly boiling salted water, stirring occasionally with a wooden spoon, until al dente. Drain, transfer to a heated serving bowl, add the sauce, mix well, sprinkle with parsley, and serve immediately.

SPAGHETTI AL MARE DI SARDEGNA   *Italy*
Spaghetti with Seafood, Sardinian Style

In this elaborate and impressive dish, the spaghetti is cooked, then wrapped in parchment or aluminum foil and baked together with a rich tomato and seafood sauce to amalgamate flavors. This can also be prepared in individual servings.   SERVES 4 TO 6

*One 5-ounce can baby clams,
     with juice, or 2 pounds fresh
     baby clams*
3 tablespoons olive oil
3 garlic cloves, finely chopped
*8 to 12 medium shrimp, shelled
     and deveined*
*1 small squid, cleaned (p. 17),
     cut into 1-inch pieces*
½ cup dry white wine

¼ cup Tomato Sauce (see recipe)
¼ cup whipping cream
*4 tablespoons chopped fresh
     parsley*
Freshly ground pepper to taste
Salt to taste
*8 to 12 mussels, scrubbed, beards
     removed*
1 pound spaghetti
3 tablespoons capers

If using fresh clams, place 1 cup of water in a large saucepan, bring to a boil, add the clams, and steam, covered, shaking occasionally, until open, about 4 minutes. Strain ½ cup of the cooking liquid through a wad of cotton placed in the neck of a funnel, and set aside. When cool enough to handle, remove the flesh and discard the shells. If using canned clams, drain, reserving ½ cup of the clam juice.

Heat the oil in a skillet, add the garlic, and sauté over medium heat for 30 seconds. Add the shrimp and sauté for 2 minutes, until the shrimp are almost cooked. Remove the shrimp and set aside.

Add the squid to the skillet and cook 2 minutes. Add the ½ cup clam juice (or cooking liquid) and the wine. Simmer for 5 minutes, until squid is soft and the liquid evaporated. Add the baby clams, tomato sauce, cream, parsley, and pepper. Taste and adjust for salt, then simmer for 1 or 2 minutes to heat through. Set aside.

Bring ½ cup of water to a boil in a saucepan, add the mussels, cover, and steam, shaking the pan occasionally, until open, about 3 minutes. Remove the mussels from the liquid with a slotted spoon and when they are cool enough to handle, remove from the shells and set aside.

Preheat the oven to 450°F.

Bring 4 quarts of salted water to a rapid boil, add the spaghetti, and cook, stirring occasionally, until *very* al dente. Drain and set aside.

Place a large sheet of parchment paper or aluminum foil in a baking dish, distribute the spaghetti over it and top the spaghetti with the tomato mixture. Arrange the shrimp and mussels on the spaghetti and sprinkle with the capers. Cover with another sheet of parchment or foil, seal the borders, and bake for 5 minutes.

Remove from the oven, cut the paper, and serve immediately, steaming hot.

PASTA CON TONNO E OLIVE   *Italy*
Pasta with Tuna and Olives

A simple but absolutely scrumptious dish. If you've got the ingredients on hand, you can have a terrific pasta dish ready in the time it takes the pasta to cook.   SERVES 4 TO 6

4 tablespoons olive oil
3 garlic cloves, chopped
2 cups crushed canned Italian
*   plum tomatoes with juice, or*
*   2 cups seeded, peeled, and*
*   minced ripe tomatoes*
1 small hot red pepper, crushed
*   or minced*
½ cup dry white wine
Two 7-ounce cans Italian tuna
*   fish, packed in oil, drained*
*   and flaked*

2 tablespoons chopped capers
15 Italian black olives, pitted,
*   rinsed well if salty, and*
*   roughly chopped*
4 tablespoons chopped fresh
*   parsley*
1 pound short, stout pasta such
*   as rigatoni*

Heat the oil in a large skillet, add the garlic, and sauté over medium heat for 1 minute, until it begins to color. Add tomatoes and pepper and cook over medium heat for 5 minutes, stirring occasionally. Add wine and allow to evaporate for a few minutes.

Blend in the tuna fish, crush lightly with a fork to obtain a coarse-textured sauce, then add the capers, olives, and parsley. Mix thoroughly and remove from the heat, but keep warm.

Meanwhile, cook the pasta in 4 quarts of boiling salted water until al dente, stirring occasionally with a wooden spoon. Drain, combine with the tuna sauce in a large heated bowl, and serve immediately.

FETTUCCINE CON SCAMPI   *Italy*
Fettuccine with Shrimp Sauce

The Tiburtina is a working-class section of Rome, picturesque in its own way, but certainly not an area of town noted for its restaurants. The Tiburtini like it that way—the small, excellent fish restaurant hidden in the heart of the district is already overcrowded and local residents dread the day when its reputation spreads. This is one of its specialties, a delicate creamy shrimp sauce with fresh, homemade pasta.   SERVES 6 TO 8

4 tablespoons butter
1 pound medium shrimp, shelled
   and deveined
⅓ cup finely chopped onion
1 tablespoon flour
1½ cups whipping cream, or 1
   cup whipping cream with ½
   cup milk

¼ cup Tomato Sauce (see recipe)
Salt and freshly ground pepper to
   taste
1½ pounds Homemade Pasta
   (see recipe), made as
   fettuccine

Heat the butter in a large skillet, add the shrimp, and sauté until cooked through, about 3 to 4 minutes. Remove with a slotted spoon and set aside.

Add the onion to the skillet and sauté until the onion begins to color, about 5 minutes. Add the flour to the onion and cook for 1 minute. Blend in the cream, a little at a time, stirring constantly with a wooden spoon, and after the sauce thickens cook for 1 minute. Add the tomato sauce, mix well, and set aside.

Reserve 6 or 8 shrimp for garnish, chop the rest finely, and add to the sauce. Season with salt and pepper. Set aside but keep warm.

Bring 5 quarts of salted water to a rapid boil, add the pasta, and cook, stirring occasionally, until al dente. Drain, place in a heated serving bowl, add the sauce, mix, decorate with the reserved shrimp, and serve immediately.

VARIATION This dish makes an excellent *pasticcio,* an Italian equivalent of a casserole. Proceed as described above. Preheat the oven to 400°F. Butter well a large baking dish and sprinkle with toasted bread crumbs. Place the cooked pasta mixed with sauce in the dish, cover with ½ cup toasted bread crumbs, dot the surface with butter, and bake until the top browns, about 20 minutes. Serve as a main course for a luncheon.

‖ *LASAGNE AI TRE FORMAGGI*   *Italy*
‖ Lasagna with Three Cheeses

In this unusual and delicious lasagna, onions and cheeses form layers with the pasta. It can be served as a main course for a brunch, luncheon, or light dinner. It is perfect for a buffet. We give the recipe using homemade pasta. You can use commercial varieties but you will never enjoy the true delicacy of this dish until you try it with fresh pasta.   SERVES 4 TO 6

Dough for Homemade Pasta (see recipe), made with 3 cups of flour
3 tablespoons unsalted butter
1¾ pounds white onions, thinly sliced
1 cup ricotta, drained if very moist

1 cup freshly grated Parmesan
1 cup whipping cream
⅓ pound grated Gruyère or Italian fontina
¼ teaspoon freshly grated nutmeg
¼ teaspoon freshly ground white pepper
1 tablespoon olive oil

Make the dough for homemade pasta, roll out to the penulti-mate setting on the machine, then cut the sheets of pasta into 4-inch lengths. The width of each sheet will, of course, be deter-mined by the width of your pasta machine. Most make sheets about 5¼ inches across. Set aside for 30 minutes on a dry, floured board to rest.

Meanwhile, heat the butter in a large skillet, add the onions, and cook, covered, over low heat, stirring frequently, for 30 min-utes. Remove the cover, cook another 5 to 10 minutes, until the onions are very tender, then set aside. Do not allow the onions to brown.

Combine the remaining ingredients, except for the oil, in a saucepan, then heat, stirring constantly, until the cheeses melt and amalgamate. Set aside.

Bring 4 quarts of salted water to a rapid boil in a large sauce-pan or stockpot and add the oil to the water. Fill a mixing bowl with cold water and place near the stove. Lay out a couple of clean, damp dishcloths on a work surface. Boil the pasta 2 sheets at a time until barely cooked. Remove from the water with a slotted spoon, place in the cold water, remove, drain, and lay out on the dishcloth.

Preheat the oven to 400°F. Butter well an 8-inch-square bak-ing dish.

Spread a thin layer of cheese mixture in the bottom of the baking dish, distribute a layer of pasta over the cheeses, allowing the pasta to overlap slightly. Distribute a thin layer of onions over the pasta and follow with another layer of cheeses. Repeat until all the ingredients are used, ending with the cheeses. Bake for 20 minutes, until the top begins to brown. Let rest for 5 minutes, then serve from the baking dish.

MACCHERONI CON LE SARDE   *Italy*
Macaroni with Sardines

When Mimi Serani first told us about this Ligurian specialty, in which pasta is combined with a rich tomato sauce, sardines, and mushrooms, we were intrigued. The combination of ingredients was unusual and, as it turned out, inspired. It takes time to prepare, but both the tomato sauce and the sardines can be cooked ahead of time.   SERVES 4 TO 6

2 ounces dried wild mushrooms, preferably porcini (Boletus edulis)

1½ cups warm water

2 anchovies preserved in salt

7 tablespoons olive oil

2 garlic cloves, finely chopped

2 large, ripe tomatoes, peeled and chopped

3 tablespoons finely chopped fresh parsley or basil

2 tablespoons capers

½ pound fresh mushrooms, washed, trimmed, and thinly sliced

4 tablespoons light seed oil for frying

¾ pound fresh sardines with heads, tails, and bones removed, filleted (p. 16)

⅔ pound short, stout pasta such as tufoli or rigatoni

1 tablespoon bread crumbs

2 tablespoons freshly grated sharp pecorino or Romano

Soak the dried mushrooms in the water for 30 minutes. Remove carefully from the water and drain. Strain the soaking liquid through a wad of cotton placed in the neck of a funnel. Reserve the liquid.

Rinse the anchovies well in cold running water to remove the salt. Remove bones and chop the anchovies finely.

Heat 5 tablespoons olive oil in a saucepan, add the garlic, and sauté over medium heat until it begins to color, about 1 minute. Add the anchovies and cook until they dissolve. Add the tomatoes, parsley or basil, and capers, and cook until the sauce begins to thicken, about 15 minutes. The sauce should be moist but not soupy. Set aside.

Heat 2 tablespoons olive oil in a saucepan, add the fresh mushrooms, and sauté over medium heat for 5 minutes. Add the reconstituted wild mushrooms, 2 tablespoons of the soaking liquid, and cook, uncovered, over low heat for 10 minutes, stirring frequently. Add more of the soaking liquid as necessary during the cooking to prevent the mushrooms from sticking to the pan. The mushrooms should be slightly moist when cooked. Set aside.

Heat the seed oil in a skillet and fry the sardine fillets until just cooked, about 1 minute or less per side. Do not overcook. Drain on paper towels and set aside. The dish can be prepared in advance to this point.

Preheat the oven to 375°F. and oil an 8-by-12-inch attractive baking dish.

Bring 4 quarts of salted water to a rapid boil in a large pan, add the pasta, and cook until just tender, about 10 minutes, stirring occasionally with a wooden spoon. The pasta should be a little underdone. Drain in a colander and transfer to a large mixing bowl. Add the tomato sauce and combine thoroughly.

Distribute half the pasta evenly over the bottom of the baking dish. Place the sardines on the pasta in a single layer. Cover evenly with the mushrooms, then top with the remaining pasta. Combine the bread crumbs and cheese, and sprinkle over the pasta. Bake until the top begins to brown, about 10 to 15 minutes. Serve immediately.

Rices and Risottos

RISOTTO AL MELOGRANO   *Italy*
Risotto with Pomegranate

This risotto, unusual but delicious, with the bittersweet flavor of pomegranate seeds highlighting the creamy taste of the risotto, harks back to the Renaissance, when the practice of cooking with fruit was quite common. Use fresh pomegranates.   SERVES 6

4 tablespoons butter
⅔ cup finely chopped onions
2½ cups Arborio rice
½ cup dry white wine
6 cups Vegetable Broth (see
    recipe)

¾ cup freshly grated Parmesan
1 cup fresh pomegranate seeds
    (about 1 pomegranate)
Salt and freshly ground pepper to
    taste

Heat the butter in a saucepan, add the onions, and sauté over low heat for 5 minutes, until wilted and translucent. Do not brown. Add the rice and cook, stirring, for 1 minute. Add the wine and cook another minute.

Add hot broth to the rice, ½ cup at a time, stirring constantly, cooking over medium heat. Do not add more broth until the previous addition is absorbed. Cooking takes about 20 to 25 minutes. When done, the rice should be creamy, slightly moist, and al dente —firm, but cooked through.

Remove from the heat, blend in the Parmesan and ⅔ cup of pomegranate seeds, taste and adjust for salt and pepper, and transfer the risotto to a heated serving bowl or individual serving plates. Sprinkle the top with the remaining seeds and serve immediately.

RISOTTO DI ZUCCA   *Italy*
Squash Risotto

Rice and squash, like wine and cheese, just seem to be made for each other. This is, at least, the impression you get in the Mediterranean, where almost every region combines them in one or more dishes. Both Paola Boni and our painter-gourmet friend Francesco Colacicchi insisted that we include this risotto—they maintain it's the best there is.   SERVES 6

3 tablespoons olive oil
3 tablespoons butter
½ medium onion, minced
2 cups golden Hubbard or butternut squash, peeled and cut into ½-inch cubes
1 medium ripe tomato, peeled, seeded, and chopped
6 cups Vegetable Broth (see recipe)

2 cups Arborio rice
½ cup dry white wine
Salt and freshly ground pepper to taste
⅔ cup freshly grated Parmesan
4 tablespoons chopped fresh parsley

Heat the oil and butter in a saucepan, add the onion, and sauté for 3 minutes over medium heat. Add the squash, reduce heat to low, and sauté, stirring constantly, for 5 minutes. Add the tomato and cook another 5 minutes until the squash begins to soften. Add some of the broth as necessary to prevent the squash from sticking.

Add the rice and mix well. Pour in the wine and cook 1 minute. Blend in the hot broth, ½ cup at a time, stirring constantly. Do not add more broth until the previous addition is absorbed. The rice takes about 20 to 25 minutes to cook. When done, it should be creamy and slightly moist—firm but cooked through. The squash will be very tender and partially disintegrated.

Taste and correct for salt and pepper. Add 4 tablespoons Parmesan and the parsley, mix well, transfer to a serving bowl, and serve immediately. Pass the remaining Parmesan for those who wish to add it.

RISOTTO GIALLO AL PEPERONI CON MARSALA   *Italy*
Saffron Risotto with Peppers and Marsala

SERVES 4

2 tablespoons butter
1½ cups Arborio rice
⅓ cup Marsala
Large pinch saffron
4 cups Vegetable Broth (see recipe)
4 tablespoons olive oil
1 red bell pepper, cored, seeded, and cut into thin strips

1 green bell pepper, cored, seeded, and cut into thin strips
2 tablespoons capers (optional)
10 to 12 black Italian olives, pitted, rinsed well if salty, and halved

Heat the butter in a large, heavy saucepan. Add the rice and cook 2 minutes, stirring, until well coated with the butter. Add the Marsala and cook until it evaporates. Blend in the saffron.

Add the hot broth, ½ cup at a time, stirring constantly, and cook over medium heat. Do not add more broth until the previous addition is absorbed. Continue until the rice is cooked, about 20 to 25 minutes. When done, the risotto should be creamy and slightly moist, the rice firm but cooked through. Place in a bowl and set aside.

Heat 2 tablespoons olive oil in a skillet, add the peppers, and sauté over medium heat, stirring constantly, for 3 or 4 minutes, until the peppers are wilted but still firm. Distribute them over the rice. Add the capers and black olives, drizzle with the remaining olive oil, and combine well. Serve at room temperature.

RISOTTO AI MUSCOLI   *Italy*
Mussel Risotto

SERVES 6

1 cup dry white wine
1 cup water
1 bay leaf
½ onion, finely chopped
3 pounds mussels, scrubbed, beards removed
3 tablespoons olive oil
3 garlic cloves, finely chopped
1 cup drained, canned Italian plum tomatoes, or 1 cup peeled and chopped ripe tomatoes

¼ teaspoon freshly ground pepper
Pinch of saffron
2½ cups Arborio rice
4 cups Vegetable Broth (see recipe)
1 tablespoon chopped fresh parsley
1 tablespoon butter

Place the wine, water, bay leaf, and onion in a large saucepan and bring to a boil. Add the mussels, and steam, covered, shaking the pan occasionally, until the mussels open, about 3 minutes. Remove the mussels with a slotted spoon and, when cool enough to handle, remove and reserve the mussels, discarding the shells. Strain the cooking liquid through a wad of cotton placed in the neck of a funnel and reserve.

Heat the oil in a heavy saucepan, add the garlic, and sauté over medium heat for 2 minutes, until it begins to brown. Add the cooking liquid, the tomatoes, pepper, and saffron. Add the rice and blend. Continue to cook over low heat, stirring constantly, until all the liquid is absorbed. Add the hot vegetable broth, ½ cup at a time, stirring constantly, until the rice is cooked. Do not add more broth until the previous addition is absorbed. When done, the rice should be creamy and moist. It takes 20 to 25 minutes for the rice to cook.

A few minutes before the rice is cooked, add the mussels, parsley, and butter. Combine well. Serve immediately.

VARIATION The same ingredients can be used as a pasta sauce. Add only 1 cup of the cooking liquid to the garlic, tomato, and saffron. Simmer for a few minutes and combine with the cooked pasta.

PILAV   *Turkey*
Rice with Nuts and Herbs

The first time we visited Turkey, we slipped across the narrow strait that separates the Greek island of Samos, our home base that summer, from the small fishing village of Kuşadasi. Our Greek friends were dismayed by our desire to visit Turkey—the food was lousy, they said, the people uncivilized, and the scenery humdrum. We wondered about their sources, since we knew they had never ventured into what they considered hostile territory, but the subject was too delicate to pursue. We went in spite of these warnings and were delighted with what we found. The food was superb, the people gracious and friendly, and the coastline stupendous. This was the dish that introduced us to Turkish food.   SERVES 4

1 cup long-grain rice
5 tablespoons olive oil
3 medium onions, finely chopped
2 tablespoons pine nuts
3 tablespoons chopped fresh
    parsley
1 heaping teaspoon ground
    allspice
Salt and freshly ground pepper to
    taste

¼ teaspoon cayenne pepper
3 tablespoons currants, soaked in
    ½ cup water for 20
    minutes, drained, water
    reserved
1 medium ripe tomato, peeled and
    minced
1½ cups hot water
12 pistachios, shelled
2 tablespoons chopped fresh mint

Rinse the rice very well in cold running water to remove excess starch. Set aside.

Heat the oil in a large saucepan, add the onions, and sauté over medium heat until they begin to color, about 5 to 7 minutes. Add the pine nuts and sauté for another 3 minutes. At this point, blend in the parsley, allspice, salt and pepper, cayenne pepper, and currants. Add the water in which the currants were soaked, the tomato, and the hot water. Cover and simmer over low heat until the rice is just tender, about 15 minutes. Add the pistachios 5 minutes before the rice is done.

Remove the pan from the heat, remove the cover, and place a clean dish towel over the top of the pan. Replace the cover and set aside until cooled, about 30 minutes.

When ready, transfer the rice to a serving platter, fluff with a fork, mix in the mint leaves, and serve at room temperature.

RIZ DE PROVENCE AUX HERBES   *France*
Rice with Herbs and Wine

Rice from the Camargue, the swampy delta of the Rhone, is short-grained and perfumed with a mild, nutty flavor. Yearly output is small and the rice is practically impossible to find outside Provence. It is the rice normally employed in this dish, but Arborio from Italy is a good substitute. The herbs should be fresh.

SERVES 4

2 tablespoons olive oil
2 shallots, minced
2 garlic cloves, minced
1½ cups Camargue or Arborio
    rice
1 cup dry white wine
2 cups water
6 tablespoons butter

½ teaspoon minced fresh
    rosemary, or ¼ teaspoon
    crumbled dried rosemary
1 teaspoon minced fresh sage
2 teaspoons fresh thyme leaves
⅓ cup chopped fresh basil
¼ cup chopped fresh parsley
Salt and freshly ground pepper to
    taste

Heat the olive oil in a saucepan, add the shallots and garlic, and sauté over medium heat for 2 minutes. Add the rice, sauté for 3 minutes, until well coated with the oil, then add the wine. Blend well, add water, cover, and cook until al dente, about 20 minutes.

While the rice cooks, place the butter and seasonings in a heated serving bowl. When cooked (all the liquid should be absorbed), pour the rice into the bowl, stir well to combine, and serve hot.

PATLICANLI PILAV   *Turkey*
Eggplant Pilav

One of the most popular rice dishes in Turkey, the eggplant is first browned, then cooked with rice, herbs, and spices. It is served cold, ideal as the first course for a summer buffet. Although traditionally the eggplant is fried, we prefer to broil or bake it on a prepared griddle. The pilav is, as a result, much lighter and more easily digested. This makes a hearty first course and can also be served as a side dish.   SERVES 4

1 cup long-grain rice
Salt to taste
¾ pound small eggplants
4 tablespoons olive oil
½ cup finely chopped onion
2 cups Vegetable Broth (see
*   recipe) or water*

Freshly ground pepper to taste
1 teaspoon ground allspice
2 tablespoons pine nuts, lightly
*   toasted*
2 tablespoons currants
1 tablespoon finely chopped fresh
*   dill*

Place the rice in a bowl, add 2 cups of hot water, a pinch of salt, stir, and allow to sit until cooled. Drain and set aside.

Cut the eggplants into lengthwise strips approximately ½-inch thick, sprinkle with salt, and place in a colander to drain for 30 minutes. When ready, wipe dry with a paper towel, then broil or bake on an oiled cast-iron griddle until browned on both sides. Cut into cubes and set aside.

Heat the olive oil in a large saucepan, add the onion, and sauté over medium heat until the onion begins to color, about 5 minutes.

Add the rice and continue to cook, stirring constantly, for another 5 minutes. Add vegetable broth or water, salt and pepper, and allspice. Bring to a rapid boil, lower heat, and add the remaining ingredients, including the reserved eggplant. Cover, reduce heat to low, and simmer until the rice is tender and the liquid is absorbed, about 15 minutes. Remove from the heat, remove the cover, place a clean dish towel over the pan, replace the cover, and allow to sit for 20 or 30 minutes, until cooled. Fluff the rice. Serve at room temperature.

PAELLA DE VERDURAS   Spain
Vegetable Paella

It's not always easy, as we discovered, to find a purely vegetable *paella* in Spain—the Spanish like their rice dishes with fish and meat—but when you do, you're in for a treat. This dish comes, as one might expect, from Valencia, the major rice-growing area of the country and, reputedly, the best place in the world to eat *paella.* It makes a splendid first course and can be served as the main dish for a luncheon or light supper.   SERVES 4 TO 6

4 tablespoons olive oil
1 large onion, finely chopped
2 garlic cloves, finely chopped
2 large ripe tomatoes, peeled and
    chopped
½ pound green beans, trimmed
2 medium carrots, peeled and cut
    into sticks about 2 to 3
    inches long by ¼ -inch
    square
2 tablespoons water

½ cup fresh or frozen peas
2 green or red bell peppers,
    peeled, seeded, and cut into
    ¼ -inch strips (p. 13)
3 tablespoons chopped fresh
    parsley
2 cups Italian or Spanish rice
4 cups Vegetable Broth (see
    recipe)
Large pinch saffron

Heat the olive oil in a *paella* pan or a large, low-sided saucepan that can be used in the oven. Add the onion and garlic and sauté over medium heat for 5 minutes, until the onion begins to color. Add the tomatoes, the green beans, and the carrots and cook for a few minutes uncovered. Add about 2 tablespoons of water, cover, and simmer over low heat for 10 minutes, until the vegetables begin to soften. Add the peas, if fresh, peppers, and parsley. Cook, covered, another 2 minutes. Uncover, add rice, peas, if frozen, boiling hot vegetable broth, and saffron. Cook, stirring constantly, until the liquid is almost absorbed, about 5 to 10 minutes. Some liquid should remain.

Place the pan, uncovered, in the oven and bake for 10 to 15 minutes, until the rice is cooked and all the liquid absorbed. Remove from the oven and allow to sit 10 minutes, partly covered, before serving.

SEPIA MAA ARROS   *Morocco*
Cuttlefish with Rice, Moroccan Style

Tangier has one of the best fish markets on the Mediterranean, in part because it draws supplies from the Atlantic as well as the Mediterranean. We were there one day with our friend Toni, choosing dinner, when the fishmonger suggested we take the big cuttlefish lying on his counter. To persuade us that it was fresh, he gave it a poke and the cuttlefish, very much alive, began to squirm. We were, of course, convinced and brought it home to Fatima. She prepared it with rice, herbs, and spices, a dish that is perfect as a first course or even as the main course for a light dinner.

SERVES 4 TO 6

3 tablespoons olive oil
4 garlic cloves, chopped
1½ cups minced onions
1½ teaspoons ground ginger
1½ teaspoons ground cumin
*1 teaspoon freshly ground black
  pepper*
*½ cup chopped fresh coriander
  leaves*

*3 large ripe tomatoes, peeled,
  seeded, and chopped, or 1½
  cups drained canned Italian
  plum tomatoes*
4 cups water
*1 pound cuttlefish, cleaned (p.
  17), cut into 1-inch pieces*
1 cup Arborio rice
1 cup fresh or frozen peas
Salt to taste

Heat the oil in a large low-sided saucepan, add the garlic and onions, and sauté 3 minutes. Add the spices, the coriander, and tomatoes. Simmer 3 or 4 minutes, add 2 cups of water, the cuttlefish, cover, and simmer, stirring occasionally, until tender, about 40 minutes.

Add the rice, fresh peas, salt, and 2 more cups of water. Stir to combine, cover, and cook, stirring occasionally, until the rice is tender, about 20 minutes. If using frozen peas, blend in after 10 minutes. Add more water, if necessary, to prevent the rice from sticking. The rice, when cooked, should be moist and creamy. Serve immediately.

RIŽA SA RIBLIOM JUHOM, SKAMPI, I MUŠULE   *Yugoslavia*

Rice with Fish Broth, Shrimp, and Mussels

As you might expect, two staples of the Mediterranean diet, rice and fish, are bound to find their way into the same pot. This recipe, provided by a Yugoslavian friend, comes from the Dalmatian coast, but similar ones exist in Spain, Italy, and Lebanon. It makes an elegant, delectable first course.   SERVES 4 TO 6

3 cups Fish Stock (see recipe)
½ pound shrimp, shelled and
    deveined
½ pound mussels, scrubbed,
    beards removed
2 tablespoons olive oil
½ cup finely chopped onion

1½ cups Arborio rice
½ cup dry white wine
Salt and freshly ground white
    pepper to taste
2 tablespoons butter
1 tablespoon chopped fresh
    parsley

Bring the stock to a boil in a saucepan, add the shrimp, cook 1 minute, and remove with a slotted spoon. Add the mussels and cook until open. Remove with a slotted spoon and set aside with the shrimp. Keep warm. Strain the stock through a wad of cotton placed in the neck of a funnel and return to the saucepan over low heat.

Heat the oil in a large heavy saucepan, add the onion, and

sauté over medium heat for 5 minutes, until transparent. Add the rice and mix well. Pour in wine and simmer until absorbed. Add the fish stock, ½ cup at a time, stirring constantly, until the rice is firm but cooked through. Do not add stock until the previous addition is absorbed. When done, the risotto should be creamy and moist.

Remove from the heat, taste, and adjust for salt and pepper, add the butter, and transfer to a heated serving bowl. Distribute the shrimp and mussels on top, sprinkle with parsley, and serve hot.

Soups

SOPA DE AJO   *Spain*
Garlic Soup

The best garlic soup we ever had was in a small restaurant in Seville. The secret, we discovered, after much trial and error, was the quality of the stock. So if you want a first-rate soup all you need is lots of garlic and a rich, flavorful vegetable broth.   SERVES 4

4 tablespoons olive oil
1 cup French bread, cut into
    small cubes
8 garlic cloves, roughly chopped
½ cup canned Italian plum
    tomatoes, with juice, or ½
    cup peeled, seeded, and
    chopped ripe tomatoes

2 tablespoons chopped fresh herbs
    such as parsley, basil, or
    thyme
Pinch of saffron
1 quart Vegetable Broth (see
    recipe)
Salt and freshly ground pepper to
    taste
1 extra-large egg, beaten

Heat the oil in a large, heavy saucepan, add the bread cubes, and fry until browned on all sides. Remove, drain on paper towels, and set aside. Add the garlic to the same oil and sauté over low heat until tender, about 1 minute. Do not allow the garlic to brown.

Add the tomatoes and herbs to the pan and cook over medium heat until the sauce just begins to thicken, about 5 to 7 minutes. When ready, add the saffron and broth and simmer over low heat for 20 minutes. Taste and adjust for salt and pepper.

When ready to serve, add the beaten egg to the broth in a thin stream, stirring the broth constantly to distribute the egg. Serve hot in a heated soup tureen. Place the bread cubes in the tureen or in individual soup bowls.

VARIATION There are infinite variations to this basic soup. An interesting one is to omit the beaten egg and, instead, poach 4 eggs, place them in the individual soup bowls, and eat them with the soup. The dish is then quite substantial and can serve as the main course for a luncheon.

SOPA DE AJO BLANCO CON PASAS *Spain*
Cold Garlic Soup with Almonds and Raisins

In this unusual and delightful cold soup, garlic is ground together with almonds and raisins and mixed with milk. We first had it in Málaga, on the Costa del Sol, where this and similar dishes are very popular. The soup is rich—a little goes a long way—and should be served with a light main dish. It's perfect for a summer buffet.

SERVES 6

¾ cup diced fresh bread, crusts removed, cut into ½-inch cubes

1 cup blanched almonds, lightly toasted

2 garlic cloves, peeled

1 cup raisins, soaked in 2 cups warm water for 30 minutes, drained

1 quart milk

2 tablespoons raisins, soaked in 2 tablespoons medium-dry sherry for 30 minutes

Soak the bread in water to cover in order to soften, then squeeze out excess liquid. Place the bread and almonds in a blender or food processor along with the garlic and 1 cup raisins and process until the ingredients are very finely ground. Combine thoroughly with the milk, add the 2 tablespoons of whole raisins with the sherry, and chill well. Since the ingredients tend to settle, stir before serving. Serve very cold.

YOĞURT CORBASI   *Turkey*
Yogurt Soup

Of the many yogurt soups one finds in Turkey, this is our favorite. It's easy to prepare and, because the yogurt is added at the very end, there is no danger that the yogurt will curdle. Although served hot, it's wonderfully refreshing, ideal for a warm summer evening.   SERVES 4

4 cups Vegetable Broth (see
   recipe)
¼ cup long-grain rice
½ cup water
2 tablespoons flour
5 tablespoons butter

2 tablespoons fresh chopped mint
   leaves, or 1 tablespoon dried
   mint leaves, plus a few
   whole leaves for garnish
1 egg yolk
1 cup yogurt
1½ teaspoons cayenne pepper

Heat the vegetable broth in a large saucepan, add the rice, and cook until almost done, about 18 minutes.

Mix the water into the flour, blend well, and add to the rice broth to thicken, stirring constantly to prevent lumping. Add 2 tablespoons of butter and the mint. Cook another 1 or 2 minutes, until the rice is done.

Place the egg and yogurt in a heated soup tureen and beat together with a wire whisk. Ladle in the boiling soup, a little at a time, stirring constantly. Garnish with the whole mint leaves. Melt the remaining butter and mix it with the cayenne. Place in a bowl and serve for those who wish to sprinkle it over the soup to add some bite. Serve hot.

SIGUK DOMATES
Cold Tomato Soup

Turkey

SERVES 6

*3 cups peeled, seeded, and
   chopped ripe tomatoes, or 3
   cups canned Italian plum
   tomatoes, with juice*
1 medium onion, chopped
1 cup Vegetable Broth (see recipe)
3 tablespoons lemon juice

*Salt and freshly ground pepper to
   taste*
1 cup yogurt
2 tablespoons chopped fresh basil
*2 tablespoons chopped fresh
   parsley*
2 tablespoons olive oil

Place the tomatoes and onion in a saucepan, bring to a boil, lower the heat, and simmer for 10 minutes. Add the vegetable broth and remove from the heat. Allow to cool for 15 minutes, then place in a blender and purée until smooth. Add the lemon juice, and salt and pepper, blend another second, and transfer to a mixing bowl. Depending on the capacity of your blender, you may prefer to do this in batches.

Whip the yogurt until smooth and add to the cool tomato mixture. Combine well. Stir in the basil, parsley, and olive oil, and chill until ready to serve.

MINESTRA FIORI DI ZUCCA
Zucchini Flower Soup

Italy

If you have zucchini plants, you will also have an abundance of flowers. Use them for this delightful, very easy-to-prepare vegetable soup. Our friend Francesco Colacicchi gave us the recipe, one he picked up in Calabria.   SERVES 4 TO 6

3 tablespoons olive oil
½ cup finely chopped onion
2 garlic cloves, roughly chopped
2 cups peeled and diced potatoes
½ pound zucchini flowers,
    washed and cut in half
    lengthwise
1 bay leaf
½ teaspoon oregano
4 cups Vegetable Broth (see
    recipe)

2 cups tightly packed spinach or
    Swiss chard, well washed
    and roughly chopped
2 tablespoons chopped fresh basil
1 cup scrubbed and diced zucchini
¼ teaspoon freshly ground black
    pepper.
Salt to taste

Heat the oil in a saucepan, add the onion and garlic, and sauté over low heat for 5 minutes, until the onion is transparent. Do not brown. Add the potatoes and cook, stirring, for 2 minutes. Add the flowers, bay leaf, oregano, and the broth. Bring to a boil, reduce heat, and simmer covered for 30 minutes.

Add the spinach or Swiss chard, basil, zucchini, pepper, and salt. Simmer covered another 15 minutes, until the vegetables are cooked. Remove the bay leaf. Serve warm or at room temperature.

OLLA GITANA   *Spain*
Sweet and Sour Vegetable Soup

In this remarkably good and unusual soup from Algeciras, squash and pears provide the sweetness, vinegar the sour contrast.

SERVES 4 TO 6

½ cup dry chick-peas, or 1 cup
    canned chick-peas
1 tablespoon flour
3 cups water
6 tablespoons olive oil
1 dried bell pepper (p. 14)
    (optional)
2 garlic cloves, roughly chopped
1 slice hearty white or
    whole-wheat bread
6 blanched almonds, lightly
    toasted
Pinch of saffron
½ cup finely chopped onion
1 large ripe tomato, peeled and
    chopped

1 tablespoon sweet paprika
¼ pound green beans, trimmed
    and cut into 2-inch segments
¼ pound butternut squash, peeled
    and cut into ½-inch cubes
2 medium half-ripe Bartlett pears,
    peeled, cored, and cut into
    eighths
About 4 to 6 cups Vegetable
    Broth (see recipe)
Salt and freshly ground pepper to
    taste
1½ tablespoons white wine
    vinegar

Soak the chick-peas for 8 hours or overnight in 2 cups of water with 1 tablespoon of flour. When ready, rinse, and simmer, covered, in 3 cups of water until tender, about 1½ hours. As an alternative, cook in a pressure cooker for 30 minutes. Drain, reserving the cooking liquid. Set the chick-peas aside. If using canned chick-peas, rinse with cold water, and set aside.

Heat 4 tablespoons olive oil in a large saucepan, add the dried bell pepper, fry lightly, and remove. Add the garlic and bread and fry until they begin to brown. Remove from the oil with a slotted spoon, then grind all three together with the almonds, saffron, and 2 tablespoons oil in a mortar or food processor until a fine paste is formed. Set aside.

Reheat the oil, add the onion, and sauté over medium heat until it begins to color, about 5 minutes. Add the tomato, paprika, green beans, and squash. Cover and simmer over low heat until the vegetables are barely tender, about 10 minutes. Do not overcook. Add the pears, combine well, cook another minute. Add the chick-peas, the water in which the chick-peas cooked, and enough vegetable broth to make 6 cups of liquid. If using canned chick-peas, use 6 cups vegetable broth. Bring to a boil, cook 2 minutes, adjust for salt and pepper, remove from the heat, and set aside.

Combine the vinegar with the garlic-almond paste and ¼ cup

of the soup broth. Mix well and blend into the soup. Heat through and serve hot in a heated soup tureen.

AIGO BOULIDO   *France*
Provençal Sage Soup

Sage in Provençal herbal lore has miraculous, health-giving properties. One proverb maintains that with sage in the garden, you have no need of a doctor, while another states that boiled water in which the principal ingredient is sage will save your life *(l'eau bouille sauve la vie)*. Medicinal properties aside, the soup is delicious and very easy to prepare. You do need fresh sage.   SERVES 4

4 cups Vegetable Broth (see
   recipe)
6 to 8 garlic cloves, crushed
1 large sprig fresh sage, about 10
   leaves
1 small sprig fresh or ¼ teaspoon
   dried thyme
1 bay leaf
2 tablespoons olive oil

1 cup peeled and diced potatoes
1 cup vermicelli noodles
1 egg yolk
4 slices French or whole-wheat
   bread, toasted
1 cup Aïoli (see recipe)
   (optional)
4 tablespoons freshly grated
   Parmesan

Place the broth in a saucepan, add the garlic, sage, thyme, bay leaf, and olive oil. Bring to a boil, reduce the heat, and simmer, covered, 15 minutes. Add the potatoes and cook another 15 minutes, until the potatoes are tender. Remove the herbs, add the vermicelli noodles, and cook until the noodles are al dente.

Place the egg yolk in a soup tureen, add 1 cup of hot broth, a little at a time, stirring constantly, then add the rest of the soup. Place a slice of bread in each soup bowl and serve warm, accompanied by the *aïoli* and Parmesan.

PANCOTTO
Cooked Bread
Italy

In spite of its uninspired name, *pancotto* is an excellent soup. It is a simple peasant dish created to make use of stale bread. If you don't have stale bread, dry it in the oven at low heat to simulate the real thing. The soup can be prepared in advance; in fact, it's better the second day.   SERVES 4 TO 6

5 tablespoons olive oil
1 large onion, finely chopped
3 garlic cloves, finely chopped
1 teaspoon fresh rosemary, or ½
    teaspoon dried rosemary
Pinch dried oregano
2 tablespoons chopped fresh
    parsley
2 tablespoons chopped fresh basil
2 cups canned Italian plum
    tomatoes, with juice
½ medium cabbage, finely sliced
    (about 2 cups)

½ cup freshly grated Parmesan
½ cup freshly grated Romano or
    sharp pecorino
Salt to taste
¼ teaspoon coarsely ground black
    pepper
¼ teaspoon cayenne pepper
    (optional)
3 cups stale whole-wheat or white
    bread
5 cups Vegetable Broth (see
    recipe) or water

Heat the olive oil in a large, heavy saucepan, add the onion, garlic, rosemary, and oregano, and sauté over medium heat for 3 to 4 minutes, until the onion just begins to color. Add the parsley and basil, cook another minute, then blend in the tomatoes and cabbage and cook, stirring occasionally, for 5 minutes. Add 2 tablespoons of Parmesan, 2 tablespoons of Romano or pecorino, and the remaining ingredients. Mix well, cover, and simmer over low heat, stirring occasionally, for 30 minutes. About 5 minutes before the soup is done, blend in the remaining Parmesan and Romano or pecorino. Serve hot in a warm soup tureen.

POTAJE VALENCIANO   *Spain*
Valencian Chick-pea and Spinach Soup

Valencia is justly famed for its rice creations but there is, of course, more to the cuisine of Valencia than rice. This dish, one of the many excellent vegetable soups found in the area, recalls, through the felicitous combination of chick-peas and spinach, the Arabic influence on Valencian food. The entire soup can be made in advance but do not add the egg yolks and lemon juice until you are ready to serve it.   SERVES 6

1 cup dry chick-peas
1 tablespoon flour
1 bay leaf
1 stalk celery with leaves
2 medium onions
1 carrot, peeled and cut into 4
*   pieces*
6 whole peppercorns
1 pound spinach, well washed,
*   tough stems removed*
4 tablespoons olive oil
2 garlic cloves, finely chopped

2 tablespoons finely chopped fresh
*   parsley*
1 heaping tablespoon sweet
*   paprika*
¼ teaspoon freshly ground black
*   pepper*
Salt to taste
About 4 cups Vegetable Broth (see
*   recipe)*
2 egg yolks
Juice of 1 lemon

Soak the chick-peas in 4 cups of water with the flour for 8 hours or overnight. Drain, rinse, and cook with 6 cups of water, the bay leaf, celery, 1 onion cut in half, the carrot, and peppercorns until tender, 1½ hours in a covered saucepan, 30 minutes in a pressure cooker. Remove the vegetables with a slotted spoon and discard. Set aside the chick-peas and the cooking liquid.

Place the spinach in a saucepan without adding water, bring to a boil, lower the heat, and cook, uncovered, until the spinach is tender, about 5 minutes. Drain, chop, and set aside.

Chop the remaining onion finely. Heat the oil in a large saucepan, add the onion, and sauté over medium heat until it begins to soften, about 3 minutes. Add the garlic, sauté another minute, add the parsley, paprika, pepper, salt, spinach, chick-peas, and the cooking liquid plus enough vegetable broth to make 6 cups of liquid. Combine well and simmer, covered, over low heat for 10 minutes. Remove and discard the bay leaf.

When ready to serve, combine the egg yolks, lemon juice, and ¼ cup of the soup broth in a mixing bowl and mix well. Bring the soup to a boil, remove from the heat, and, stirring constantly with a wooden spoon, blend in the egg-and-lemon mixture. Pour into a warm soup tureen and serve hot.

SOBBA DEL BOULBOULA AU L'FOULE   *Morocco*
Bulgur and Bean Soup

The addition of paprika and fresh coriander leaves does wonders for this simple, nourishing mixture of broth, bulgur, and beans. Canned beans can be used for this recipe. Rinse before adding to the broth. If using dried beans, remember to soak 8 hours or overnight before cooking.   SERVES 4 TO 6

*6 cups Vegetable Broth (see
    recipe)
¾ cup coarse bulgur wheat
1 tablespoon sweet paprika
½ teaspoon turmeric*

*½ teaspoon cayenne pepper
1 cup cooked white beans
3 tablespoons chopped fresh
    coriander leaves*

Bring the broth to a boil, add the bulgur, paprika, turmeric, and cayenne pepper. Simmer, covered, for 30 minutes, then blend in the beans and coriander leaves. Cook another 3 to 5 minutes. Serve hot.

HARIRA   *Morocco*
Vegetable Soup

Harira is the traditional first course served in Morocco to break the day-long fast observed during the month of Ramadan. As one might expect, there are almost as many versions of *harira* as families in Morocco, although all are made with lamb. Fatima made a

meatless version that captures the rich flavor and zest of the original. The secret lies in long, slow cooking, so give yourself plenty
of time. The soup will keep a few days in the refrigerator and will,
in fact, improve with age.   SERVES 8 TO 10

½ cup dry chick-peas
⅓ cup flour plus 1 tablespoon
3 onions, minced
3 tender celery stalks with leaves,
    minced
1 cup minced fresh parsley
1⅓ cups minced fresh coriander
    leaves
2 teaspoons freshly ground black
    pepper
1 tablespoon sweet paprika
1 teaspoon turmeric
1 teaspoon ground ginger

1 teaspoon ground cinnamon
3 tablespoons butter
2½ quarts cold water plus 1 cup
2 pounds fresh, ripe tomatoes,
    peeled, seeded, and finely
    chopped, or 3 cups canned
    Italian plum tomatoes, with
    juice
1 tablespoon tomato paste
½ cup lentils
Salt to taste
Juice of 2 lemons
2 extra-large eggs

Soak the chick-peas 8 hours or overnight in 3 cups of water
with 1 tablespoon of flour.

Place the onions, celery, parsley, 1 cup of coriander leaves,
pepper, paprika, turmeric, ginger, cinnamon, and butter in a large
stockpot. Add 2½ quarts of cold water and bring slowly to a boil.
Simmer, covered, for 20 minutes. Add the tomatoes and tomato
paste. Simmer another 10 minutes.

Drain and rinse the chick-peas, add them with the lentils to the
pan, partially cover, and simmer for 1½ hours, until the chick-peas
are tender. Stir occasionally. Taste and adjust for salt, then blend
in the remaining coriander leaves.

Mix 1 cup of cold water into ⅓ cup flour and blend until
smooth. Add to the soup slowly in a thin stream, stirring constantly. Cook another 5 minutes, stirring frequently to prevent
lumping, to thicken the soup.

When ready to serve, add the lemon juice. Beat the eggs in a
separate bowl, then add to the simmering soup, stirring constantly.
Remove from the heat and serve hot.

SOBBA DEL ADESS
Lentil Soup
Morocco

To select one lentil soup to include in this book was a little like choosing our favorite Greek island—a virtually impossible task. We finally settled on a sensational, spicy soup from Morocco, light and easy to prepare. It is excellent the next day.

SERVES 4 TO 6

1 cup lentils
1 large ripe tomato, peeled and
    chopped, or ½ cup canned
    Italian plum tomatoes, with
    juice
1 cup chopped onions
4 scallions, green parts included,
    chopped
3 garlic cloves, chopped
1 bay leaf
4 tablespoons chopped fresh
    parsley

5 tablespoons chopped fresh
    coriander leaves
2 teaspoons ground ginger
2 teaspoons turmeric
2 teaspoons sweet paprika
2 tablespoons olive oil
2 tablespoons peanut oil
1 teaspoon freshly ground black
    pepper
Salt to taste
5 cups water
1 tablespoon ground cumin

Combine all the ingredients except the cumin in a large saucepan with the water. Bring to a boil and simmer on low, covered, for 1½ hours. Discard the bay leaf.

Remove 1 cup of soup and pureé it. Return to the pan, heat through, sprinkle cumin on top, and serve hot.

MACCU
Purée of Fava Bean Soup
Italy

An ancient rustic soup from Sicily, *maccu* is thick and nourishing. It can be made with fresh or frozen lima beans or, preferably, dried fava beans. The soup is usually consumed cold but it is equally good hot.

SERVES 4 TO 6

2 cups dried or fresh lima beans
    or dried fava beans
6 cups water
4 tablespoons fresh dill, or 2
    tablespoons dried dill
½ cup egg noodles, cut into
    1-inch pieces
4 tablespoons olive oil

½ cup roughly chopped onion
1 medium ripe tomato, peeled,
    seeded, and chopped, or ½
    cup drained canned Italian
    plum tomatoes
Salt and freshly ground pepper to
    taste

If using dried beans, soak 8 hours or overnight in 4 cups of water. Drain and remove outer skins. If using fresh lima beans, omit this step.

Place 6 cups of water in a large saucepan, add the beans, and simmer, covered, for 1½ hours, until the beans disintegrate. Stir occasionally. Add the dill and cook another 10 minutes. Add the pasta and cook until al dente, stirring frequently to prevent the pasta from sticking. Add additional water if too thick, although it should have the consistency of thick split pea soup.

Meanwhile, heat the olive oil in a skillet, add the onion, and sauté over medium heat until golden, about 10 minutes. Add the tomato and cook another 5 minutes.

When the pasta is cooked, add the onion-and-tomato mixture to the soup. Season with salt and pepper, stir, and serve either warm or at room temperature. Pass additional olive oil for those who wish to add a tablespoon to their soup.

VARIATION Sauté 1 cup thinly sliced golden Hubbard or butternut squash in 2 tablespoons olive oil until tender, about 10 minutes, and add to the soup when adding the dill. Proceed as above.

CREMA DI ASPARAGI AL MASCARPONE   *Italy*
Cream of Asparagus with Mascarpone

SERVES 4

2 tablespoons butter
1 pound asparagus, washed,
    tough parts of stems trimmed
    or removed
3 cups Vegetable Broth (see
    recipe)
¼ cup Arborio rice
Pinch of nutmeg

1 cup whipping cream
¼ pound Mascarpone
Salt and freshly ground pepper to
    taste
1 extra-large egg
¼ cup freshly grated Parmesan
1 tablespoon chives, cut into
    small segments

Heat the butter in a skillet, add the asparagus, cover, and cook over low heat, stirring frequently, until tender, about 10 minutes. Cut off 1 inch of the tips and reserve

Place the asparagus stems in a blender or food processor with a cup of vegetable broth and purée. Place in a saucepan, add the remaining broth, and bring to a boil. Add rice and nutmeg, and cook 15 to 20 minutes, until the rice is done. Allow to cool for 10 minutes, then return to the blender or food processor and pulse a few times. The rice should not be entirely puréed. Depending on the size of your blender or processor, you may wish to do this in two batches.

Combine the cream with the Mascarpone and add to the hot soup. Blend over low heat, taste, and adjust for salt and pepper. The soup can be prepared ahead of time to this point.

When ready to serve, beat the egg together with the Parmesan in a small mixing bowl and pour into a heated soup tureen. Add a ladleful of hot soup to the egg mixture, a little at a time, beating constantly with a wire whisk. Add the remaining soup, incorporate the asparagus tips, sprinkle with chives, and serve hot.

SOUPE AU POTIRON   *France*
Provençal Squash Soup

All winter long, the food markets of Provence feature *potirons*—
huge, tan-skinned, orange-fleshed pumpkins, as beautiful as they
are delicious. This recipe was given to us by Madame Mascargue,
one of the vendors in the Antibes market who kept us supplied with
potirons from her garden. There is no squash in North America as
sweet and richly flavored as those we found in Provence but golden
Hubbard or butternut with a little sugar makes a good substitute.

SERVES 4 TO 6

3 tablespoons olive oil
2 cups cleaned and roughly
   chopped leeks, with some
   green
2 garlic cloves, roughly chopped
2 pounds golden Hubbard or
   butternut squash, peeled,
   seeded, and cut into cubes
1 teaspoon sugar (optional)
5 cups water

Bouquet garni made with thyme,
   sage, rosemary, and bay leaf,
   tied together (p. 11)
1 celery stalk, with leaves,
   roughly chopped
2-inch piece of lemon zest
Salt and freshly ground pepper to
   taste
2 tablespoons chopped chives
1 cup Crème Fraîche (see
   recipe)

Heat the oil in a large saucepan, add the leeks and garlic, and
sauté 5 minutes until the leeks wilt. Add the squash and sugar,
lower the heat, and sauté 5 more minutes, stirring frequently with
a wooden spoon.

Add the water and all the remaining ingredients except the
chives and *crème fraîche*. Simmer for 30 minutes.

Remove and discard the bouquet garni, allow to cool for 10
minutes, then transfer the soup to a blender or food processor,
and purée. Depending on the size of your blender or processor,
you may wish to do this in two batches. Return to the saucepan and
heat through.

Serve hot, sprinkled with chives. Pass the *crème fraîche* for those
who want to add a tablespoon or two to their soup.

CRÈME DE FENOUIL
Cream of Fennel Soup

France

SERVES 6

3 large fennel bulbs, cut into
   wedges
Bouquet garni made with thyme,
   rosemary, sage, and bay leaf,
   tied together (p. 11)
4 cups Vegetable Broth (see
   recipe)
2 tablespoons olive oil
4 shallots, roughly chopped

2 garlic cloves, roughly chopped
1 cup canned Italian plum
   tomatoes, with juice, or 1
   cup peeled, seeded, and
   chopped ripe tomatoes
1 cup light cream
Salt and freshly ground pepper to
   taste
2 tablespoons chervil, chopped

Place all but 1 fennel wedge in a large saucepan, add the bouquet garni and broth, and cook, covered, for 25 minutes, until the fennel is very tender.

Meanwhile, heat the oil in a large, low-sided saucepan, add the shallots and garlic, and sauté 2 minutes. Add the tomatoes and cook 10 minutes, stirring occasionally.

When the fennel is cooked, remove with a slotted spoon, and transfer to the tomato mixture. Remove the bouquet garni from the broth and discard. Simmer the fennel for 5 minutes in the tomato mixture, then add the broth in which it was cooked.

Remove the soup from the heat, allow to cool for 10 minutes, then purée the soup in a blender or food processor. Depending on the size of your blender or processor, you may wish to purée in two batches. Return to the saucepan, add the cream, salt, and pepper, and heat through.

Chop the remaining fennel wedge, combine with the chervil, and set aside. Pour the soup into a heated tureen, sprinkle the chopped fennel and chervil on top, and serve hot.

SOUPE AUX PETITS POIS   *France*
Fresh Cream of Pea Soup

This is a great spring soup, a delicious purée of peas, leeks, and onions enriched with a little *crème fraîche.* You can use frozen peas but fresh ones are preferable.   SERVES 4

2 cups shelled peas, fresh or
    frozen
2 medium well-washed and
    chopped leeks, with some
    green
1 cup chopped onions
½ cup chopped potatoes
3 shallots, chopped
Bouquet garni made with thyme,
    rosemary, bay leaf, and sage,
    tied together (p. 11)

1 teaspoon sugar
Salt and freshly ground pepper to
    taste
5 cups water
½ cup Crème Fraîche (see
    recipe)
1 extra-large egg yolk

Combine the vegetables and all the remaining ingredients, except the *crème fraîche* and egg yolk, in a large saucepan with the water.

Bring to a boil and cook, covered, for 45 minutes, stirring occasionally until the vegetables are very tender. If using frozen peas, add for the final 15 minutes of cooking.

Remove the bouquet garni and discard. Remove from the heat, allow to cool for 10 minutes, then purée the soup in a blender or food processor, return to the saucepan, and keep warm. Depending on the size of your blender or processor, you may wish to purée the soup in two batches. Combine the *crème fraîche* and egg yolk in a small mixing bowl and pour into a soup tureen. Add the soup, mix thoroughly, and serve. The soup can also be served cold.

SOUPE AUX MOULES
Mussel Soup

France

A delicious and substantial soup, we often serve it as a main dish for a light dinner along with salad and dessert.   SERVES 4

1 cup dry white wine
3 pounds small mussels, scrubbed, beards removed
3 tablespoons olive oil
1 onion, finely chopped
2 garlic cloves, finely chopped
½ cup canned Italian plum tomatoes, with juice, or ½ cup peeled and minced ripe tomatoes

Pinch of saffron
Bouquet garni made with thyme, rosemary, and bay leaf, tied together (p. 11)
Salt to taste
1 cup spaghettini or vermicelli broken into 1-inch segments
2 tablespoons chopped fresh parsley
Freshly ground pepper to taste

Combine wine and 1½ cups of water in a large saucepan. Bring to a boil, add mussels, cover, and steam, shaking the pan occasionally, until the mussels open, about 3 to 4 minutes. Remove the mussels with a slotted spoon and set aside to cool. Strain the cooking liquid through a wad of cotton placed in the neck of a funnel and reserve. When cooled, remove the flesh and discard the shells.

Heat the oil in a large saucepan, add the onion and garlic, and sauté over medium heat until golden. Add the tomatoes, saffron, bouquet garni, the cooking liquid, and enough water to make 5 cups, bring to a boil, season with salt, then add the pasta and cook until al dente, about 10 minutes.

Remove the pan from the heat, discard the bouquet garni, and add the mussels. Sprinkle with parsley, season with pepper, and serve immediately.

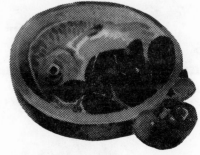

SOUPE DE POISSON CÔTE D'AZUR   *France*
Fish Soup of the Côte d'Azur

Many of the best Mediterranean fish soups derive directly from the stockpots of fishermen. They sell the best of their catch and keep the rest, the ugly, firm-fleshed rock fish, for their own consumption. Mixed with herbs, spices, vegetables, and a little wine, these fish make a great soup. In this recipe, the fish is cooked long and slowly, then passed through a fine sieve, so that only the flavor and none of the fish remains. It is served with toasted bread rubbed with garlic and Rouille, a spicy red pepper sauce. As for the type of fish, red mullet, scorpion fish, sea trout, porgy, snapper, and whiting are all fine.   SERVES 6 TO 8

4 tablespoons olive oil	*One 2-inch piece of orange rind*
2 leeks, with some green, washed	*Pinch of cayenne pepper, or 1*
* and sliced*	* small dried hot pepper,*
1 medium onion, roughly chopped	* crushed*
10 garlic cloves	*1 teaspoon chopped fresh dill*
2 pounds fresh fish, washed,	*Salt and freshly ground pepper to*
* scaled, with heads and tails*	* taste*
* included, cut into pieces*	*8 cups cold water*
1 medium ripe tomato, peeled,	*12 to 18 slices French bread,*
* seeded, and cubed*	* lightly toasted*
Generous pinch saffron	*1 cup* **Rouille** *(see recipe)*
1 bay leaf	*1 cup freshly grated Parmesan*

Heat the oil in a large, heavy saucepan, add the leeks, onion, and 4 garlic cloves, chopped. Sauté until vegetables begin to color, about 7 minutes. Add the fish and tomato and cook another 2 to 3 minutes. Add the saffron, bay leaf, orange rind, cayenne pepper, dill, salt, pepper, and cold water. Bring to a boil and simmer, covered, for 30 minutes.

Pass all the soup ingredients, including the heads, tails, and bones, through a food mill fitted with a fine disk.

Return the soup to the saucepan, heat through, and transfer to a heated tureen. Serve hot accompanied by the toast, 6 remaining whole garlic cloves, *rouille,* and Parmesan. Each guest, according to taste, rubs the toast with garlic and adds it to his or her soup along with some of the *rouille* and Parmesan.

PSAROSOUPA AVGOLEMONO   *Greece*
Fish Soup with Egg-Lemon Sauce

This is one of the most popular soups in Greece, fish stock and rice flavored with lemon juice, thickened with eggs. We often serve it as the first course at a dinner party.   SERVES 4 TO 6

6 cups water
2 pounds fish (whiting, red mullet, porgy, sea trout), washed and scaled, heads and tails included
2 medium onions, quartered
1 cup peeled and cubed potatoes
2 celery stalks, leaves included, chopped

½ cup long-grain rice
2 tablespoons chopped fresh parsley
2 extra-large eggs
Juice of 2 lemons
Salt and freshly ground pepper to taste

Place water in a saucepan, add the fish, bring to a boil, and cook 3 minutes. Remove any scum that accumulates on the surface of the stock, then add the onions, potatoes, and celery. Cover and simmer 1 hour.

Pass the soup, including fish heads, bones, and tails, through a food mill fitted with a fine disk, return the soup to the saucepan, add the rice and parsley, and simmer, covered, 15 to 20 minutes, until the rice is cooked.

While the rice cooks, place the eggs in a heated soup tureen and beat with a wire whisk until frothy. Pour the lemon juice into the eggs in a thin stream, beating constantly.

When the rice is cooked, add 2 ladles of the hot stock to the egg-and-lemon mixture a little at a time, beating constantly. Pour in the remaining soup, stirring constantly. Season with salt and pepper and serve immediately.

SOPA DE PESCADO CATALUÑA   *Spain*
Catalonian Fish Soup

This soup is usually made with monkfish but it works well with any white, firm-fleshed fish, such as halibut, cod, or hake. The soup is extremely easy to prepare and delicately flavored, suitable for all occasions.   SERVES 4

1 pound monkfish, skin and
    membrane removed, or other
    firm-fleshed fish fillets
2 tablespoons olive oil
1 large onion, finely chopped
12 blanched almonds, lightly
    toasted
1 tablespoon pine nuts
3 garlic cloves
Large pinch saffron
1½ cups peeled, seeded, and
    chopped ripe tomatoes, or
    1½ cups drained canned
    Italian plum tomatoes

½ cup dry white wine
5 cups Fish Stock (see recipe)
Salt and freshly ground pepper to
    taste
3 tablespoons chopped fresh
    parsley
2 slices hearty homemade bread,
    toasted and cut into bite-size
    pieces

Wash the fish and cut into 1-inch cubes. Set aside. Heat the oil in a large saucepan, add the onion, and sauté over medium heat until the onion begins to color.

Meanwhile grind the almonds, pine nuts, garlic, and saffron together in a mortar to form a smooth paste. Set aside.

When the onion is ready, add the tomatoes, fish, wine, fish stock, almond paste, and salt and pepper. Cover and simmer for 20 minutes.

Blend in the parsley and bread and simmer another 5 minutes. Serve hot.

SOPA DE PESCADO MÁLAGUEÑA **Spain**
Málagan Fish Chowder

It was a hot day in late spring, perfect, we decided, for lunch on a terrace overlooking the Mediterranean. It was also ideal for this wonderful sherry-spiked soup, a specialty of the restaurant Antonio Martín in Málaga. SERVES 4 TO 6

3 cups Fish Stock (see recipe)
12 to 18 medium shrimp (3 per
*   person), with shells*
12 to 18 small clams (3 per
*   person), scrubbed*
1 cup peeled and cubed potatoes
½ pound white fish (halibut,
*   grouper, or monkfish, skin*
*   and membrane removed)*
*   fillets, cut into 4 or 6 pieces*

1 cup milk
1 cup whipping cream
⅓ cup good dry sherry
Salt and freshly ground white
*   pepper to taste*

Place the fish stock in a saucepan, bring to a boil, add the shrimp, and simmer, covered, 2 to 3 minutes, until cooked. Remove with a slotted spoon and, when cooled, peel. Add the clams, cover, and cook until open. Remove with a slotted spoon and set aside.

Strain the stock through a wad of cotton placed in the neck of a funnel. Return the stock to the saucepan, add the potatoes, and simmer, covered, until almost cooked, about 10 minutes. Add the fish and simmer, covered, 5 minutes. Add the milk, cream, and sherry, heat through, taste and adjust for seasoning. Keep hot.

Distribute the shrimp and clams in individual soup bowls, add the hot fish chowder, and serve immediately.

Tarts, Croquettes, and Other Dishes

TARTE AUX POIREAUX ET POMMES DE TERRE   *France*
Leek and Potato Tart

This dish can serve as a substantial first course or as the main dish for a light supper, accompanied by soup and salad. It improves with age and can be made at least one day ahead of time. Serve at room temperature.   SERVES 4 TO 6

Pâte Brisée *(see recipe) made*
   with:
   2½ cups unbleached
   all-purpose flour
   6 ounces (1½ sticks) unsalted
   butter
   ¼ teaspoon salt
   2 extra-large eggs

1½ tablespoons lemon juice
1 pound new potatoes
1 pound leeks, with some green
Salt and freshly ground pepper to
   taste
Pinch of nutmeg
¼ cup Crème Fraîche *(see*
   recipe)

First make the *pâte brisée.* Roll into a ball, wrap with wax paper, and place in the refrigerator for at least 1 hour.

When ready to prepare the tart, preheat the oven to 400°F. and butter an 8-inch flan pan with a removable bottom.

Wash the potatoes, cut in half, and boil until almost cooked, about 15 minutes. Drain and set aside. Wash the leeks and cut into pieces about ¼-inch thick. Steam for 5 minutes, until just tender, drain, and set aside.

Divide the dough into 2 balls, one with two-thirds of the dough, the other with one-third. Roll the larger ball into a circle about ⅛-inch thick and fit it snugly into the bottom and sides of the flan pan, allowing extra dough to drape over the edges. Prick the bottom in several places with the tines of a fork.

Cut the potatoes into thin slices and cover the bottom of the flan pan with a single layer of potatoes. Place the leeks over the potatoes and cover the leeks with the remaining potatoes. Sprinkle lightly with salt, pepper, and nutmeg. Spread 2 tablespoons of *crème fraîche* over the potatoes.

Roll out the remaining dough ⅛-inch thick. Wet the edges of the dough and drape the newly rolled dough over the top of the flan pan. Secure the edges by pressing with your fingers or the tines of a fork. Trim off any excess dough.

Cut a hole in the center of the top about ¾ inch in diameter and place a 1-inch-high rolled piece of foil in it to act as a chimney. Prick the top in several places with the tines of a fork. Place the flan in the oven and bake for 15 minutes at 400°F. Reduce the heat to 375°F. and bake for another 20 minutes. When done, remove from the oven, remove the chimney, and pour the remaining *crème fraîche* into the hole. Set aside to cool. Remove the sides of the pan before serving.

VARIATION The flan can be made more substantial by adding thin slices of Gruyère. Distribute them over the leeks before adding the final layer of potatoes.

INFARINATA   *Italy*
Cornmeal with Vegetables

It was a bitterly cold January day in Florence. The north wind, the *tramontana,* was fierce and a ghostly sun hovered heatless in a pale sky. We had spent most of the morning supervising olive picking on the farm and were ready for a hearty, warming meal. Cornmeal dishes are perfect on such occasions and nothing could have been better than the robust soup of black cabbage, beans, and cornmeal that was served as the first course. That evening the leftovers were cut into squares and fried—which of the two versions we preferred was a toss-up. In this recipe, we describe the latter.   SERVES 4

*½ cup dry cannelini (white
    kidney) beans
1½ cups tightly packed, finely
    sliced kale leaves, stems
    removed
½ medium onion, chopped
2 garlic cloves, thinly sliced*

*1 carrot, peeled and thinly sliced
2 tablespoons finely chopped fresh
    parsley
¾ cup coarsely ground cornmeal
Salt and freshly ground pepper to
    taste
½ cup light seed oil for frying*

Soak beans 8 hours in 3 cups water. Bring 4 cups of water to a boil in a large saucepan. Add the kale, onion, garlic, carrot, parsley, and beans, drained and rinsed. Cook, covered, until the kale is tender, about 40 minutes. Add the cornmeal to the mixture in a thin stream, stirring constantly. Continue to cook, uncovered, over low heat, stirring frequently, until the cornmeal is cooked, about 30 minutes. Remove from the heat and set aside.

Wet a large wooden, marble, or Formica work surface with water, and, with the assistance of a wet knifeblade or spatula, spread the hot cornmeal mixture evenly over the surface. It should be about ¼-inch thick. Let cool completely.

When ready to serve, cut the cornmeal mixture into 2- to 3-inch squares. Heat the oil in a skillet, fry the squares until lightly browned on both sides, and drain on paper towels. Serve hot.

VARIATION If you decide to serve as a thick soup, increase the amount of water by 2 cups. After adding the cornmeal, continue to cook covered. To give the soup more flavor, you may wish to sauté the onion, garlic, and carrot before adding them to the soup. Serve with extra-virgin olive oil for those who wish to add it.

PIMIENTOS CON RELLENO DE PESCADO   **Spain**
Peppers Stuffed with Fish

We include here a modified version of a dish we had at the Sol-Ric restaurant in Tarragona, one that is relatively simple to prepare, very colorful, and delicious. It can also be served as an elegant main dish for a luncheon or light dinner.   SERVES 4

4 large yellow, green, or red bell
 peppers, plus ½ yellow,
 green, or red bell pepper,
 peeled and minced (p. 13)
2 medium onions
2 garlic cloves, quartered
4 sprigs parsley
1 bay leaf
Salt and abundant freshly ground
 white pepper
1 cup dry white wine
1 pound halibut or hake, skin
 and bones removed

3 tablespoons whipping cream
1 extra-large egg plus 1 egg yolk
3 tablespoons unsalted butter
1 pound ripe tomatoes, peeled and
 minced, or 1½ cups finely
 chopped canned Italian plum
 tomatoes, with juice
1 tablespoon sweet paprika
¼ teaspoon cayenne pepper
 (optional)
2 tablespoons finely chopped fresh
 parsley

Cut 1 inch off the tops of the peppers, discard the seeds and cores, and set the peppers with their tops aside.

Place 1 quartered onion in a small fish poacher or saucepan together with the garlic, parsley, bay leaf, salt and pepper, wine, and 1 cup of water. Bring to a boil and simmer, covered, for 10 minutes. Add the fish and simmer until cooked, about 8 minutes. Drain and purée the fish in a blender or food processor together with the cooked onion, garlic, 2 tablespoons of cream, and whole egg plus extra yolk. Set aside.

Preheat the oven to 375°F.

Stuff the peppers with the fish mixture and place them in a deep baking dish in which they fit snugly. Add enough water to come halfway up the sides of the peppers, cover with foil, and bake in the oven until the peppers are tender, about 35 to 40 minutes.

While the peppers cook, heat the butter in a saucepan, add the second onion, finely chopped, and sauté over medium heat until it begins to color, about 5 minutes. Add the tomatoes, paprika, cayenne pepper, and 1 tablespoon of cream, and cook, uncovered, stirring frequently, until the sauce begins to thicken, about 10 to 15 minutes. Remove from the heat, purée in a blender or food processor, return to the heat, add the minced bell pepper and parsley, combine well, and keep warm.

Distribute the tomato sauce evenly on 4 small plates. Remove the peppers from the oven, place 1 on each plate, and serve.

BUÑUELOS DE BACALAO   *Spain*
Croquettes of Salt Cod

Croquettes of cod and potatoes seasoned with garlic and parsley, fried, and served piping hot, are a specialty of Catalonia. These appetizers are among the most delicious we had in Spain.

SERVES 6

½ pound salt cod, preferably
    deboned and skinned
1 pound potatoes, unpeeled
2 garlic cloves, finely chopped
2 tablespoons finely chopped fresh
    parsley

Pinch of nutmeg
Salt and freshly ground pepper to
    taste
2 extra-large eggs, separated
½ cup light seed oil for frying

Soak the cod in cold water to cover for 24 to 36 hours, changing the water occasionally.

Place 3 or 4 cups of water in a saucepan, bring to a boil, add the cod and potatoes, cover, and simmer for 10 minutes, until the cod is very tender. Remove the cod with a slotted spoon and set aside. If using salt cod with skin and bones, remove and discard when cool enough to handle. Continue cooking until the potatoes are tender, another 20 minutes. Drain and set aside.

While the potatoes cook, combine the cod, garlic, parsley, nutmeg, salt, and pepper in a mortar and mash with a pestle. As an alternative, pass through a fine sieve. When the potatoes are ready, peel, mash, and combine them with the cod in a large mixing bowl. Add 2 egg yolks and blend thoroughly. Beat the egg whites until they form stiff peaks, then fold into the cod-potato mixture. Set aside.

Heat the oil in a skillet suitable for deep frying and, when hot, scoop up a tablespoon of the mixture and fry in the oil until browned on all sides. Drain on paper towels and keep warm until all the batter is used. It is best to fry a few croquettes at a time. Serve hot.

BOREKS I
Fried Dumplings

Turkey

These and similar preparations are extremely popular in Turkey and, for that matter, throughout the Middle East and North Africa. They come in various shapes, sizes, fillings, and doughs. The two we include here (see the following recipe as well), both Turkish, are made with a simple short dough, and are rolled into cylindrical shapes. They are superb first courses and surprisingly easy to make.   MAKES APPROXIMATELY 32 BOREKS

Pâte Brisée *(see recipe)*
1¼ *cups feta cheese*
3 tablespoons chopped fresh
     parsley

3 tablespoons chopped fresh dill
½ *cup light seed oil for frying*

Make the *pâte brisée* and place in the refrigerator for at least 1 hour.

Blend feta cheese, parsley, and dill in a mixing bowl and set aside until ready to use.

When ready, divide the dough into 4 roughly equal pieces. Take 1 piece, shape into a ball, flatten, place on a lightly floured marble or wooden work surface and roll out very thin, turning and flipping every so often to prevent sticking. Then, with a sharp knife, cut into triangular shapes, roughly 2½ inches at the base, as if you were cutting a pie. Put a little stuffing at the base of the triangle, fold the 2 bottom corners over the filling to prevent it from escaping, then roll up from the base to the apex of the triangle to form a short, stout cylinder. Wet the apex with a little water to seal. Set aside. Repeat with the remaining dough and filling until all is consumed.

Heat the oil in a skillet until medium hot—if too hot the butter in the dough will burn before the dough itself is cooked. Add a few *boreks* and fry until golden on all sides. Drain on paper towels and keep warm until all are cooked. Serve immediately.

|| *BOREKS II*   **Turkey**
|| Baked Dumplings

Similar to the preceding recipe, these are filled with a feta-spinach mixture, and baked instead of fried. They are equally delicious. The filling and the dough can both be made a day in advance.

MAKES APPROXIMATELY 32 BOREKS

Pâte Brisée *(see recipe)*

FOR THE FILLING:

1 pound spinach, washed well,
   tough stems removed
2 tablespoons olive oil
2 garlic cloves, chopped
Pinch of nutmeg
½ cup feta cheese

1 extra-large egg
2 tablespoons chopped fresh
   parsley
2 tablespoons chopped fresh dill
Freshly ground pepper to taste

1 egg yolk or 2 tablespoons butter
   at room temperature

Make the *pâte brisée*, roll into a ball, wrap with wax paper, and place in the refrigerator for at least 1 hour.

Place the spinach in a large saucepan, bring to a boil without adding water, reduce heat to low, and simmer, uncovered, until tender, about 5 minutes. Drain, squeeze all excess water out by pressing the spinach against the side of a colander with a wooden spoon, chop finely, and set aside.

Heat the oil in a skillet, add the garlic, and sauté over medium heat for 1 minute. Add the spinach and nutmeg, blend thoroughly, and sauté another 2 minutes. Remove from the heat and set aside.

Mash the feta with a fork in a mixing bowl, add the remaining filling ingredients, and combine. Add the spinach mixture, blend, and set aside.

Heat oven to 375°F. and butter a cookie sheet or the equivalent well.

Roll the dough, cut into triangles roughly 2½ inches at the base, stuff and roll into cylindrically shaped boreks as explained in the previous recipe. Place on the cookie sheet, brush with the egg yolk or butter, and bake in the oven until golden, about 15 to 20 minutes. Serve immediately.

BRIWAT BEL BED   *Morocco*
Fried Dumpling with Egg

This is a terrific, very common Moroccan dish, good as an appetizer, a first course, or even the main course for a luncheon or light dinner. The problem for us was the dough. Traditional Moroccan dough for this dish is water based and quite difficult and time-consuming to make. It is not readily available outside of Morocco and most substitutes are inferior. After some experimentation, we decided to abandon tradition entirely and to use a standard short dough with a Moroccan filling. Since this is very similar to a sophisticated *panzerotto,* an Italian delicacy, it can be thought of as an Italian first course with a Moroccan flavor. Whatever the country of origin, the dish is scrumptious.

SERVES 4

Pâte Brisée *(see recipe), half the amount*
3 tablespoons olive oil
½ large onion, finely chopped
4 tablespoons chopped fresh coriander leaves

Salt and abundant freshly ground pepper
4 medium eggs
½ to ¾ cup light seed oil

Make the *pâte brisée* and set aside in the refrigerator for at least 1 hour.

Heat the olive oil in a saucepan, add the onion, and sauté for

3 minutes. Add the coriander and continue to cook until the onion begins to color. Remove from the heat and set aside to cool.

When ready to serve, take a piece of dough roughly the size of a large golf ball and roll it into a thin disk about 6 inches in diameter. Place the dough in a shallow bowl and put a little of the onion mixture in the center of the disk, then break an egg over the stuffing, taking care to keep the yolk intact. Wet the border of the disk with water, then fold in half to form a half moon. Make 3 more dumplings.

Heat the seed oil in a skillet over medium heat. Do not overheat the oil—if it is too hot, it will burn the dough without cooking it. Add the dumplings, one at a time, brown on both sides, drain, and serve immediately.

SCACCIATA SICILIANA   *Italy*
Sicilian Pizza with Onion, Cheese, and Anchovies

In Calabria and Sicily, pizza is often made with a top as well as a bottom crust and a coarse semolina flour replaces regular finely ground flour in the dough. The result is a much more substantial pizza with a robust, flavorful crust. The range of possible stuffings is immense—the one we include here, a combination of onion, sharp cheese, and anchovies, is delicious and very easy to make. The pizza can be made in advance and reheated, although it's best if baked and served at once. Serve as an appetizer, first course, snack, or even a main dish for an informal dinner.

SERVES 6 TO 8

1½ teaspoons (½ package)
   active dry yeast
1¼ cups water
3 cups semolina flour
4 tablespoons olive oil
¼ teaspoon salt
6 ounces sharp provolone, grated
   or thinly sliced

1 medium onion, thinly sliced
8 to 10 anchovy fillets, packed in
   oil, drained and cut into
   small pieces
¼ teaspoon freshly ground black
   pepper

Dissolve the yeast in ½ cup warm water, cover, and set aside for 10 minutes.

When ready, add the flour, 2 tablespoons of olive oil, salt, and ¾ cup water. Combine well, turn onto a lightly floured work surface, and knead for 10 minutes, until a fairly firm but easily workable dough is obtained. If using a food processor, insert the metal blade, add the flour and the other ingredients to work bowl, and process until the dough clears the sides of the bowl. You may have to add a little more water but do so 1 tablespoon at a time.

Coat the dough with a thin film of olive oil, place in a large mixing bowl, cover well with a plastic wrap, and set aside to rise in a warm place for about 45 minutes, until doubled in bulk.

Preheat the oven to 400°F. and oil a 12-inch pizza pan or the equivalent.

Divide the dough into 2 equal parts, set one aside, and roll the other into a thin circle roughly the size of the pizza pan. The dough should be about ⅛-inch thick. Place the dough in the pan and push it out to the edges. Spread the cheese, onion, and anchovies over the surface of the dough, taking care to leave a ¼-inch border free of stuffing. Drizzle with 1 tablespoon of olive oil and sprinkle with the pepper.

Roll out the remaining dough as you did the first piece and use it to cover the pizza. Seal the border by pressing firmly with your fingers, paint the surface with the remaining tablespoon of oil, poke holes in the top with the tines of a fork, and set aside to rise for 20 minutes. When ready, bake for 20 to 25 minutes, until lightly browned. Cool for 10 minutes before serving.

PASTA PER PIZZA   *Italy*
Pizza Dough

Traditional pizza dough is simply bread dough with the addition of a little olive oil. We give here a recipe for dough made with white flour. If you wish to make a whole-wheat crust, substitute 1¼ cups of whole-wheat flour for half the white flour. You can also make the dough using baking powder in place of yeast. Use 2¾ teaspoons of double-acting baking powder instead of yeast. Since baking powder dough does not have to rise, preparation time is considerably reduced. The recipe makes enough dough for a 12-inch pizza.   MAKES A 12-INCH PIZZA

1½ teaspoons (½ package) active dry yeast	2½ cups unbleached all-purpose flour
1 cup warm water	2½ tablespoons olive oil
Pinch of sugar	½ teaspoon salt

Dissolve the yeast in ½ cup of warm water (110°F. to 115°F.) with the sugar in a large mixing bowl and set aside for 10 minutes.

Add the flour, 2 tablespoons of olive oil, salt, and approximately ½ cup of warm water. Mix, then turn onto a lightly floured board or marble slab and knead for 10 minutes, until a smooth, elastic, homogeneous dough is obtained. You may have to add more water, depending on the water-absorbing capacity of your flour. The dough should be very pliable but not sticky. Place in a large mixing bowl, coat with the remaining ½ tablespoon of oil, cover well with a plastic wrap, and set aside in a warm place to rise for 1 hour, until doubled in bulk.

When ready, oil lightly a 12-inch pizza pan. Knead the dough for a few minutes on a board or marble slab, roll it out to roughly the size of the pan, fit the dough in the pan, spreading it with your fingers. Use according to the recipe.

PISSALADIÈRE　　　　　　　　　　　　　　*France*
Niçoise Onion Pizza

According to a baker we know in Nice, *pissaladière* was originally a poor man's dish, made with nothing more than bread dough, onions, salt, olive oil, and, perhaps, heads and tails of anchovies. The style today is much more elaborate, with lots of anchovies and olives and occasionally other ingredients as well. He still makes them in the old way—just onions, salt, and oil—and his are the best we've eaten. We include a few anchovies and olives in the recipe below, but exclude them if you wish.

MAKES A 12-INCH PIZZA

Pizza Dough (see recipe)
2 pounds onions, finely chopped
6 tablespoons olive oil
2 or 3 anchovy fillets, packed in oil, drained and cut into small pieces (optional)

6 Niçoise olives, pitted, rinsed well if salty, quartered (optional)
Pinch of salt

Make the pizza dough and set aside to rise.

Place the onions in a saucepan with 4 tablespoons of olive oil, cover, and simmer, stirring occasionally, for 40 minutes, until the onions almost disintegrate.

Preheat the oven to 400°F. and oil well a 12-inch pizza pan or the equivalent.

When ready, roll out the dough on a board or marble slab, then transfer to the pizza pan. Allow to rest 15 minutes, covered with a clean dry dish towel. When ready, cover with the onions, distribute the anchovies and olives over the onions, drizzle with the remaining oil, sprinkle with salt, and bake for 20 minutes. Lower the heat to 375°F. and continue baking another 10 to 15 minutes, until the dough is cooked and the onions lightly browned. Remove and let cool about 10 minutes before serving. The pizza can also be served at room temperature.

COCA DE VERDURA   *Spain*
Vegetable Pizza

We weren't so surprised to find pizza in Barcelona. Italian food, after all, is almost as ubiquitous as soccer. But we were surprised to learn that this and similar flat breads dressed with vegetables were not in the least Italian, but were instead traditional dishes of the Balearic Islands. It makes an ideal first course for a simple dinner and could even serve as a main dish for a light luncheon.

SERVES 4

Pizza Dough (see recipe)
3 cups finely sliced, tightly packed
 Swiss chard, well washed
3 tablespoons olive oil
2 tablespoons chopped fresh
 parsley
1 medium onion, quartered, thinly
 sliced

3 garlic cloves, thinly sliced
1 large ripe tomato, quartered,
 thinly sliced
Salt and freshly ground pepper to
 taste

Make the pizza dough and set aside. Preheat the oven to 375°F. and oil well a 12-inch pizza pan or the equivalent.

Bring ½ cup of water to a boil in a saucepan, add the Swiss chard, and simmer over low heat until it is tender, about 7 to 10 minutes. Drain well, pressing it against the side of a colander with a wooden spoon to expel excess water. Heat 1 tablespoon of olive oil in a skillet, add the Swiss chard, and sauté for 1 or 2 minutes, stirring constantly, until the ingredients are well mixed, and the Swiss chard totally dry. Blend the parsley with the Swiss chard and set aside.

Roll out the dough, place on the pizza pan, cover with a clean dish towel and allow to rest for 20 minutes. When ready, distribute the Swiss chard evenly over the surface of the dough. Spread the onion, garlic, and tomato evenly over the Swiss chard, add salt and pepper, drizzle with the remaining oil, and bake until the dough is cooked, about 20 minutes. Serve hot or warm.

Main Dishes

The recipes in this chapter represent the full range of Mediterranean fish and vegetable dishes from elaborate fare such as Swordfish Pie from Sicily and Fish Couscous from Morocco, to simple treats such as Octopus, Provençal Style, and Baked Rice with Vegetables from Spain. Many are drawn from the vast storehouse of traditional dishes, including Cuttlefish with Spinach, Potato Omelet, and *Bourride,* while others, such as Cold Poached Salmon with Mustard Sauce, Bell Pepper Tart, and Shrimp Tagine are modern variations on ancient themes. The chapter is divided into Fish Dishes, Fish Soups, Couscous, and Vegetable and Egg Dishes.

Fish Dishes

Once, many years ago, we dined with friends at a small seafood restaurant right on the beach in Forte dei Marmi. The main course was a large, very fresh sea bass, stuffed with rosemary and wild fennel, sprinkled with rich Tuscan olive oil and coarse sea salt, then grilled over coals until the skin was crisp, the flesh steaming and succulent. For all its simplicity, it was, we agreed, a magnificent dish, one of the best we had ever eaten. Although grilled fish is, indeed, a treat and popular throughout the region, Mediterranean cooks have created a large number of superb dishes in which fish is cooked with vegetables, sautéed in wine, poached, and broiled on skewers. We include here a sample from this collection of dishes. In most recipes, we give two or three types of fish from which you can choose.

POISSON GRILLÉ
France
Grilled Fish

There are many delicious and inventive ways to prepare fish, but when it is fresh, the simplest is often the best. The French and Italians, in particular, have made a fine art out of broiling, grilling, or baking fresh fish with a few herbs and nothing else. We give a French recipe—if you wish to make it Italian, omit the fennel seeds. Actually, you can include the fennel seeds and just tell your guests it's *"nuova cucina."* Use sea bass, snapper, porgy, sea trout, or, best of all, red mullet. It is impossible to give precise cooking times in this recipe since the thickness of the fish determines how long it takes to cook. You can usually figure about 10 minutes for each inch of thickness for broiling, grilling, or baking in a hot oven. If you like to cook fish over coals, you can buy (at a good kitchen supply store) a wire rack shaped like a fish, which holds the fish and greatly facilitates turning. SERVES 4

1 whole fish weighing 2½ pounds, or the equivalent weight in smaller fish, scaled, cleaned, head and tail intact
2 garlic cloves, chopped
1 tablespoon fresh rosemary, or 1½ teaspoons dried rosemary

1 teaspoon fennel seed (optional)
3 sprigs parsley
3 tablespoons olive oil
Salt and freshly ground pepper to taste
1 lemon, cut in wedges

Wash and pat the fish dry. If using a single large fish, make 3 gashes on each side about ¼-inch deep across the fleshy part of the body. Place the fish in an oiled baking dish and stuff the cavity and the gashes with garlic, rosemary, fennel seed, and parsley. Sprinkle with olive oil and salt and pepper, and bake for 10 minutes. As an alternative, broil for 5 minutes per side, until the fish is done. You can also grill over coals, but make sure that the grill is well oiled. Serve surrounded by lemon wedges.

SARDELE NA RAŽNJU
Grilled Sardines
Yugoslavia

Many years ago, we traveled for a couple of months with Yugoslavian friends along the Dalmatian coast. During our delightful two-week stay on the island of Lastovo with their relatives, all fishermen, we had a chance to participate in a sardine fishing expedition. The boats went out at twilight, nets were strung across the path of the onrushing sardines, and about four hours later the nets, loaded with sardines, were hauled in. Around nine the next morning, the last of the sardines were finally extracted from the nets and most were packed with salt in wooden barrels for winter consumption. It was then that the feast began. The remaining fish were skewered with flat, wooden sword-shaped sticks, roasted over coals, and served with homemade *rakia,* Yugoslavian *grappa.* The honor of being king for the day, awarded to the one who consumes most, went to our friend Ivan, who managed to eat an astonishing number of sardines. Sardines prepared this way are outstanding and as easy to eat as they are to prepare.   SERVES 4

2½ pounds fresh small sardines, cleaned (p. 16), heads and tails intact

6 tablespoons olive oil
Coarse salt to taste

Place the fish on skewers or the equivalent and grill over hot coals until tender, about 2 minutes per side. Drizzle with oil, sprinkle with salt, and serve hot. The sardines can also be cooked in a broiler.

KOUTBANE DEL HOUT BE CHARMOULA
Fish Kebobs Marinated in Charmoula
Morocco

Even in the most modern kitchens in Morocco, one finds a small charcoal brazier that is used to grill kebobs and, often, to cook tagines (stews). When Fatima made these wonderful kebobs, she simply set her brazier on the sill of the kitchen window and grilled them over hot coals. They can also be cooked in a broiler. You can substitute monkfish or grouper for swordfish.   SERVES 4

Charmoula *(see recipe)*
1 pound fresh swordfish, cut into
  1½-inch cubes

1 small red bell pepper, cored,
  seeded, and cut into 1-inch
  squares, or 8 cherry tomatoes

Make the *charmoula* and set aside.

Place the fish in a mixing bowl. Pour the *charmoula* over the fish and combine well. Marinate in the refrigerator for at least 2 hours. Stir occasionally to ensure that the marinade is evenly mixed.

Distribute equal amounts of fish on 4 skewers, placing a piece of pepper or a cherry tomato at both ends. Grill or broil about 5 minutes, turning occasionally, until the fish is cooked. Serve hot.

BROCHETTES DE THON AU COULIS DE   *France*
TOMATE
Fresh Tuna Brochettes with Provençal Tomato Sauce

SERVES 4

Juice of ½ lemon
Salt and freshly ground pepper to
  taste
1½ pounds fresh tuna, trimmed,
  cut into 1-inch cubes

½ pound pearl onions, peeled
  and halved, if large
⅔ cup Provençal Tomato Sauce
  (see recipe)

FOR THE GARNISH:
3 tablespoons capers
1 or 2 dill pickles, sliced
½ Spanish onion, thinly sliced

Mint sprigs
1 lemon, cut in wedges

Combine the lemon juice with salt and pepper in a small mixing bowl. Add the tuna, mix, and set aside to marinate for 30 minutes.

Distribute the tuna pieces evenly among 4 skewers, alternating the fish pieces with small onions. Broil or grill over coals for 3 minutes per side, until the fish is cooked.

Place equal amounts of the tomato sauce in the center of 4 dining plates. Place 1 brochette diagonally across the sauce and distribute the garnish on each plate. Serve hot.

‖ *ORGOZ SISTE*   *Turkey*
‖ Grouper Kebobs

An ideal dish for a summer meal, fish kebobs prepared in this way are easy, flavorful, and delicious.   SERVES 4 TO 6

2 pounds fresh, firm-fleshed fish such as grouper, swordfish, or sea trout, deboned, cut into 1-inch cubes
Juice of 1 lemon
3 tablespoons olive oil
1 tablespoon chopped fresh dill

1 medium red onion, cut into 1-inch pieces
1 or 2 green or red bell peppers, seeded, cut into 1-inch pieces
Salt and freshly ground pepper to taste
Lemon wedges and parsley sprigs for garnish

Place the fish in a large mixing bowl, add the lemon juice, olive oil, and dill. Stir and place in the refrigerator to marinate for 1 hour.

Intersperse the fish cubes with the onions and peppers on metal or wooden skewers, season with salt and pepper, and broil or grill over charcoal for 5 minutes per side, until the fish is cooked. Do not overcook. Place the skewers on a serving platter garnished with parsley and lemon wedges and serve immediately.

VARIATION Use a mixture of hot Italian-style frying peppers or the equivalent and bell peppers on the skewers.

EL HUTH HARRA M'CHARMEL   *Morocco*
Spicy Marinated Baked Fish

In Morocco fish is almost always marinated prior to cooking and
the marinades, with minor variations, are similar. In this recipe, the
marinated fish is covered with tomato slices and baked slowly in a
medium oven until flavors meld and the fish is very tender. It's a
wonderful dish for a dinner party.   SERVES 4

4 garlic cloves, minced
Juice of 1½ lemons
1 teaspoon turmeric
1 tablespoon sweet paprika
1 teaspoon ground cumin
½ teaspoon cayenne pepper
½ teaspoon salt
½ cup chopped and tightly
*   packed fresh coriander leaves*

2¼ pounds whole red snapper or
*   porgies, scaled, cleaned, head*
*   and tail included*
2 teaspoons peanut oil
½ cup fresh parsley leaves
1 large ripe tomato, peeled and
*   cut into thick slices*

Combine the garlic, lemon juice, turmeric, paprika, cumin,
cayenne pepper, salt, and 3 tablespoons coriander leaves in a mixing bowl. Spread over the fish and allow to marinate for at least
1 hour at room temperature.

Preheat the oven to 375°F. and oil well a baking dish large
enough to hold the entire fish.

Place the marinated fish in the baking dish with the marinade
and sprinkle the peanut oil over it. Stuff the cavity with the remaining coriander leaves and the parsley. Cover with tomato slices and
bake for 45 minutes. Serve warm.

EL HOUT BEL HAMED M'RAKED   *Morocco*
Fish Baked with Preserved Lemons

In this Algerian specialty, adapted from Irene and Lucienne Karsenty's *Cuisine Pied-Noir,* fish is coated with *charmoula,* placed on a
bed of preserved lemons, and baked until tender. It's a brilliantly
flavored dish and very easy to prepare.   SERVES 4

2 preserved lemons or limes (p.
    15), rinsed and cut into
    ½-inch wedges
2¼ pounds whole red snapper or
    porgies, scaled, cleaned, head
    and tail included

2 tablespoons chopped fresh
    coriander leaves
1 tablespoon Charmoula (see
    recipe)
½ cup olive oil
1 tablespoon sweet paprika

Preheat the oven to 400°F. and oil lightly a baking dish large enough to hold the fish.

Place two-thirds of the preserved lemons or limes on the bottom of the baking dish. Make incisions ¼-inch deep in the sides of the fish, then place it on top of the lemons or limes. Stuff the cavity with coriander leaves and coat the top with *charmoula*. Mix the oil with paprika and drizzle over the fish. Cover the fish with the remaining lemons or limes, and bake for 15 minutes. Baste a few times with its own juice as the fish cooks. Serve hot.

LENGUADO AL PLATO   Spain
Sole with Sherry

A simple but very satisfying way to prepare sole, turbot, or flounder. The ingredients can be laid out ahead of time, but cook the fish just before serving.   SERVES 4 TO 6

4 tablespoons white raisins
¾ cup dry sherry
2 pounds sole, turbot, or flounder
    fillets
6 tablespoons bread crumbs
4 tablespoons unsalted butter

Juice of 2 lemons
Salt and freshly ground pepper to
    taste
20 black olives, pitted, rinsed and
    chopped

Soak raisins in sherry for 20 minutes. Drain, reserving both the raisins and the sherry.

Dredge the fish in bread crumbs and set aside.

Heat the butter in a large skillet, add the fish, a few pieces at a time, brown lightly on both sides over medium-high heat, and set aside. When all pieces are browned, return them to the skillet, add the lemon juice, reserved sherry, and salt and pepper. Cover and simmer over low heat for 5 minutes. Halfway through the cooking, add the olives and raisins. Serve immediately with the sherry-lemon sauce.

SOGLIOLE AL MARSALA   *Italy*
Sole with Marsala

You can use fillets of any flat, delicately flavored fish such as sole, turbot, or flounder for this dish. It requires last-minute preparation but takes almost no time. The dish has an inherent sophistication that makes it suitable for an elegant party despite its simplicity.   SERVES 4 TO 6

2 pounds fish fillets
½ cup unbleached all-purpose
*   flour*
5 tablespoons unsalted butter
½ cup dry white wine
½ cup Marsala

Juice of ½ lemon
3 tablespoons chopped fresh
*   parsley*
Salt and freshly ground pepper to
*   taste*
6 lemon wedges for garnish

Dredge the fillets lightly in the flour. Heat the butter in a skillet and brown the fillets over high heat, cooking about 1 minute per side, until just cooked through. Do not overcook. Remove fillets, place on a serving platter and keep warm.

Lower the heat to medium, add the wine and Marsala to skillet, and simmer until the sauce begins to thicken. Add 1 tablespoon of flour if necessary to aid thickening. Blend in the lemon juice and parsley, season with salt and pepper, and pour over the fillets.

Serve immediately garnished with lemon wedges.

LOUP À LA SAUCE AU VIN DE BOURGOGNE
Sea Bass with White Wine Sauce   *France*

Typical of *nouvelle cuisine* in its simplicity, elegance, and delicacy of flavor, fresh sea bass or sea trout is broiled, then served on top of a light sauce, surrounded by steamed zucchini and fresh tomatoes. It's easy to prepare, impressive, and delicious. The sauce should be made with a good white Burgundy and the same wine should be served at the meal.   SERVES 4

1½ pounds fillet of sea bass or sea trout, skinned	*2 medium firm tomatoes, peeled and seeded*
3 tablespoons olive oil	*2 egg yolks*
Salt and freshly ground pepper to taste	*Juice of 1 lemon*
2 small zucchini, scrubbed and trimmed	*¼ cup cold water*
	½ cup white Burgundy wine
	⅓ cup unsalted butter, melted

Sprinkle the fish with oil and salt and pepper, and set aside.

Cut the zucchini in quarters lengthwise, then cut into 1½-inch-long segments. Steam until just tender, about 5 minutes. Drain, set aside, but keep warm. Slice the tomatoes thinly and set aside.

To prepare the sauce, place the egg yolks in a saucepan with the lemon juice and cold water. Beat with a wire whisk to combine, then cook over very low heat, beating constantly with the whisk until the sauce thickens. This takes about 5 minutes. Then pour in the wine, a little at a time, beating constantly. The sauce should be creamy and smooth. Preparation to this point can be done in advance. Cover the sauce and set aside.

When almost ready to serve, broil the fish in a hot broiler for about 2 minutes per side, until just cooked through. Precise time will depend on the thickness of the fish. Warm the sauce over low heat, beating constantly with a whisk. Remove from the heat and set aside. Heat the butter to bubbling, then add to the sauce a little at a time, beating constantly with a whisk. Adjust for salt and pepper.

Distribute the sauce on individual heated dinner plates. Place pieces of fish in the center of each plate, decorate with the zucchini and tomato slices, and serve immediately.

RAPE ALLA MARINERA   *Spain*
Monkfish with Clams and Shrimp

SERVES 6

2 pounds monkfish, cut into
   steaks
2 tablespoons bread crumbs,
   lightly toasted
4 tablespoons olive oil
1 large onion, minced
2 garlic cloves, minced
1 large ripe tomato, peeled,
   seeded, and minced

1 tablespoon sweet paprika
Large pinch saffron
Salt and freshly ground pepper to
   taste
¾ cup dry white wine
12 to 18 baby clams, scrubbed
½ pound medium shrimp, shelled
   and deveined

Dredge the fish steaks in bread crumbs. Heat the oil in a large, low-sided saucepan, add the fish, and brown lightly on both sides over medium-high heat. Remove the fish and set aside.

Add the onion and garlic to the saucepan and sauté over medium heat until golden, about 10 minutes. Add the tomato and sauté another 10 minutes until the sauce begins to thicken. Blend in the paprika, saffron, and salt and pepper. Transfer the sauce to a blender or food processor and purée. Return to the saucepan, add the wine, and reduce by half.

In a small saucepan, bring 1 cup of water to a boil, add the clams, and steam, covered, shaking occasionally, until the clams open wide, about 5 minutes. Remove and set aside.

Place the fish steaks on the tomato sauce in the large, low-sided saucepan, then add the shrimp and clams. Cover and simmer about 5 minutes, until all the seafood is cooked. Serve immediately.

MERLUZA CON ALMENDRAS **Spain**
Hake with Almonds

In this richly flavored dish, the fish is first fried lightly, then baked with raisins, almond paste, hazelnuts, garlic, and parsley. It is relatively simple to prepare and absolutely delicious.   SERVES 6

2 pounds hake or cod, cut into 6
   steaks
Salt and freshly ground pepper to
   taste
Juice of ½ lemon
4 tablespoons flour
¼ cup light seed oil
2 garlic cloves
2 tablespoons parsley

12 blanched almonds, lightly
   toasted
12 blanched hazelnuts, toasted
¼ teaspoon ground cinnamon
12 raisins, soaked in warm water
   for 20 minutes, drained
¼ cup dry white wine
1 hard-boiled egg, thinly sliced,
   for garnish

Season the fish steaks with salt, pepper, and lemon juice. Dredge fish in the flour. Heat the oil in a skillet, add the fish and fry for a few minutes on each side. Drain on paper towels and set aside. Reserve 2 tablespoons of the cooking oil.

Grind the garlic, parsley, almonds, hazelnuts, and cinnamon into a smooth paste in a mortar. Combine with the reserved cooking oil and set aside.

Place the fish in a large saucepan. Coat with the nut paste, dot with raisins, add the wine, and simmer, covered, for 10 minutes. Transfer to a serving dish, garnish with the egg slices, and serve hot.

TAGINE DEL HOUT METHOUN BE **Morocco**
SALSA HARRA
Tagine of Fish Balls in Pungent Sauce

Abdillah, a Moroccan friend, offered us this recipe when he heard we were writing a cookbook. It's a dish his mother makes for

simple family meals, a stew of fish balls in a richly flavored sauce.
You can use halibut, whiting, sea trout, or even sardines.

SERVES 4 TO 6

*1 pound fish fillets, finely chopped
    or passed through a meat
    grinder*
4 garlic cloves, minced
½ teaspoon turmeric
*2 teaspoons plus 1 tablespoon
    sweet paprika*
*½ cup chopped fresh coriander
    leaves*
1 teaspoon ground ginger
1 teaspoon ground cumin
1 extra-large egg, beaten

*Salt and freshly ground pepper to
    taste*
3 tablespoons olive oil
1 cup grated onion
*3 medium ripe tomatoes, peeled,
    seeded, and chopped, or ¾
    cup canned Italian plum
    tomatoes, with juice*
1 tablespoon tomato paste
½ cup chopped fresh parsley
½ teaspoon cayenne pepper
½ cup water
Juice of 1 lemon

Place the fish in a mixing bowl, add 2 garlic cloves, turmeric,
2 teaspoons paprika, ¼ cup coriander leaves, ginger, cumin, and
the egg. Blend well, season with salt and pepper, and set aside.

Heat the oil in a large skillet, add the onion and remaining 2
cloves garlic, and sauté over medium heat for 2 to 3 minutes. Add
the tomatoes and tomato paste, parsley, remaining coriander, and
cayenne pepper. Blend, then add water and simmer over low heat
for 25 minutes, stirring occasionally, until the sauce thickens.

Shape the fish into balls the size of walnuts and place them on
a wet plate until ready to use.

Five minutes prior to serving, add the lemon juice to the
tomato sauce, season with salt and pepper, and bring to a simmer.
Place the fish balls in the sauce, cover, and simmer for 4 minutes.
Serve hot directly from the skillet.

ROTOLI DI PESCE SPADA   *Italy*
Swordfish Rolls with Pecorino

Every area in Sicily has its favorite filling for swordfish fillets and its preferred way to cook them. The one we include here is made with a delicious mixture of pecorino, garlic, and parsley spread thinly over the fish fillets and grilled or sautéed with tomato sauce. Fresh tuna can be substitued for the swordfish.   SERVES 4

1 extra-large egg, beaten
2 tablespoons bread crumbs
2 tablespoons sharp pecorino, grated
2 garlic cloves, finely chopped
3 tablespoons finely chopped fresh parsley

3 tablespoons olive oil
Salt and freshly ground pepper to taste
1½ pounds swordfish, cut into ¼-inch-thick fillets about 4 inches long
1 cup Tomato Sauce (see recipe)

Combine the egg, bread crumbs, cheese, garlic, parsley, and 2 tablespoons oil in a mixing bowl. Add salt and pepper and set aside.

Place the fish fillets on a work surface, spread the cheese mixture evenly over them, roll them loosely into cylinders, and tie with string. Heat the remaining tablespoon of oil in a saucepan large enough to hold the fish in a single layer, add the tomato sauce, dilute it with 1 or 2 tablespoons of water, and bring to a simmer. Add the fillets, cover, and simmer over low heat until the fish is cooked, about 10 minutes. Add water, a little at a time, as necessary during cooking. Remove the string and serve fish hot, surrounded by the tomato sauce.

VARIATION Brush the fish rolls with olive oil and cook in a broiler or over hot coals. Serve on a bed of curly endive with lemon wedges.

SAUMON FROID À LA SAUCE MOUTARDE   *France*
Cold Poached Salmon with Mustard Sauce

A great dish for a summer buffet, the salmon is surrounded with steamed vegetables such as carrots, green beans, and zucchini.

SERVES 6

FOR THE COURT BOUILLON:

1 celery stalk with leaves

1 onion, cut in half

1 bay leaf

1 cup dry white wine

½ teaspoon black peppercorns

2 pounds fresh salmon, in 1 piece

FOR THE SAUCE:

1 egg yolk

1½ tablespoons Dijon mustard

½ cup light seed oil

Salt and freshly ground pepper to taste

1 tablespoon warmed white wine vinegar

¾ cup whipping cream, lightly whipped

¼ cup Provençal Tomato Sauce (see recipe)

2 tablespoons dry white wine

3 tablespoons chopped fresh chives

¼ teaspoon cayenne pepper (optional)

To make the court bouillon, place all the ingredients in a fish poacher or saucepan large enough to hold the salmon, bring to a boil, and simmer, covered, for 10 minutes. Remove the celery, onion, bay leaf, and peppercorns with a slotted spoon, add the salmon, and simmer, covered, for 5 minutes. Remove from the heat and allow the salmon to cool, covered, in the court bouillon.

Meanwhile make the sauce. Place the egg yolk in a mixing bowl, add the mustard, and beat with a wire whisk for 2 minutes. Add the oil, a little at a time, beating constantly with the whisk. The sauce should have the consistency of mayonnaise. Add salt and pepper and the vinegar and combine thoroughly.

Blend in the whipped cream, tomato sauce, wine, 2 tablespoons of chives, and cayenne pepper, if desired.

Drain the salmon and place on a serving platter or cut into

slices and place on individual plates. Spread a thin coating of sauce over the fish, sprinkle with the remaining chives, and serve. Serve the remaining sauce in a sauceboat.

NOTE: You can make the sauce in a food processor or blender if you wish. Place a whole egg in the work bowl and, with the machine running, add the oil, then the mustard. Pulse in the remaining ingredients.

TONNO E FAGIOLI   *Italy*
Tuna with Cannelini Beans

This is one of the secret marvels of the Tuscan kitchen, an unpretentious but absolutely delicious dish, a combination of beans, tuna, onion, garlic, and tomatoes. It is sort of a Tuscan equivalent of chili. The dish is best if made with dried beans, soaked 8 hours or overnight, and cooked, but, in a pinch, you can use canned.

SERVES 4 TO 6

3 cups cooked cannelini (white kidney) beans or cranberry beans, or 1½ cups dried beans

3 tablespoons olive oil

1 cup chopped onions

1 garlic clove, chopped

Two 7-ounce cans Italian tuna fish, packed in oil, drained

1 cup fresh tomatoes, peeled, seeded, and chopped, or 1

cup canned Italian plum tomatoes, drained

2 large fresh sage leaves, or ¼ teaspoon dried sage

1 tablespoon chopped fresh basil (optional)

1 dried hot pepper, crushed

Salt and freshly ground pepper to taste

2 tablespoons chopped fresh parsley

If using dried beans, soak overnight in 4 cups of water with the addition of 1 tablespoon of flour. Rinse, place in a large saucepan, add 6 cups of water, bring to a boil, reduce the heat, and simmer, covered, until tender, about 2½ hours. As an alternative, cook the beans in a pressure cooker for 25 minutes. Drain and set aside until ready to use.

Place the oil in a large skillet, add the onions, and sauté until wilted, about 5 minutes. Add the garlic, and sauté another minute. Add the tuna, break into small pieces with a fork or wooden spoon, simmer 2 minutes, then add the beans and all the remaining ingredients except the parsley. Blend well, then simmer for 5 minutes, stirring occasionally. Sprinkle with parsley and serve hot.

FILETS DE POISSON AUX CÈPES   *France*
Fish Fillets Baked in Parchment with Wild Mushrooms

One of our favorite restaurants on the Côte d'Azur is La Reserve in Cros-de-Cagnes. The food is excellent and the atmosphere warm and friendly. The owners have a peculiar schedule for that part of the world—the restaurant is closed Saturday night, all day Sunday, and July and August. Shutting down in the summer is roughly the equivalent of closing Disneyworld during the Christmas holidays. For regulars, of course, it's a great schedule and that's exactly what the owners have in mind. This is one of their specialties, an ingenious, delicious blend of wild mushrooms and fresh fish. Use sea trout, sea bass, snapper, or porgy fillets.

SERVES 4

1 ounce dried cèpes (Boletus
    edulis)
*4 fish fillets, each approximately
    ⅓ pound*
*2 sprigs fresh thyme, or 1
    teaspoon dried thyme*
¼ cup finely sliced shallots
½ pound fresh mushrooms,

*cultivated shiitake,
chanterelles, cèpes, or oyster
mushrooms, if available,
sliced*
4 lemon slices
4 tablespoons butter
*Salt and freshly ground pepper to
    taste*

Soak the dried mushrooms in 1 cup warm water for 30 minutes. Remove from the water, taking care not to stir up sand and dirt that may have fallen to the bottom of the bowl. Chop finely and set aside.

Preheat the oven to 400°F.

Place each of the fillets on buttered parchment paper or foil, distribute the chopped mushrooms and the remaining ingredients equally over the fillets, season with salt and pepper, seal, place on a cookie sheet, and bake for 10 to 15 minutes, depending on the thickness of the fillets.

Serve hot, placing an unopened parchment or foil package on each diner's plate.

NASELLO CON PATATE   *Italy*
Hake with Potatoes

This and the following recipe are just two of many ways in which fish and potatoes are combined in Mediterranean cuisine. They are, however, ones that we find particularly satisfying.

SERVES 4

2 pounds new potatoes, washed well, thinly sliced with the peel

1 large onion, thinly sliced

12 black Italian olives, pitted, rinsed well if salty, and cut in half

4 fresh halibut, hake, or grouper steaks, about 1½ pounds

6 anchovy fillets, packed in oil, drained

2 tablespoons chopped fresh basil

2 tablespoons chopped fresh parsley

Freshly ground pepper to taste

3 tablespoons olive oil

Preheat the oven to 375°F. Oil well a baking dish large enough to hold the fish in a single layer.

Place half of the potatoes in a layer on the bottom of the baking dish. Cover with a layer of onions. Distribute the olives over the onions and place the fish steaks on this bed. Spread the anchovy fillets over the fish, sprinkle with the basil and parsley, cover with the remaining potatoes, and add pepper. Drizzle with the olive oil, cover the baking dish with aluminum foil, and bake for 20 minutes. Remove the foil and bake uncovered for another 20 to 30 minutes, until done. Serve hot.

EL HOUT BEL BATATA   *Morocco*
Baked Fish with Potatoes

We set out from Tangier on a glorious spring day with Peter
Winchester, an architect friend from Oxford who wanted to inves-
tigate the ruins of an ancient Roman port city he had heard about.
We found it, quay still intact, nestled in a half moon bay, deserted
except for the tent of a shepherd and a few goats. Above the bay,
just off the road, was a makeshift café. We had lunch there, perched
on a hill overlooking the bay, the sea, and in the distance, Gibral-
tar. We were served this wonderful, simple dish. You can use fresh
sea trout, whiting, or porgy. It is customary to cook and serve the
fish whole, head and tail intact, resting on a bed of potatoes, but
you can also use fish steaks.   SERVES 6

2 tablespoons olive oil	¼ cup chopped fresh coriander
2 tablespoons peanut oil	leaves
1 tablespoon sweet paprika	Salt to taste
½ teaspoon freshly ground black	One 3¼ pound whole fish, or 2
pepper	pounds steaks
¼ teaspoon cayenne pepper	1½ pounds potatoes, peeled and
(optional)	thickly sliced
1 teaspoon ground cumin	1 medium onion, thinly sliced
3 garlic cloves, crushed	1 medium ripe tomato, peeled,
¼ cup chopped fresh parsley	seeded, and sliced
	1 lemon, thinly sliced

Blend together in a mixing bowl the oils, paprika, pepper,
cayenne pepper, cumin, garlic, parsley, coriander, and salt. Coat
the surface and cavity of the fish with the paste and marinate for
1 hour.

Preheat the oven to 375°F. and oil well a baking dish large
enough to hold the fish in a single layer.

Layer the potatoes and onions in the baking dish. Add ½ cup
of water, cover with foil, and bake 30 minutes. Remove from the
oven and place the fish on the potato-and-onion bed. Distribute
the tomato and lemon slices on top and around the fish, add more

water if necessary (there should be enough to baste with), and bake, basting 2 or 3 times, for 35 to 45 minutes, depending on the thickness of the fish. Serve hot.

FILET DE SOLE À LA CRÈME DE POIREAUX

Sole with Leeks   *France*

Delicious and easy to prepare, this dish can be made with other filleted fish, such as flounder, monkfish, or turbot.   SERVES 6

4 tablespoons butter
4 leeks, cut into slices 2 inches
    long, with some green
Salt and pepper to taste
1½ cups Crème Fraîche *(see*
    recipe)

3 tablespoons lemon juice
½ cup flour
2 pounds fish fillet, cut into
    2-inch pieces
2 tablespoons chopped fresh
    parsley

Melt 2 tablespoons of butter in a skillet and add the leeks. Sauté for 2 minutes, then add ¼ cup water and salt and pepper. Cover and simmer for 5 minutes.

Mix together the *crème fraîche* and lemon juice. Pour it over the leeks and heat through.

Meanwhile, heat the remaining butter in another skillet. Flour the fish and brown it in the butter, 2 minutes on each side.

Place the hot leeks on a heated serving platter or on individual dishes. Place the fish fillets on top, sprinkle with parsley, and serve hot.

LOTTE AUX ENDIVES

Monkfish with Belgian Endives   *France*

In this elegant dish, the slightly bitter flavor of braised endives brings out the delicate sweetness of the monkfish. We have found that the dish is equally good whether the monkfish is baked, broiled, or sautéed, so cook it the way you find most convenient.

SERVES 6

2 pounds monkfish, skin and
    outer membrane removed, cut
    into 1½-inch cubes
2 tablespoons olive oil
Juice of 1 lemon
3 tablespoons butter
2 pounds Belgian endives, hard
    core removed, cut diagonally
    into 1-inch segments

¾ cup whipping cream
Grated zest of ¼ lemon
1½ tablespoons sugar
Salt and freshly ground pepper to
    taste
1 tablespoon chopped fresh chervil
    or parsley

Place the monkfish in a mixing bowl, add the oil and half the lemon juice. Mix well and set aside to marinate ½ hour.

Heat the butter in a skillet, add the endives, and sauté 1 minute. Add the cream, lemon zest, sugar, and salt and pepper. Combine, cover, and simmer, stirring occasionally, for 20 minutes.

If baking the monkfish, preheat the oven to 400°F. Place the monkfish pieces in a baking dish and bake for 5 minutes, until cooked. Do not crowd the pieces. Alternatively, broil until browned on both sides (about 1 minute per side) or sauté in 2 tablespoons of olive oil until lightly browned, about 1 minute per side.

Place the endives on 6 individual dinner plates or one large, heated serving platter. Place the monkfish on the endives, drizzle with the remaining lemon juice, sprinkle with the chervil or parsley, and serve at once.

TAGINE DEL HOUT BEL HOMESS   *Morocco*
Tagine of Fish Steaks with Chick-peas

You can use whiting, sea trout, snapper, or halibut steaks in this simple but delicious tagine.   SERVES 6

1½ cups dried chick-peas
1 tablespoon flour
Salt to taste
Freshly ground pepper
3 tablespoons olive oil
6 garlic cloves, minced

2¼ pounds fish steaks, roughly 2 inches thick
2 tablespoons sweet paprika
2 teaspoons ground cumin
1 tablespoon chopped fresh coriander leaves
1 small hot pepper, finely chopped

Soak the chick-peas in 5 cups of water for 8 hours or overnight with flour. Rinse, drain, place in a saucepan with 4 cups of water, bring to a boil, season with salt and pepper, and simmer covered until tender, about 1½ hours. As an alternative, cook in a pressure cooker for 35 minutes. Drain the chick-peas and set aside. Reserve 1 cup of the cooking liquid. You can also use canned chick-peas. You will need 3 cups. Rinse before using.

Heat the oil in a *tagine*, or an enamel or stainless steel saucepan. Distribute the garlic on the bottom of the pan and cover with the fish steaks. Reduce the heat to low and sprinkle with paprika, cumin, coriander leaves, salt, ½ teaspoon pepper, and the hot pepper. Cover and simmer for 30 minutes. The heat should be such that the oil just barely sizzles.

Add the chick-peas to the pan, placing them in the spaces between the fish steaks. Pour the chick-pea liquid over the fish and stir the peas delicately to combine with the fish sauce. If using canned chick-peas, add water or vegetable broth. Simmer, covered, for the first 10 minutes, then uncover and continue to cook 5 minutes more. Serve hot.

TAGINE DE SARDINE M'CHARMEL   *Morocco*
Tagine with Stuffed Sardines

Country *souks* in Morocco are like festive, open-air department stores where local farmers purchase everything from luxury fabrics and jewelry to soap, spices, magic potions, farm and kitchen implements, and the services of barbers, tailors, dentists, blacksmiths, and shoemakers. They are, in most cases, held once each week, with many towns named by the day on which their *souk* is held. On one outing, we were drawn to the food tents by the irresistible aroma of fried sardines. They were as good as they smelled, packed into pita-type bread and laced with a spicy tomato sauce. Fatima, on hearing of our culinary adventure, volunteered an equally delectable tagine of stuffed sardines. We include both versions here, the tagine as the main entry, the sandwich as a variation. They are both suitable for an informal meal with family and friends.

SERVES 6 TO 8

6 garlic cloves, chopped
1 cup chopped fresh parsley
1½ cups chopped fresh coriander
    leaves
2 teaspoons dried oregano
3 teaspoons ground cumin
½ teaspoon cayenne pepper
½ teaspoon peppercorns
¼ cup olive oil
⅓ cup lemon juice
Salt to taste
2 pounds sardines, heads
    removed, cleaned, deboned,
    and butterflied (p. 16)

3 large potatoes, peeled and
    thickly sliced
¾ pound green beans, cut into
    2-inch pieces
2 small onions, thickly sliced
2 medium ripe tomatoes, peeled,
    seeded, and roughly chopped,
    or ½ cup drained canned
    Italian plum tomatoes
1 cup water
1 lemon, cut into wedges

Preheat the oven to 350°F.

Place the garlic, parsley, coriander, oregano, cumin, cayenne pepper, and peppercorns in a mortar and pulverize until the ingredients are well ground. As an alternative, grind in a blender or food processor. Add the oil and lemon juice, a little at a time, grinding constantly, until a paste is formed. Add salt to taste. Distribute two-thirds of the paste over the inner surface of half the butterflied sardines, then place the remaining sardines over the stuffed ones, thus forming sandwiches with the paste in the middle. Set aside for 30 minutes.

Oil generously a *tagine,* or an enamel or stainless steel saucepan and place the potatoes in the bottom. Cover with the beans, then the onions. Place the sardines on the onions, spread the remaining paste over the sardines, cover with the tomatoes, sprinkle with additional salt, and add the water. Cover the pan and bake for 1 hour, basting occasionally with juices in the pan. Remove the cover and bake another 15 to 20 minutes to reduce the sauce. The fish should be moist but not swimming in liquid. Serve hot with lemon wedges.

VARIATION Stuffed sardines are delicious dredged in flour and fried. Prepare the sardines as described above, then dredge and fry in light seed oil, drain on paper towels, and serve hot in pita bread dressed with *Harissa* (see recipe).

SARDINES FARCIES ANTIBOISE   *France*
Stuffed Sardines, Antibes Style

When we asked what went into the stuffing for his sardines, the cook at La Socca, a small restaurant in Antibes, answered, *"Au bout du doight,"* which means "Whatever is handy." And that was, indeed, the case, since each time we had his stuffed sardines the flavor was slightly different. This recipe is one of his particularly successful versions.   SERVES 6

2½ pounds small sardines, heads removed, cleaned, deboned, and butterflied (p. 16)
5 tablespoons olive oil
8 tablespoons bread crumbs, lightly toasted
2 egg yolks
2 tablespoons milk
¼ cup lemon juice

5 garlic cloves, minced
4 tablespoons minced fresh parsley
1 teaspoon fresh thyme leaves, or ½ teaspoon dried thyme
Pinch of rosemary leaves
2 teaspoons fennel seed
½ teaspoon black peppercorns, crushed in a mortar
Salt to taste

Preheat oven to 450°F. and oil well a large baking dish, preferably of metal but attractive enough to bring to the table. Place half the butterflied sardines, skin side down, in the baking dish.

Combine in a small mixing bowl 3 tablespoons olive oil, 7 tablespoons bread crumbs, and all the remaining ingredients. Spread 1 tablespoon of the stuffing on top of each sardine. Cover each with another sardine, making a sandwich with the stuffing in the middle. Press down gently. Drizzle the remaining oil over the sardines, then sprinkle with the remaining bread crumbs.

Bake for 15 to 20 minutes, until the bread crumbs are well browned. Serve sizzling hot.

TAGINE DEL FOULE OU L'HOUT   *Morocco*
Tagine of Fava Beans and Fish

Fava beans are popular all over the Mediterranean. When they are young and tender, they are often eaten raw with salt or, as in Tuscany, with sharp pecorino. They are cooked with artichokes, lamb, peas, or simply with garlic. However, until our most recent visit to Morocco, we had never eaten fava beans cooked in the pod. The pods, we discovered, impart an intense, earthy flavor that is difficult to capture with the beans alone. It is not always easy to find fresh, tender fava beans but it is well worth the effort. The pods should be no more than ½ inch across and about 5 inches long. They should be firm and pale green, with no blemishes.

SERVES 4 TO 6

2 tablespoons olive oil
2 tablespoons peanut oil
4 garlic cloves, chopped
¼ cup chopped fresh parsley
¼ cup chopped fresh coriander
    leaves
½ tablespoon sweet paprika
½ teaspoon cayenne pepper
1½ teaspoons turmeric
1 teaspoon ground ginger

2 pounds fresh fava beans in the
    pod, washed, trimmed, and
    cut into 2-inch segments
Salt to taste
1 cup peas, fresh or frozen
2 pounds cod, halibut, or grouper
    fillets
1 tablespoon ground cumin
1 large ripe tomato, peeled,
    seeded, and cut into thick
    slices
1 lemon, cut into wedges

Heat the oils in a *tagine,* or an enamel or stainless steel saucepan, and add the garlic, parsley, coriander, paprika, cayenne pepper, turmeric, and ginger. Sauté over low heat for 5 minutes, stirring frequently. Add the beans, salt, and enough water to come

1 inch above the vegetables. Simmer, covered, without stirring for 30 minutes. Add the peas and simmer 15 more minutes if fresh, 5 minutes if frozen.

Preheat the oven to 375°F.

Sprinkle the fish with cumin, wedge the pieces among the beans, and distribute tomato slices over and around the fish. Sprinkle with salt and bake for 15 minutes, covered. Remove the cover and bake another 15 minutes. Serve hot with lemon wedges.

IMPANATA DI PESCE SPADA Italy
Swordfish Pie

In this impressive Sicilian classic, swordfish is sautéed with onions, olives, celery, capers, and tomatoes, then baked in a pastry shell together with fried zucchini. It takes time to prepare, but is well worth the effort. The dough usually contains sugar but we prefer it without. The filling and the dough can be made in advance, but it is best to bake the pie just prior to serving.   SERVES 6

Pâte Brisée *(see recipe) made*
 with:
  3 cups unbleached all-purpose
   flour
  Pinch of salt

⅜ pound unsalted butter
2 extra-large eggs plus 1 egg
 yolk
1½ tablespoons lemon juice

FOR THE FILLING:
8 tablespoons olive oil
1 large onion, finely chopped
½ cup chopped tender celery
 stalks
½ cup pitted and chopped green
 olives
2 tablespoons chopped capers

2 tablespoons chopped fresh
 parsley
5 tablespoons Tomato Sauce (see
 recipe)
1 pound fresh swordfish, diced
Freshly ground pepper to taste
5 small zucchini, washed and
 sliced

Make the *pâte brisée* and place in the refrigerator to rest at least 1 hour.

To make the filling, heat 4 tablespoons of olive oil in a large, low-sided saucepan, add the onion, and sauté over medium heat until golden, about 10 minutes. Add the celery, olives, capers, and parsley, and cook another 2 minutes. Blend in the tomato sauce, and cook over low heat, stirring frequently, for 5 minutes. Add the swordfish and pepper and simmer, uncovered, stirring frequently, for 10 minutes. Set aside.

Heat the remaining oil in a skillet, add the zucchini, and fry until browned on both sides. Drain on paper towels and set aside.

Preheat the oven to 350°F. and butter well an 8-inch spring-form pan.

. Roll out two-thirds of the dough ⅛ inch thick on a floured board and use it to line snugly the bottom and sides of the spring-form pan. Allow excess dough to drape over the edges of the pan. Prick the dough with a fork and distribute half the swordfish mixture in the pan. Cover with the zucchini, then top with the rest of the swordfish mixture. Roll out the remaining dough ⅛ inch thick and use it to cover the top of the pan, allowing a ½ inch overlap. To ensure a good seal, join the top to the sides, using water as a sealer, and pinching the dough with your fingers. Press firmly all around with the tines of a fork. This will reinforce the seal and give an attractive pattern to the border. Prick the top with a fork.

Bake for 50 minutes, until the top of the pie is browned. Remove from the oven, allow to cool 15 minutes, then remove the sides of the springform pan and serve.

BALIK PILÂKISI   *Turkey*
Cold Swordfish Steaks with Vegetable Sauce

This is a wonderful dish for a summer buffet. It is ideally suited for fresh swordfish, but any firm-fleshed fish will do.   SERVES 6

4 tablespoons olive oil
1 cup chopped onions
4 garlic cloves, chopped
¾ cup chopped carrots
1 cup peeled and chopped new
    potatoes
¾ cup peeled and chopped celery
    root
1½ cups chopped canned Italian
    plum tomatoes, with juice, or
    1½ cups peeled, seeded, and
    chopped ripe tomatoes

2 tablespoons chopped fresh
    parsley
2 pounds fresh swordfish steaks
Salt and freshly ground pepper to
    taste
1 lemon, thinly sliced
Fresh dill sprigs for garnish

Heat the oil in a large, low-sided saucepan. Add the onions, garlic, carrots, potatoes, and celery root and sauté over medium heat, stirring constantly, until the vegetables begin to color, about 5 minutes. Add the tomatoes and cook, stirring frequently, until the sauce just begins to thicken, about 10 to 15 minutes. It should be moist to provide liquid in which to cook the fish. Add the parsley, combine, and move the sauce to one side of the pan.

Place the fish on the bottom of the pan, cover with the sauce, sprinkle with salt and pepper, and distribute half the lemon slices over the fish. Cover the saucepan and simmer over low heat until the fish is cooked, about 15 minutes for 1-inch-thick swordfish steaks. Add water, a tablespoon at a time, if necessary, as the fish cooks. When cooked, remove from the heat, remove the cover, and allow to cool in the pan.

When ready to serve, transfer the fish to a serving platter, cover with the sauce, discard the lemon slices that cooked with the fish and replace them with those that remain, garnish with dill, and serve at room temperature.

TIAN DE MORUE AUX EPINARDS   *France*
Gratin of Salt Cod with Spinach

SERVES 4 TO 6

1 pound salt cod, preferably skinned and deboned	*5 tablespoons olive oil*
	1 large onion, finely chopped
1½ pounds spinach, well washed	*4 garlic cloves, finely chopped*
1 cup bread crumbs, lightly toasted	*½ teaspoon freshly ground black pepper*
1 cup milk	*2 tablespoons chopped fresh dill*

Soak the cod for 24 to 36 hours in water to cover, changing it three or four times.

Drain the cod, pat dry, place the cod in a saucepan, add cold water to cover, bring to a boil, remove from the heat, and let sit 15 minutes. Drain, then flake the fish with a fork. Set aside.

Place the spinach in a saucepan without adding water, and simmer, covered, until tender, about 5 to 7 minutes. Drain, removing excess water by squeezing with your hands or by pressing the spinach against the sides of a colander with a wooden spoon. Chop finely and set aside.

Preheat oven to 450°F. and oil well an 8-by-12-inch baking dish.

Mix all but 2 tablespoons of bread crumbs with the milk. Heat 3 tablespoons of olive oil in a skillet, add the onion and garlic, and sauté over medium heat until golden, about 5 minutes. Add the bread-crumbs-and-milk mixture and, after 1 minute, the spinach. Sauté 2 minutes more, stirring constantly. The mixture should have the consistency of thick paste. Off the heat, add the cod, pepper, and dill, and mix well.

Place the mixture in the baking dish, sprinkle the top with the remaining bread crumbs, and drizzle with the remaining oil. Bake for 10 to 15 minutes, until the top is lightly browned. Serve hot.

BACCALÀ CON LE OLIVE   *Italy*
Salt Cod with Olives

When we asked Mimi Serani, a close friend, which among the many
Italian salt cod dishes she particularly liked, she singled out this
one. The hot pepper and olives perk up an otherwise bland fish
and make this a delightful, rustic dish.   SERVES 4

1½ pounds salt cod, preferably   *½ cup Italian pickled vegetables*
   skinned and deboned   *or dill pickles, thinly sliced*
3 tablespoons flour   *½ cup Italian black olives,*
¼ cup olive oil   *pitted, rinsed well if salty,*
3 garlic cloves, chopped   *and roughly chopped*
½ cup chopped onion or leeks   *2 tablespoons capers*
1 cup Tomato Sauce (see recipe)   *2 tablespoons chopped fresh*
1 dried hot pepper, crushed   *parsley*

Soak the cod for 24 to 36 hours in water to cover, changing
it three or four times.

Drain the cod, pat dry, and cut into 2-inch-square pieces.
Dredge with flour and set aside. Heat the oil in a skillet and fry the
cod over medium-high heat until golden, about 2 to 3 minutes per
side, depending on thickness. Remove and drain on paper towels.
Set aside.

Sauté the garlic and onion or leeks in the same oil until
golden, about 5 to 7 minutes. Add the tomato sauce and hot
pepper, cover, and simmer 15 minutes. Add the pickled vegetables
or pickles, olives, and capers. Combine well, cover, and simmer 5
minutes. Add 1 or 2 tablespoons of water to the sauce if it is too
thick. Add the cod to skillet, sprinkle with parsley, cover, heat
through, and serve immediately.

GAMBAS AL AJILLO   *Spain*
Garlic Shrimp

After weeks of traveling and living on restaurant food, we were
delighted to return to our apartment in Antibes. We were starved

for simple, straightforward fare with strong, basic flavors. We went
to the market, found fresh shrimp, and cooked them Spanish style,
with garlic, oil, and hot peppers. It's a terrific dish, maybe the best
way of all to prepare shrimp. In Spain, it is usually served as a *tapas*,
but it makes a delicious, light main dish.   SERVES 4 TO 6

6 tablespoons olive oil

6 garlic cloves, thinly sliced

1 to 2 dried hot peppers, minced

2 pounds extra large shrimp,
    shells and heads intact

3 tablespoons chopped fresh
    parsley

Salt and freshly ground pepper to
    taste

3 tablespoons lemon juice
    (optional)

3 tablespoons dry sherry
    (optional)

Heat the oil in a large skillet, add the garlic and red pepper,
and sauté over medium heat for 1 minute. Add the remaining
ingredients and sauté 5 minutes over medium-high heat until
shrimp are cooked. Serve hot. Each diner removes the heads and
shells of the shrimp before eating them.

TAGINE DE "CREVETTES"   *Morocco*
Shrimp Tagine

SERVES 4

3 tablespoons peanut oil

3 tablespoons olive oil

3 cups finely chopped onions

4 garlic cloves, chopped

Pinch of saffron, crushed, soaked
    in ½ cup water

¼ cup finely chopped fresh
    parsley

1 tablespoon sweet paprika

¼ teaspoon cayenne pepper

1 teaspoon ground cumin

2 green or red bell peppers, cored,
    seeded, and thinly sliced

Salt to taste

1 pound large shrimp, shelled
    and deveined

Heat the oils in a *tagine*, or an enamel or stainless steel saucepan, add the onions and garlic, and sauté until golden. Add the
saffron and water, parsley, paprika, cayenne pepper, and cumin,
and sauté over low heat for 5 minutes.

Heat the oven to 350°F.

Add the peppers and salt to the saucepan and combine. Cover and bake for 30 minutes.

Remove from the oven, place the shrimp in the sauce, cover, and bake another 15 minutes. Remove the cover, raise the oven temperature to 450°F., and cook, uncovered, for 15 minutes, until a light crust forms over the shrimp. Serve hot.

GARIDES ME SPANÁKI   *Greece*
Shrimp with Spinach

In this dish, the spinach can be prepared in advance but the shrimp should be cooked just before serving.   SERVES 4

6 tablespoons olive oil
1 large onion, finely chopped
2 large ripe tomatoes, peeled and
    minced
1 green bell pepper, seeded and
    diced
1½ pounds fresh spinach, well
    washed and roughly chopped

Juice of 2 lemons
Salt and freshly ground pepper to
    taste
1½ pounds shrimp, shelled and
    deveined
Lemon wedges for garnish

Heat 4 tablespoons of oil in a large, low-sided saucepan. Add the onion and sauté over medium heat for 5 minutes, until it begins to color. Add the tomatoes and bell pepper and continue to cook, uncovered, for about 10 minutes, until the sauce begins to thicken. Add the spinach, lemon juice, and salt and pepper, and simmer, uncovered, stirring occasionally, another 10 minutes, until the spinach is tender. Set aside.

Heat the remaining oil in a skillet, add the shrimp, and sauté over medium heat for 3 minutes, stirring constantly, until the shrimp are cooked. Combine with the spinach in a saucepan, heat through, and serve immediately, garnished with lemon wedges.

GARIDES ME RIZI   *Greece*
Shrimp with Rice

In this Greek classic, the shrimp are first poached in a court bouillon, then combined with rice just before serving. It is a delicately flavored dish, suitable as either a main course or a first course for an elegant dinner party.   SERVES 4

2 sprigs parsley
1 tender celery stalk, with leaves
1 bay leaf
1 small onion, halved
8 whole peppercorns
½ cup dry white wine
2 cups water
1 pound shrimp in shells
3 tablespoons olive oil
½ cup finely chopped onion

½ cup drained canned Italian plum tomatoes
¾ cup parboiled or Carolina long-grain rice
Salt and freshly ground pepper to taste
12 Kalamata olives, pitted and quartered
1½ tablespoons lemon juice
1 lemon quartered, for garnish

Combine the parsley, celery, bay leaf, onion halves, peppercorns, and white wine in a large saucepan with the water. Bring to a boil and simmer, covered, for 10 minutes. Add the shrimp, return to a boil, then simmer, covered, for 3 minutes. Remove the shrimp with a slotted spoon and set aside until cool enough to handle. Strain the broth, reserving the liquid and discarding the vegetables. When cooled, peel the shrimp, discard the shells, and set aside.

Heat the olive oil in a saucepan, add the chopped onion, and sauté over medium heat for 2 or 3 minutes until the onion softens. Add the tomatoes and cook another 10 minutes, until the sauce begins to thicken. Add the rice and salt and pepper, combine with the sauce, blend in 2 cups of the shrimp broth, and simmer, uncovered, for 12 minutes. Add the shrimp, cover, and simmer until the rice is cooked, about 8 minutes. Add the olives and lemon juice, mix well, and serve immediately garnished with lemon quarters.

SAINT-JACQUES ET LÉGUMES AU SAFRAN   **France**

Scallops with Saffron and Vegetables

A friend who lives near Montpellier served this marvelous, simple, and beautiful dish one evening, assuring us that it was much easier to prepare than its elegance and taste suggested. She was right. It's great for dinner parties.   SERVES 4 TO 6

¼ cup unsalted butter

1½ pounds sea or bay scallops

¼ pound small green beans, trimmed and cut into 2-inch segments

3 medium carrots, peeled, halved, and cut into very thin 2-inch sticks

1 small turnip, peeled and cut into 2-inch sticks

2 small leeks, white parts only, washed, cut in half, and then cut into 2-inch-long slivers

¾ cup dry white wine

1 pinch saffron, soaked in ¼ cup warm water

¼ teaspoon dried thyme, or ½ teaspoon fresh thyme leaves

Salt and freshly ground pepper to taste

¼ cup whipping cream

Juice of ½ lemon

Heat the butter in a skillet. Pat the scallops dry with a paper towel and sauté until lightly browned on both sides, about 3 minutes. If using frozen scallops, thaw first and drain. Remove from the skillet, set aside, but keep warm.

In the same skillet, add the vegetables, wine, saffron and water, thyme, and salt and pepper. (If the green beans are tough, steam first until barely tender, about 5 minutes, then add to the skillet.) Combine, cover, and cook 5 minutes, until the vegetables are just tender. Add the cream, lemon juice, and scallops, and heat through. Serve the scallops on a bed of the vegetables dressed with the sauce.

SEPPIE IN ZIMINO   *Italy*
Cuttlefish with Spinach

This is a classic Tuscan dish, a delicately flavored, easy-to-prepare
stew of cuttlefish and spinach. It is equally good if Swiss chard is
substituted for spinach. Some argue, in fact, that Swiss chard is the
appropriate green vegetable to use. You can also replace the cuttlefish with squid.   SERVES 4

6 tablespoons olive oil
6 garlic cloves
¼ cup finely chopped onion
1 medium carrot, finely chopped
1 medium celery stalk, finely
    chopped
1 dried hot pepper, crushed
3 tablespoons finely chopped fresh
    parsley
1½ pounds cuttlefish, cleaned (p.
    17), cut into ½-inch slices,
    tentacles included

1 cup dry white wine
½ cup peeled, seeded, and
    chopped fresh tomatoes, or
    ½ cup drained canned
    Italian plum tomatoes
10 ounces fresh spinach or Swiss
    chard, stems removed, well
    washed
1 lemon cut into wedges

Heat 4 tablespoons olive oil in a heavy saucepan, preferably
earthenware, add 4 minced garlic cloves, and the onion, carrot,
celery, and hot pepper, and sauté 5 minutes. Add the parsley, fish,
wine, and tomatoes, combine, cover, and simmer over low heat for
30 minutes, until the fish is tender. Add water if necessary.

Meanwhile, place the spinach in a saucepan, and simmer, covered, until tender, about 5 to 7 minutes. Do not add water. If using
Swiss chard, bring 1 cup of water to boil in a saucepan, add the
chard, and simmer, covered, until tender, about 15 to 20 minutes.
Drain and squeeze out excess water with your hands or by pressing
the greens against the side of a colander with a wooden spoon.
Chop roughly and set aside.

Heat the remaining oil in a skillet, add 2 whole garlic cloves
and spinach or chard, and sauté 2 or 3 minutes, stirring constantly.
Set aside.

When the cuttlefish is cooked, add the spinach or chard and

cook another 10 minutes, stirring occasionally. Cook without a cover if very moist, otherwise cover. When cooked, the dish should resemble a stew. Serve warm with lemon wedges.

CALAMARI RIPIENI ALLA SICILIANA   *Italy*
Stuffed Squid, Sicilian Style

Almost all the countries bordering the Mediterranean have a stuffed squid dish. This is an absolutely fabulous way to prepare it. The rich stuffing of pine nuts, currants, and garlic and the delicate flavor of the squid are perfectly balanced by the light tomato sauce.   SERVES 4

1½ pounds squid, sacs 4 to 5
   inches in length

FOR THE STUFFING:
4 garlic cloves, minced
4 tablespoons minced fresh parsley
¼ pound mushrooms, minced
4 tablespoons bread crumbs
4 tablespoons pine nuts

4 tablespoons currants, soaked in
   warm water for 10 minutes,
   drained
Salt and freshly ground pepper to
   taste

FOR THE SAUCE:
2 tablespoons olive oil
½ cup grated onion
1 cup peeled, seeded, and chopped
   ripe tomatoes, or 1 cup
   canned Italian plum
   tomatoes, with juice

1 cup dry white wine

Clean the squid according to directions (p. 17). Use only the sacs.

Make the stuffing by combining all the ingredients in a mixing bowl. Stuff the squid sacs loosely, using a teaspoon. Close the opening with small skewers or toothpicks. Set aside.

In a skillet large enough to hold all the squid, heat the oil, add the onion, and sauté for 5 minutes, until transparent. Add the tomatoes and cook another 5 minutes. Place the squid in the pan and sauté 1 minute on each side. Add the wine, cook uncovered for a few minutes, then cover and cook over low heat for 20 minutes, until the squid are tender.

Remove the squid from the sauce and keep warm. When ready to serve, heat the sauce and place it on the bottom of a heated serving platter. Slice the squid and distribute it over the sauce, overlapping the slices, and serve hot.

POULPE À LA PROVENÇALE   *France*
Octopus, Provençal Style

This stew, a rich blend of octopus, wine, tomatoes, peppers, and potatoes, is typical of the Côte d'Azur. Like all good stews, the flavor improves with a little age, so make it a day in advance if you can. Serve over boiled rice.   SERVES 4

3 tablespoons olive oil
4 garlic cloves, chopped
1 cup chopped onions
1 pound octopus, cleaned (p. 18), cut into 2-inch pieces
1 red or green bell pepper, cored, seeded, and cut into ½-inch-square pieces
Pinch of saffron
½ cup dry white wine
1½ cups peeled, seeded, and chopped ripe tomatoes, or 1½ cups drained canned Italian plum tomatoes

¼ teaspoon freshly ground black pepper
1 sprig fresh thyme, or ½ teaspoon dried thyme
1 bay leaf
2 cups peeled and cubed new potatoes
Salt to taste
1 cup water
½ cup Italian or Niçoise black olives, pitted, rinsed well if salty, and quartered
1 tablespoon chopped fresh parsley

Heat the oil in a skillet, add the garlic and onions, and sauté until lightly browned, about 7 minutes. Add the octopus and sauté another 2 minutes. Add half the bell pepper pieces, the saffron, wine, tomatoes, pepper, and thyme, and bring to a boil. Transfer to an earthenware, enamel, or stainless steel saucepan. Cover with aluminum foil, then cover with the lid to form a tight seal. Simmer over low heat for 1 hour.

Remove the lid and foil, add the bay leaf, the remaining pieces of pepper, potatoes, salt, and the water. Mix well, cover with the lid, and simmer 15 to 20 minutes, until the potatoes are tender. When adding salt, take care since the olives may be salty. Remove and discard the bay leaf, blend in the olives, sprinkle with parsley, and serve hot directly from the pan.

VARIATION In Sicily, the dish is made without potatoes, olives, and saffron but with 2 more bell peppers.

ZARZUELA DE MARISCOS　　　　　*Spain*
Catalonian Seafood Plate

In this delightful seafood specialty of Catalonia, the fish are cooked separately, then combined and served with a richly flavored tomato sauce. Vary the ingredients as you wish—with lobster, it becomes a very elegant and impressive main dish.　　　SERVES 6

¾ pound grouper, halibut, or monkfish steaks, cut into 2-inch-square pieces

2 tablespoons flour

8 tablespoons olive oil

½ pound medium or large shrimp, with shells

½ pound jumbo shrimp, with shells

12 baby clams, scrubbed

1 medium onion, minced

3 garlic cloves, minced

1 fresh or dried hot pepper, chopped if fresh or crushed if dried

1 large ripe tomato, peeled and minced

2 teaspoons sweet paprika

Pinch of saffron, ground in a mortar, soaked in 2 tablespoons white wine

Salt and freshly ground pepper to taste

1 cup dry white wine

2 tablespoons chopped fresh parsley

1 lemon cut into wedges for garnish

Dredge the fish pieces with flour. Heat 4 tablespoons oil in a large, low-sided saucepan, add the fish, and sauté over medium heat until browned on all sides, about 5 minutes. Remove and set aside. Add the medium shrimp and cook 3 minutes. Remove and set aside. Add the jumbo shrimp, 1 or 2 tablespoons of water, and cover. Simmer until tender, about 10 minutes. Remove shrimp and set aside. In a saucepan, bring 1 cup of water to a boil, add the clams, cover, and steam until opened, about 3 to 5 minutes. Remove, discard half the shell from each clam, and set the clams aside.

In the same saucepan in which the fish was cooked, heat the remaining oil, add the onion and garlic, and sauté until golden, about 5 minutes. Add the hot pepper, tomato, paprika, saffron and its wine, and salt and pepper. Simmer, uncovered, for 5 minutes. Add the cup of wine and simmer another 10 minutes.

Arrange the fish and the seafood attractively in a large earthenware, enamel, or stainless steel saucepan. Cover with the sauce, cover the saucepan, and simmer over very low heat for 5 minutes. Sprinkle with the parsley, garnish with the lemon wedges, and serve.

Fish Soups

In Kuşadasi, a village on the Turkish coast where we stayed for a while one summer, fishermen would arrive early in the morning with their catch, sell the choice fish, then repair to a local restaurant where the chef, an ex-fisherman, would blend together tails, heads, small rockfish, herbs, spices, and vegetables in a big stockpot to make a first-class fish soup. With minor variations, we have witnessed similar scenes on Lastovo in Yugoslavia, in Antibes, Syracuse in Sicily, Málaga, and Tangier. Mediterranean fish soup is, for the most part, a modest, hearty meal for fishermen.

We chose two to include among main dishes, one a typical

fisherman's fish soup, *cacciucco* from Leghorn, the other, a sensuous, elegant *bourride* from Provence. Both can be made with fish available in North America and both make sensational meals.

We decided not to include *bouillabaisse,* the famous Marseilles fish soup, because it cannot be made without scorpion fish *(rascasse),* a species not always available in North America.

‖ CACCIUCCO ALLA LIVORNESE   *Italy*
‖ Fish Soup, Leghorn Style

A good *cacciucco* is made with inexpensive fish and is always spicy. You should use three varieties of fish: a rockfish such as scorpion fish, redfish, or rockfish; fish steaks or fillets from a large fish such as dogfish, grouper, or halibut; and mollusks and crustaceans.

SERVES 8 TO 10

6 tablespoons olive oil
8 garlic cloves, roughly chopped
6 fresh sage leaves, or 1½
    teaspoon dried sage
⅔ pound squid, cleaned (p. 17),
    cut into 1-inch pieces
1 teaspoon black peppercorns,
    crushed in a mortar
1 or 2 dried hot peppers, crushed
1 medium onion, chopped
1 medium carrot, chopped
1 celery stalk, chopped
¼ cup chopped fresh parsley
1 cup dry white wine
2 cups ripe seeded, peeled, and
    chopped tomatoes, or 2 cups
    canned Italian plum
    tomatoes, with juice

4 cups water
4 pounds rockfish or the
    equivalent, cleaned, scaled,
    and cut into pieces, heads
    and tails included
2 pounds fish steaks, cut into
    2-inch pieces
1 pound large shrimp, unpeeled
1 pound mussels, scrubbed, beards
    removed
1 pound small clams, scrubbed
Salt to taste
8 to 10 slices Italian bread,
    toasted and rubbed with
    garlic
2 lemons cut into wedges

Heat the oil in a large, heavy, low-sided saucepan, add the garlic and sage, and sauté for 1 minute. Add the squid and sauté

5 minutes over low heat. Remove the squid and set aside. Add the black peppercorns and crushed hot pepper, the onion, carrot, celery, and parsley. Sauté over medium heat for 5 minutes. Add the wine, tomatoes, water, and the rockfish. Cover and simmer 30 minutes.

When it is cooked, transfer the rockfish with a slotted spoon to a large plate. Remove as many bones as possible from the fish. Set it aside and return the bones, heads, and tails to the broth. Pass the bones and broth through a food mill equipped with a medium disk. Return to the pan and set aside. The soup can be made in advance up to this point.

Twenty minutes prior to serving, bring the broth to a boil, add the fish steaks and shrimp, and cook over low heat for 10 minutes. Add the mussels and clams, cover, and cook 3 to 5 minutes until the mollusks open. Add the squid and the reserved rockfish. Heat through, taste, and adjust for salt.

Serve the *cacciucco* in a heated tureen. The bread should be placed in the individual soup bowls and the soup ladled over it. Serve accompanied by lemon wedges.

BOURRIDE   *France*
Provençal Fish Soup with Aïoli

Bourride, once savored, is a dish you are unlikely to forget. Use at least two kinds of fish, preferably three, chosen from snapper, turbot, sea bass, and monkfish. With a light appetizer, a salad, and dessert, it makes a fabulous meal.   SERVES 6

4 cups water

2 cups high-quality dry white wine

2 leeks, white parts only, cut into disks

1 medium onion, sliced

1 tender celery stalk, with leaves, roughly chopped

1 carrot, peeled and sliced

2 tablespoons roughly chopped fresh parsley

¼ teaspoon fresh or dried thyme

One 3-inch piece orange peel, thinly sliced

2 bay leaves

1 tablespoon minced fresh dill

Salt and freshly ground white pepper to taste

2 pounds fish heads, tails, and trimmings

1 pound small new potatoes, cut into ½-inch cubes

2 small zucchini, scrubbed, cut into ½-inch slices

2 pounds fish fillets, cut into 1½-inch cubes

1½ cups Aïoli (see recipe)

3 egg yolks

2 tablespoons lemon juice

12 slices French bread, toasted

Make a court bouillon with the water, the wine, leeks, onion, celery, carrot, parsley, thyme, orange peel, bay leaves, dill, and salt and pepper. Add fish heads, tails, and trimmings and simmer for 40 minutes. When cooked, drain through a sieve or fine colander, reserve the liquid, and discard the rest.

Place the potatoes in a saucepan, add water to cover, bring to a boil, lower heat, and simmer, covered, until cooked but still firm, about 15 minutes. Drain and set aside. Steam the zucchini until just tender, drain, and set aside.

Fifteen minutes prior to serving, poach the fish fillets in the court bouillon for 5 to 8 minutes, until tender but not overcooked. Remove with a slotted spoon, set aside, but keep warm.

Place ½ cup of *aïoli* in a large saucepan, and, stirring constantly with a whisk over very low heat, add the hot court bouillon, a ladleful at a time. Continue until all but 1 cup of the bouillon is added. Do not allow it to boil.

Mix the egg yolks with the lemon juice, then dilute with the reserved cup of bouillon. Pour the egg mixture, a little at a time, into the bouillon, stirring constantly. Heat through but do not boil. Distribute the fish pieces in 6 individual shallow soup bowls. Do the same with the potatoes and zucchini, add the hot broth, and serve immediately with the bread and remaining *aïoli*. One usually slathers the bread with the *aïoli* and adds it to the soup. The *bourride* can also be served in a heated soup tureen.

Couscous

Couscous, the great North African specialty, refers both to hard grains of flour-coated semolina and to the stew of meat, fish, and/or vegetables that is eaten with the grain. Couscous is a creation of the Berbers, the pre-Arabic residents of the region, but is now as much a part of Moslem cuisine in North Africa as the minaret is part of the landscape. And, like all great dishes, couscous has made its way to other areas in the Mediterranean, including Italy, where it has taken on a distinctly Italian flavor. A skilled hand and lots of time are needed to roll couscous and, while some Moroccan women still do it at home, it has become common to buy it ready-made. The best couscous we ever had was a hand-rolled whole-wheat variety made by the aunt of our friend Mohammed, but most commercial varieties are very good.

Couscous dishes come in as many varieties as Arabic mosaics but all have one thing in common—the grains are cooked by the aromatic vapors of a rich broth or stew with which they are eaten. In Morocco, the grains are piled in a cone in the center of a large plate with a big crater dug out of the middle—something like a neatly exploded volcano. The stew is placed in the crater and the whole is eaten directly from the platter, each diner digging like a steam shovel into the portion in front of him, taking care not to infringe on his neighbor's space. Broth is served separately in a pitcher and is used to moisten the grains and the stew.

Master Recipe for Preparing Couscous

Couscous has the undeserved reputation of being very difficult to prepare. It does take know-how and a *couscousière* but the former is easily obtained and the latter can be improvised from some very standard kitchen utensils.

Couscous is cooked by steaming and a *couscousière* is nothing more than a specialized steamer. If you intend to make couscous frequently, buy one. Otherwise, try one of the following. A large pot with a steaming basket is perfect for couscous. You can also use a fine sieve or colander fitted on top of a large pot. The only problem with this latter device is that the vapors from the stew may escape from the sides and not pass through the sieve or colander and, therefore, leave the grains uncooked. To prevent this, wet with a water-and-flour paste a piece of cheesecloth whose length is equal to the circumference of the pot and squeeze out excess paste. Then lay the cloth across the rim of the pot. Set the sieve or colander on top and you have a perfect seal. Of course, you must reset the seal each time you remove the sieve or colander.

STEP 1. RINSING AND DRYING: The objective here is to wash excess starch off the grains and to wet them to facilitate steaming. Place the couscous in a large mixing bowl, cover completely with cold water, stir briefly with your fingers, then drain in a fine sieve or colander. Place the grains on a large shallow platter or metal pan and allow to dry for about 15 minutes. During this time break up lumps with your fingers a couple of times. The grains must not be allowed to stick to one another.

STEP 2. FIRST STEAMING AND DRYING: This is the first stage of the cooking process. Place the top of the *couscousière* or steam basket or colander over the stew that is simmering in the pot below. Spread about ½ inch of grains in the bottom of the basket and, when steam begins to rise through the grains, add the rest. Steam uncovered for 30 minutes. Remove the basket from the pot and place the grains on the large platter or pan. While stirring the grains with one hand to aerate, sprinkle with 1½ to 2 cups of water (for 3 cups of raw grains). The water should be added a little at a time. Do not add more than the grains can absorb. Make sure no lumps form. Add salt at this time. You may, if you wish, stir the grains with a wooden spoon in the beginning, since they will be hot. However, finish with your fingers.

Let the grains sit for 15 minutes to swell, aerating once or twice. The couscous, to this point, can be prepared a few hours in advance. Cover with a damp cloth if it is left for more than 1 hour. Remember to break up the grains with your fingers before going on to Step 3. Remove the pot from the stove.

STEP 3. SECOND STEAMING: This is the second and final stage. Twenty minutes before serving, bring the stew in the pot to a simmer, replace the steamer, sealing if necessary, add the couscous and steam for 20 minutes. Place the grains on a large serving platter, break up lumps, and blend in 2 to 3 tablespoons of butter or broth. Shape the grains into a cone with a crater in the center, place the stew in the crater, and serve immediately.

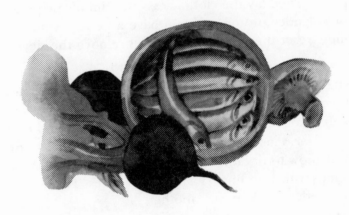

SECSOU BEL HOUT   *Morocco*
Fish Couscous

Fish couscous, quite common in Tunisia and even in Trapani in Sicily, is virtually unknown in Morocco. We were told by friends that we might find a Moroccan version in Al Hocema, a small resort on the Mediterranean near the Algerian border, but we opted instead for a recipe that we got from Fatima. She uses red mullet, bream (a Mediterranean porgy), and sea bass, an excellent combination with only one drawback—the fish are bony. When we make it, we use grouper, halibut, sometimes even monkfish, and purchase heads and cuttings for the stock separately. Whatever you do, use two or three different kinds of fish.   SERVES 6 TO 8

2 pounds fish heads, tails, and
    trimmings
¼ cup olive oil
1 celery stalk with leaves, roughly
    chopped
1 onion, roughly chopped
2 medium, ripe tomatoes, peeled
    and chopped
1 tablespoon tomato paste
Salt to taste
½ teaspoon freshly ground black
    pepper
1 teaspoon cayenne pepper
1 tablespoon sweet paprika
3 cups couscous

Pinch of saffron
3 large carrots cut in 2-inch
    segments
1 pound turnips, peeled and cut
    into 1½-inch cubes
2 medium onions, cut in wedges
1 cup chick-peas, soaked
    overnight, peeled (see note)
½ cup raisins
2½ pounds fish steaks
3 tablespoons butter
1 tablespoon cinnamon
1 cup Harissa (see recipe)
    (optional)

Place the heads, tails, and trimmings in the bottom of a *cous-cousière* together with the oil, celery, chopped onion, tomatoes, tomato paste, salt, pepper, cayenne pepper, and paprika. Cover with 2½ quarts of water, bring to a boil, and simmer covered for 30 minutes.

While the stock simmers, wash and dry couscous (see instructions, Step 1). Pass the stock, fish parts, and vegetables through a food mill equipped with a fine disk. Return to the bottom of the *couscousière,* add the saffron and carrots, and cook for 15 minutes. Blend in the turnips, onion wedges, chick-peas, and raisins, and bring to a boil, adding water if necessary to cover the vegetables. Simmer for 20 minutes. While it simmers, do the first steaming, then the drying of the couscous (see instructions, Step 2).

To this point, the dish can be prepared a few hours in advance.

Twenty minutes before serving, add the fish steaks to the stock and simmer for about 20 minutes. Steam the couscous a second time (see instructions, Step 3).

Place the couscous on a serving platter. Incorporate the butter and 2 or 3 tablespoons of fish stock while aerating the couscous and breaking up lumps that may have formed.

Shape the couscous into a cone with a well in the center. Remove the fish pieces from the stock with a slotted spoon and place them in the well. Cover with the drained vegetables and sprinkle with cinnamon. Place the stock in a pitcher and serve separately. The stock is used to moisten the couscous and the stew. Pass *harissa* for those who want it.

NOTE: It takes time to peel chick-peas, but it's worth the extra effort. After soaking the chick-peas, make an incision along a chick-pea with the thumbnail of the left hand (reverse if you are left-handed), then squeeze the chick-pea between the thumb and index finger of your right hand. The skin will remain between your fingers, while the chick-pea will shoot into your left hand. With a little practice, you will become an expert chick-pea peeler. Peeled chick-peas cook in about half the time of unpeeled ones. If you decide not to peel them, cook them separately in 4 cups of water for 40 minutes, drain and add as the recipe calls for them.

SECSOU BEL BESSLA OU ZBIB   *Morocco*
Onion Couscous with Raisins

The spectacular array of sweet and pungent flavors make this couscous a very special eating experience.   SERVES 6 TO 8

3 cups couscous
6 tablespoons peanut oil
6 tablespoons olive oil
2½ pounds yellow onions, 1 cup
    chopped, the rest thinly sliced
½ cup finely chopped fresh
    coriander leaves
Generous pinch of saffron
½ tablespoon freshly ground
    black pepper
2 teaspoons powdered ginger
1 teaspoon turmeric
½ teaspoon salt
5 cups Vegetable Broth (see
    recipe)

6 cups water
1 cup dried chick-peas, soaked
    overnight, preferably peeled,
    (see Note above)
⅓ cup chopped fresh parsley
¼ teaspoon cayenne pepper
¼ teaspoon freshly ground
    nutmeg
1 tablespoon sugar
1 cup blond raisins
1 tablespoon cinnamon
2 tablespoons butter
1 cup Harissa (see recipe)
    (optional)

Rinse and dry the couscous grains (see instructions, Step 1).

Prepare the broth by heating 3 tablespoons of peanut oil and 3 tablespoons olive oil in the bottom of a *couscousière*. Add the chopped onions and sauté for 5 minutes, until the onions become translucent. Add the coriander leaves, saffron, pepper, ginger, turmeric, and ¼ teaspoon of salt. Blend together, then stir in vegetable broth, 5 cups of water, and the chick-peas. Bring to a boil, cover, and simmer for 1 hour.

Meanwhile, heat the remaining oils in another large, heavy, low-sided saucepan. Add the sliced onions and parsley, and sauté over high heat until the onions are lightly browned. Stir frequently, scraping the bottom of the pan to loosen browned bits. Add 1 cup of liquid from the chick-pea broth, 1 cup of water, cayenne pepper, and nutmeg. Cover and simmer ½ hour.

When the chick-peas have cooked 30 minutes, do the first steaming and drying of the couscous in the top part of the *couscousière* (see instructions, Step 2).

Add the remaining salt, and the sugar, raisins, and ½ tablespoon of cinnamon to the sliced onions. Cover and simmer over very low heat for another 30 minutes, adding broth as necessary to keep the onions moist. Do not stir the onions or they will disintegrate. Instead, shake the pan occasionally to prevent sticking or prod gently with a wooden spoon.

Remove the chick-peas from their broth with a slotted spoon, place in a bowl, and keep warm. To this point, the dish can be prepared a few hours in advance.

Do the second steaming of the couscous (see instructions, Step 3), then transfer to a large serving platter. Add the butter in small pieces and combine well, breaking up lumps with the tines of a fork. Make a large cone of couscous in the center of the platter, then form a wide crater in the middle of the cone and place the chick-peas at the bottom of the crater. Pour the hot onions over the chick-peas, making sure that the onions remain in the crater and not on the sides of the cone. Sprinkle the remaining cinnamon over the couscous. The cinnamon is traditionally distributed over the grains in lines running down the side of the cone from top to bottom like rays of sunshine.

Serve the dish at once, passing the hot chick-pea broth in a pitcher for those who want to moisten and flavor the grains. Pass the *harissa* as well for those who want to add a little zip to the couscous.

SECSOU BEL KHODRA   *Morocco*
Couscous with Vegetables

The vegetables can be varied with the seasons, but it is traditional to use a number of root vegetables. The mixture described here is particularly suited for fall and winter.   SERVES 8 TO 10

3 cups couscous
6 tablespoons butter
1 medium onion, cut into 8 pieces
1 large pinch saffron, crushed
    and soaked in 1 cup water
1½ teaspoons black peppercorns,
    crushed in a mortar
3 medium carrots, cut into 2-inch
    segments
1 cup peeled, seeded, and
    quartered ripe tomatoes, or 1
    cup canned Italian plum
    tomatoes, with juice
1 or 2 fresh or dried hot peppers,
    finely chopped if fresh,
    crushed if dried
3 cups Vegetable Broth (see
    recipe)
3 cups water

1 cup chick-peas, soaked
    overnight, preferably peeled
    (see Note, p. 208)
2 medium artichokes
Juice of 1 lemon
2 large or 3 small fennel bulbs,
    cut into eighths
½ cup tightly packed chopped
    fresh coriander leaves
1½ pounds butternut squash, cut
    into 2-inch pieces
3 medium turnips, cut into 2-inch
    pieces
½ small head of cabbage, cut
    into 2-inch-thick wedges
Salt to taste
1 cup Harissa (see recipe)
    (optional)

Rinse and dry the couscous (see instructions, Step 1).

Place 3 tablespoons butter in the bottom of a *couscousière*, add the onion and sauté over medium heat until golden, about 10 minutes. Add the saffron and its water, peppercorns, carrots, tomatoes, hot peppers, vegetable broth, and the 3 cups water. Cover and simmer for 1 hour. After 30 minutes, do the first steaming and drying of the couscous (see instructions, Step 2). If using peeled chick-peas, add after 45 minutes. If using unpeeled chick-peas, add with the saffron, peppercorns, carrots, etc.

While the vegetables cook, prepare the artichokes. Remove all but the most tender outer leaves, cutting away the stem and any green at the base to expose the tender white flesh of the heart. Trim the pointed leaves, quarter, remove the chokes, rub with a lemon, and place in water acidulated with lemon juice until ready to use.

When the broth has cooked for an hour, drain the artichokes and add them to the chick-pea mixture along with the fennel bulbs and coriander leaves, adding water to cover if necessary. Simmer for 15 minutes. The dish can be prepared a few hours in advance up to this point.

Thirty minutes prior to serving, remove 2 cups of broth and place in a small saucepan. Add the squash pieces and cook until tender, about 10 minutes. Set aside but keep warm.

Add the turnips, cabbage, and salt to the chick-pea mixture and simmer for 20 minutes, until the vegetables are tender. While cooking, do the second steaming of the couscous (see instructions, Step 3).

When ready, place the couscous on a large serving platter. Add the remaining butter cut into small pieces and 1 cup of broth. Combine well, breaking up lumps with the tines of a fork. Distribute the grains around the rim of the platter, leaving a large crater in the center.

Remove the vegetables from the broth with a slotted spoon and place them in the crater. Cover the vegetables with the drained squash. Pour the broth and the liquid from the squash into a pitcher and serve along with the couscous to moisten the grains and the vegetables. Serve *harissa* for those who want to add it.

VARIATION To make a less elaborate couscous, omit the artichokes, fennel, and cabbage, use turmeric instead of saffron, and increase the quantity of chick-peas to 1½ cups.

Vegetable and Egg Dishes

Until recently, meat was expensive and scarce in the Mediterranean, per capita incomes were low, and, not surprisingly, cooks developed the art of turning inexpensive ingredients such as eggs, vegetables, and pasta into substantial, delectable main dishes. We have included a selection of tarts and flans, baked pasta, vegetable, and egg recipes, for the most part traditional, that are easy to prepare, often elegant, and consistently good.

A word on Mediterranean omelets might be useful. Unlike the conventional French omelet, they are cooked flat like pancakes until browned on one side and almost firm on top, then flipped and browned on the other. They tend to be hearty, rustic dishes, drier than normal omelets, and good to eat warm or at room temperature. The easiest way to make an omelet of this sort is to brown the bottom, then place a plate over the pan and invert so that the omelet drops onto the plate. Slip the omelet back into the pan, uncooked side down, return the pan to the heat, and cook until browned.

CROSTATA DI PEPERONI   *Italy*
Bell Pepper Tart

Peppers, tomatoes, and onions, a classic Mediterranean combination, make a delectable filling for a savory tart. We serve this as a main dish for a buffet, light dinner, or luncheon.

SERVES 4 TO 6

Pâte Brisée *(see recipe)*
4 tablespoons olive oil
1 large onion, diced
1 small fresh or dried hot pepper, finely chopped if fresh, crushed if dried
1½ cups undrained canned Italian plum tomatoes

3 large red bell peppers, seeded, cored, and cut into ½-inch squares
2 garlic cloves, thinly sliced
Salt and freshly ground pepper to taste
2 extra-large eggs plus 1 egg white, beaten
⅓ cup freshly grated Parmesan

Make the *pâte brisée* and partially bake the pastry as described in the master recipe. Set aside until needed.

Heat the oil in a large saucepan, add the onion, and sauté over medium-low heat for about 5 minutes, until the onion is translucent. Do not brown. Add the hot pepper and sauté another minute. Blend in the tomatoes and continue to cook, stirring frequently, for 7 minutes. Add the bell peppers, garlic, and salt and pepper. Combine and simmer, covered, over low heat for 10 minutes, stirring occasionally. Uncover and cook for another 5 minutes, until most of the liquid evaporates and the peppers are very tender. Remove from the heat and allow to cool.

Preheat the oven to 375°F.

Combine the peppers with the eggs and Parmesan, transfer the filling to the pastry shell, and bake until the filling is firm, about 30 to 35 minutes. Allow to cool 10 minutes, then remove the tart from its pan. Serve warm or at room temperature.

KOLOKITHÁKIA ME FETA   *Greece*
Zucchini and Feta Flan

The rich, lemony flavor of feta makes a perfect foil for the delicate taste of zucchini in this wonderful flan. Serve warm or at room temperature. The flan can be assembled and baked in advance.

SERVES 6

1¾ pounds zucchini, washed and
    trimmed
½ pound feta cheese, soaked in
    cold water for 10 minutes,
    drained
2 tablespoons finely chopped fresh
    dill

2 tablespoons finely chopped fresh
    parsley
3 extra-large eggs, beaten
¼ cup freshly grated Parmesan
Freshly ground pepper to taste
Pinch of nutmeg

Steam the zucchini until tender, about 15 minutes. Place the zucchini in a colander and press with a wooden spoon to remove excess liquid. Chop finely, then set aside.

Preheat the oven to 375°F. and butter well an 8-by-8-inch baking pan or Pyrex baking dish.

Place the feta in a large mixing bowl, and, using a fork or wooden spoon, mash until a fairly smooth, homogeneous paste is formed. Blend in the remaining ingredients, then add the zucchini, and combine thoroughly.

Pour the mixture into the baking pan and bake for 30 minutes, until the flan is firm and a toothpick inserted into the center of the flan comes out dry. Serve hot or at room temperature.

FLAN D'AUBERGINE   *France*
Eggplant Flan

SERVES 6

3 pounds eggplants, peeled, cut
    into ½-inch-thick rounds
3 tablespoons olive oil
4 garlic cloves, chopped
5 shallots, chopped
Pinch of thyme

2 tablespoons chopped fresh basil
Salt and freshly ground pepper to
    taste
½ cup Crème Fraîche (see
    recipe)
4 extra-large eggs, beaten

Sprinkle the eggplant with salt and place in a colander to drain for 30 minutes. Rinse and wipe dry with a paper towel, cut into cubes, and set aside. Heat the oil in a large skillet, add the garlic and shallots, and sauté for 1 minute. Add the eggplant, thyme, basil, and salt and pepper. Cook, uncovered, over low heat until the eggplant is very tender, about 20 minutes. The eggplant should be dry.

Preheat the oven to 400°F. and butter a 6-cup gratin dish or the equivalent. Purée the eggplant in a food mill, using a blade with holes small enough to trap the seeds. As an alternative, purée in a food processor or blender and pass through a sieve. Add the *crème fraîche* and the eggs to the purée, combine well, and pour into the buttered baking dish. Place this dish in a larger ovenproof dish, add enough water to the larger dish to come halfway up the sides of the smaller, and bake in the water bath until firm, about 45 minutes. The flan is best served at room temperature.

FLAN D'ASPERGES   *France*
Asparagus Flan

A light main course with a touch of elegance, the flans are cooked in individual ramekins and served surrounded with asparagus spears.   SERVES 4

*1 pound asparagus, washed,
    inedible parts of stalks
    removed*
1½ cups milk
Pinch of cayenne pepper
¼ teaspoon freshly grated nutmeg

*Salt and freshly ground white
    pepper to taste*
4 extra-large eggs, beaten
½ cup whipping cream
3 tablespoons butter

Cut off and reserve 2 to 3 inches of the tips of the asparagus. Cut the stem into 1-inch pieces and place in a pan with the milk. Add the cayenne pepper, nutmeg, and salt and pepper, and simmer until the asparagus is cooked, about 10 minutes. Allow to cool for a few minutes, then purée in a blender or food processor. Transfer to a mixing bowl, add the eggs and cream, and combine thoroughly.

Preheat the oven to 400°F. and butter well 4 individual ramekins approximately 4 inches in diameter.

Distribute the asparagus mixture evenly among the ramekins

and place them in a large baking dish. Add enough water to the larger dish to come halfway up the sides of the ramekins, and bake 20 to 30 minutes, until the mixture is firm.

While the flans bake, heat the butter in a skillet, add the asparagus tips and sauté over low heat until tender but still firm, about 10 minutes.

When cooked, remove the flans from the water bath and allow to cool 15 minutes. Slip a knife along the edges of the ramekins to loosen the flans, then unmold onto individual heated dinner plates. Garnish with the asparagus tips, and serve hot.

TYRÓPITA   *Greece*
Cheese and Herb Pie

One summer we rented a ramshackle little house on a beach near Pagóndas on the Aegean island of Samos. A short way down the beach was a small taverna run by Maria and her husband, Costas. Like most locals, we were regular customers, unable to resist either Maria's cooking or the setting, a vine-covered terrace a few feet from the sparkling Aegean. With a bit of flattery and nagging, we could usually get her to break out of the souvlaki-keftas routine and make something special. Her *tyrópita* was superb, good feta and lots of fresh herbs. It's very easy to prepare, once you learn to handle phyllo dough, and can be served either as a first or main course.   SERVES 4 TO 6

*1 pound good feta cheese, soaked
  in fresh water for 15 minutes
  if very salty, creamed*
*4 tablespoons mixed chopped fresh
  herbs such as basil, parsley,
  dill, or chives*
Pinch of oregano

*4 scallions, white parts only,
  chopped*
2 extra-large eggs, beaten
Freshly ground pepper to taste
10 sheets phyllo (see Note)
*2 tablespoons unsalted butter,
  melted*

Preheat the oven to 350°F. and butter well an 8-by-8-inch baking dish.

Combine the feta cheese, herbs, scallions, eggs, and pepper in a mixing bowl and set aside.

Lay out phyllo sheets and melted butter. With a pastry brush, coat the top sheet lightly with butter. Line the bottom of the baking dish with it, allowing excess to drape over the sides of the dish. Paint the next sheet with some melted butter, and lay in pan on top of first. Repeat until 5 sheets are used.

Spread the cheese mixture over the phyllo, then cover with the remaining 5 sheets, spreading butter on each before adding the next one. Trim the phyllo with scissors or a sharp knife and bake until golden and crisp, about 40 minutes. Serve warm or at room temperature.

NOTE: Phyllo sheets, a tissue-paper-thin dough used in many Greek and Middle Eastern dishes, are extremely difficult to make at home but relatively easy to find already made in well-stocked specialty food stores. The dough comes in large sheets, each about 17-by-13 inches, with 25 or 30 per package. It is usually frozen and needs to be thawed 8 hours in the refrigerator before use. Unused dough, if sealed well in plastic wrap, can be refrozen. Phyllo dough tends to dry very quickly when exposed to air so you must prepare all ingredients for the filling before the dough is unpacked. Remove from the package only the number of sheets you need for the recipe, repack the remainder, and refreeze. Keep the dough covered with a damp dish towel during preparation.

MOUSSAKÁ *Greece*
Eggplant Moussaka with Lentils

Many years ago a friend prepared a vegetarian moussaka for us in which she replaced the ground meat with lentils. It was a splendid dish, better than the traditional one. Once you've tried it we think you will agree with our assessment. You can, to avoid excessive last-minute work, cook the lentils and eggplant in advance. The béchamel sauce is best made just before using. The dish can also be made a day in advance and reheated.   SERVES 6

1½ pounds eggplant

FOR THE LENTILS:

4 tablespoons olive oil
1 cup finely chopped onions
1 medium carrot, peeled, finely chopped
2 garlic cloves, finely chopped
2 tablespoons finely chopped fresh parsley

Béchamel *(see recipe) made with:*
  2 tablespoons butter
  2 tablespoons flour

1 cup green or brown lentils
Salt and freshly ground pepper to taste
¼ teaspoon cayenne pepper
¼ teaspoon ground cinnamon
3 cups Vegetable Broth (see recipe), or water

1¼ cups milk
¼ teaspoon salt
¼ cup freshly grated Parmesan

Peel the eggplant, cut into ¼-inch-thick slices, sprinkle with salt, and place in a colander to drain for 30 minutes.

Meanwhile, heat the olive oil in a saucepan, add the onions, carrot, garlic, and parsley, and sauté 5 minutes over medium heat. Add the lentils, salt, pepper, cayenne pepper, cinnamon, and broth or water. Simmer, covered, stirring occasionally, until the lentils are tender, about 35 minutes. Add water, a little at a time, as necessary during the cooking. All the water should be absorbed when the lentils are cooked. Purée half the lentil mixture in a blender or food processor, combine with the whole lentils, and set aside.

Rinse the eggplant slices in cold water to remove salt, pat dry with paper towels, then broil or bake on an oiled cast-iron griddle until golden on both sides. Set aside.

Preheat the oven to 375°F. and oil well an 8-by-8-inch baking dish.

Make the béchamel sauce, add half the Parmesan, and keep warm.

Cover the bottom of the baking dish with a layer of eggplant. Distribute the lentils on top of the eggplant, cover with the remaining eggplant slices, spread the béchamel sauce evenly over the eggplant slices, then top with the rest of the Parmesan. Bake until browned lightly on top, about 30 minutes. Serve hot.

PASTICCIO DI MACCHERONI
Baked Macaroni with Zucchini

Italy

SERVES 6

3 tablespoons olive oil
1 pound zucchini, scrubbed,
    trimmed, cut into ¼-
    inch-thick slices
¾ cup Tomato Sauce (see recipe)
½ cup dry white wine
1 celery stalk, chopped
2 tablespoons chopped fresh
    parsley
½ teaspoon dried oregano

¼ cup bread crumbs, lightly
    toasted
¾ pound short, stout pasta such
    as penne
2 tablespoons butter
1 cup cubed mozzarella
1 cup freshly grated Parmesan
1 cup grated sharp provolone
2 extra-large eggs, beaten
Salt and freshly ground pepper to
    taste

Heat the oil in a large skillet, pat the zucchini with paper towels to dry, add the zucchini, and sauté over medium heat until browned on both sides, about 5 minutes. Drain on paper towels and set aside.

Place the tomato sauce in a saucepan, add the wine, celery, parsley, and oregano, and simmer for 5 minutes. Set aside.

Preheat the oven to 375°F. and oil well a 9-inch springform pan. Sprinkle the interior of the pan with bread crumbs. To eliminate excess crumbs, invert the pan and shake.

Bring 4 quarts of salted water to a rapid boil, add the pasta, and cook, stirring occasionally with a wooden spoon, until al dente. Do not overcook the pasta—in fact, it is preferable to undercook it slightly. Drain and place in a large mixing bowl. Add the butter, tomato sauce, cheeses, eggs, and zucchini. You can, if you wish, reserve ½ cup of zucchini to decorate the top of the *pasticcio*. Mix well, season with salt and pepper, and transfer to the springform pan. If you have reserved any, place the rest of the zucchini on the top. Bake for 40 minutes, until the top begins to brown.

Remove from the oven and allow to cool 10 minutes. Run a sharp knife along the border of the *pasticcio* to loosen it from the pan, unmold, and serve hot. Cut in wedges like a cake.

MELITZANES GEMISTES   *Greece*
Stuffed Eggplant

Stuffed vegetables are immensely popular in Greece, Turkey, and
the Middle East. We've developed a cheese variation of the traditional ground meat stuffing that is particularly good with eggplant.
Use small eggplants with firm, glossy skins. The dish can be prepared ahead of time. The same stuffing can be used with peppers.

SERVES 6

6 small eggplants
8 tablespoons olive oil
1 large onion, finely chopped
2 garlic cloves, finely chopped
3 tablespoons finely chopped fresh
    parsley
½ teaspoon dried oregano
¼ teaspoon cayenne pepper
Freshly ground black pepper to
    taste
2 tablespoons pine nuts

½ pound feta cheese, soaked for
    10 minutes in cold water,
    drained
2 extra-large eggs, beaten
1 pound ripe tomatoes, peeled and
    minced, or 1½ cups drained
    and minced canned Italian
    plum tomatoes
2 tablespoons lemon juice
Pinch of sugar
Salt to taste
2 cups water

Cut off the tops of the eggplants (stem end) about ¼ inch
below the top, and reserve. Scoop out the pulp with a serrated
spoon or the equivalent, taking care to leave the skin of the eggplants unbroken. Sprinkle the insides of the skins with salt and
place upside down in a colander to drain for 1 hour. Place the pulp
in a mixing bowl filled with lightly salted water and set aside for
1 hour. When time is up, rinse eggplant pulp in cold water, then
squeeze out excess liquid. Chop finely.

Heat 6 tablespoons of olive oil in a saucepan, add the onion,
garlic, parsley, oregano, cayenne pepper, and black pepper, and
sauté over medium heat for 5 minutes, until the onions begin to
color. Add chopped eggplant pulp to the onion mixture, and continue to cook over medium-low heat for 10 minutes. Add the pine
nuts, then transfer to a large mixing bowl and set aside.

Place the feta in a mixing bowl and mash with a fork or

wooden spoon until a fairly smooth, homogeneous paste is obtained. Add the eggs and mix well. Blend into the eggplant-onion mixture and set aside.

Rinse the insides of the eggplant skins, then fill with the cheese stuffing, close with the reserved tops, and place standing upright in a deep pot in which they fit snugly. Add the tomatoes, lemon juice, sugar, salt, water, and the remaining olive oil to the pot. Cover, and simmer until the eggplants are very tender, about 45 minutes. Transfer the eggplants to a serving dish, reduce the liquid in the saucepan, if necessary, to a fairly dense sauce, then pour around the eggplants. Serve the eggplants whole, warm or at room temperature.

INVOLTINI DI MELANZANE CON MOZZARELLA   *Italy*
Eggplant Rolls Stuffed with Mozzarella

Paola's brother Alberto picked up this recipe during one of his many summer sojourns in Sardinia. It's easy to prepare, attractive, and delicious. You can serve it as a light main course, or as a substantial appetizer, and it's very good for buffets. The ingredients can be assembled and arranged beforehand, but it is best to bake the eggplant rolls just before serving.   SERVES 4 TO 6

⅓ cup light seed oil for frying
4 or 5 small eggplants, about 2
    pounds, unpeeled, sliced
    lengthwise ¼-inch thick
3 garlic cloves, chopped
4 tablespoons chopped fresh
    parsley

½ pound mozzarella, thinly sliced
3 tablespoons chopped capers
Salt and freshly ground pepper to
    taste
2 tablespoons olive oil
1 tomato, sliced
Parsley sprigs for garnish

Preheat the oven to 325°F. and oil lightly an attractive 8-by-8-inch baking dish.

Heat the seed oil in a skillet, add the eggplant slices, a few at a time, and fry until lightly browned on both sides. Drain on paper towels, then transfer to a work surface.

Distribute the garlic, parsley, mozzarella, and capers on the eggplant slices, sprinkle with salt and pepper, roll each of them loosely from top to bottom, fasten with toothpicks, and place in the baking dish. Drizzle with olive oil and bake for 20 minutes. Serve hot from the baking dish, garnished with fresh tomato slices and parsley sprigs.

ROTOLO DI TONNO CON PATATE   *Italy*
Tuna and Potato Loaf

A cold dish, ideal for a summer dinner party or buffet, the potato and tuna can be mixed together a day in advance and decorated a few hours before serving. It's impressive, yet very easy to prepare.   SERVES 6 TO 8

2 pounds new potatoes	6 anchovy fillets, packed in oil,
½ cup milk	drained
3 tablespoons butter	2 hard-boiled eggs, sliced or
Two 7-ounce cans Italian tuna	quartered
fish, packed in oil, drained	6 radishes, scrubbed, trimmed,
2 tablespoons grated onion	and sliced
Salt and freshly ground pepper to	½ small cucumber, scrubbed,
taste	and sliced
1 cup Mayonnaise (see recipe)	6 parsley sprigs
For garnish:	¼ cup Italian pickled
4 tablespoons capers	vegetables, preferably with
	hot peppers, or dill pickles

Bring 1 quart of water to boil, add the potatoes, and cook, covered, until tender, about 20 to 25 minutes. Drain and, when cool enough to handle, peel. Mash with a ricer or potato masher. Place the mashed potatoes in a saucepan, and, over low heat and stirring constantly with a wooden spoon, add the milk and butter, a little at a time. Cook 3 or 4 minutes.

Purée the tuna in a food mill, blender, or food processor. Place purée in a mixing bowl, add the potatoes and onion, and blend thoroughly. Season with salt and pepper.

Transfer the ingredients to a serving platter and, using a spatula, shape into a loaf, a fish, or any other form that captures your fancy. Coat the surface with mayonnaise, then decorate with the remaining ingredients. Serve cold.

‖ *ARROZ AL HORNO* **Spain**
‖ Baked Rice with Vegetables

Arroz al horno, a Valencian specialty, is, like most Spanish rice dishes, often cooked with sausages or other meats. We have developed this variation, which enhances the delicate flavor of the rice. A good main dish for a luncheon or light dinner, it can also be used as a first course.   SERVES 4 TO 6

3 tablespoons olive oil
½ cup finely chopped carrots
1 cup finely chopped onions
3 garlic cloves, finely chopped
1 cup peeled, seeded, and finely
    chopped ripe tomatoes
1 cup short-grain Italian rice

Pinch of saffron
1 teaspoon sweet paprika
Salt and freshly ground pepper to
    taste
1 cup cooked chick-peas
2¼ cups boiling water

Preheat the oven to 375°F. Oil lightly an attractive 8-by-8-inch or 9-by-9-inch baking dish. Heat the oil in a large saucepan, add the carrots, onions, and garlic, and sauté over medium heat for a few minutes. Add the tomatoes and continue cooking, stirring occasionally, until relatively dry, about 10 minutes. Add the rice and cook, stirring constantly, for a few minutes, until the rice becomes translucent.

Add the spices and seasoning and the chick-peas. Blend in the boiling water. Combine thoroughly and boil for a minute or two.

Transfer to the baking dish and bake 20 minutes. Remove from the oven, allow to sit for 5 minutes, then serve.

VARIATION Carrots are often omitted and thinly sliced potatoes are added. The rice is often baked with an entire head of garlic in the center. The garlic is purely ornamental.

UOVA TONNATE   *Italy*
Poached Eggs with Tuna-Mayonnaise Sauce

Vitello tonnato is a classic summer dish, a wonderful combination of
veal with a tuna-mayonnaise sauce. This dish, in which poached
eggs replace the veal, is equally delicious and very easy to prepare.
Serve as the main course for a luncheon or as part of a buffet. The
dish can be prepared a few hours in advance and kept in the
refrigerator.   SERVES 4

2 tablespoons white wine vinegar	4 tablespoons capers
½ teaspoon salt	1 or 2 Italian pickled vegetables
8 extra-large eggs	or dill pickles, sliced
1¼ cups Italian tuna fish,	2 tablespoons pickled red bell
packed in oil, drained	peppers, sliced into strips
1 cup Mayonnaise (see recipe)	4 parsley sprigs

Bring 4 cups of water to a boil, add the vinegar and salt,
reduce heat to low, and break the eggs, 1 or 2 at a time, into the
water, and simmer 2 to 3 minutes. Remove with a slotted spoon
and place on a serving platter. If the edges of the whites are
ragged, trim. When cooked, the whites should be firm, but the
yolks runny. Set aside.

Purée the tuna in a food mill, blender, or food processor, and
transfer to a mixing bowl. Add the mayonnaise and capers, and
combine thoroughly.

When ready to serve, spoon the mixture over the eggs, garnish with the pickles, peppers, and parsley. Serve at room temperature. If made in advance, store in the refrigerator but remove at
least 30 minutes before serving.

CAZUELA DE ESPINACAS   *Spain*
Spinach Casserole with Eggs

We first had this classic of Andalusian cuisine in a modest restaurant in Granada. It is nothing more than the inspired combination

of spinach sautéed with garlic, tomato sauce, and sweet paprika
then baked with eggs. SERVES 2

1 pound spinach

3 tablespoons olive oil

3 garlic cloves, chopped

½ cup Tomato Sauce (see recipe)

2 teaspoons sweet paprika

Salt and freshly ground pepper to taste

4 extra-large eggs

Wash the spinach well to eliminate all the grit and sand. Place
in a saucepan without adding water and cook over medium heat,
without covering, until just tender, about 5 minutes.

When ready, drain spinach very well, compressing into a ball
and squeezing with your hands or pressing it against the side of a
colander with a wooden spoon. Chop roughly and set aside.

Preheat the oven to 350°F.

Heat oil in a saucepan, add the garlic, and cook until it just
begins to color. Add spinach, tomato sauce, paprika, and salt and
pepper. Combine well. The mixture should be moist—add water
if necessary.

Distribute the spinach evenly among 2 small ramekin dishes
or the equivalent, break 2 eggs over each one, taking care not to
break the yolk, then bake until the whites just solidify, about 5
minutes. Serve hot.

VARIATION Use asparagus instead of spinach. Steam 1 pound asparagus, cut into 1-inch segments, until cooked but still very firm,
and set aside. Sauté 3 chopped garlic cloves in 4 tablespoons of
olive oil with 1/2 cup croutons for 1 or 2 minutes, until the garlic
begins to brown. Remove, season with 1 tablespoon sweet paprika
and salt and pepper to taste, then chop finely or mash together in
a mortar. Combine thoroughly with the asparagus, distribute
evenly in 2 small ramekins, top each with 2 eggs and bake for 5
minutes in a preheated oven. Serve hot.

TAGINE BEL BED BE SALSA HARRA   *Morocco*
Eggs Poached in Pungent Sauce

Every Mediterranean country has a similar dish but none is quite as satisfying as the Moroccan version, in which eggs are poached in a tomato sauce flavored with paprika, coriander, cumin, caraway, and cayenne pepper. A quick, simple meal, excellent for informal dinners. The sauce can be made in advance but the eggs should be cooked just before serving. Serve with crusty bread.

SERVES 4

3 tablespoons olive oil	*1 teaspoon caraway seeds*
3 tablespoons peanut oil	*½ teaspoon cayenne pepper*
6 garlic cloves, chopped	*4 large ripe tomatoes, peeled,*
2 tablespoons paprika	*seeded, and chopped, or 2*
1½ teaspoons ground cumin	*cups canned Italian plum*
½ cup chopped fresh parsley	*tomatoes, with juice*
½ cup chopped fresh coriander	*½ cup water*
leaves	*8 extra-large eggs*

Heat the oils in a large skillet, add the garlic, sauté 1 minute, then add all the remaining ingredients except the eggs. Simmer on low heat, stirring occasionally, for 20 minutes.

When ready to serve, break the eggs above the skillet and drop into the simmering sauce. Cover for 2 or 3 minutes, until the whites are firm and a film has formed over the yolks. Serve hot directly from the skillet.

UOVA ALLA POLENTA FRITTA   *Italy*
Fried Polenta with Eggs

In this simple but delightful dish, eggs sunny-side up are placed on fried polenta, seasoned with Parmesan and herbs, baked briefly, and served. It's a perfect way to use leftover polenta. We calculate 2 eggs per person.

SERVES 4

6 cups water
½ teaspoon salt
Freshly ground pepper to taste
1½ cups coarse cornmeal
7 tablespoons olive oil
8 extra-large eggs

4 tablespoons freshly grated
  Parmesan
2 tablespoons chopped fresh
  parsley
2 tablespoons chopped fresh chives

Place water in a large, heavy saucepan, add salt and pepper, bring to a boil, and add the cornmeal in a thin stream, stirring constantly with a wooden spoon to prevent lumps from forming. Reduce heat to low, and cook, stirring frequently, for at least 30 minutes.

Wet with water a large work surface, preferably of marble, and, when the cornmeal is cooked, spread it over the surface to a thickness of about ½ inch. To facilitate the spreading, use the blade of a large kitchen knife or spatula that you keep wet. Set aside for at least 1 hour, until completely cool and firm.

Preheat the oven to 400°F. and oil lightly a 9-by-15-inch baking dish.

Cut the cornmeal into 8 circles about 4 inches in diameter. Heat 4 tablespoons of oil in a skillet, add the cornmeal, and fry until browned, approximately 1 to 2 minutes per side. Drain on paper towels, then place side by side in the baking dish.

Heat the remaining oil in a skillet and fry the eggs sunny-side up, 1 or 2 at a time. The whites should be cooked and the yolks runny. Take care not to break the yolks. Place the eggs on the cornmeal, sprinkle with Parmesan, parsley, and chives, and bake for 2 minutes. Serve hot.

FRITTATA DI FIORI DI ZUCCA   *Italy*
Zucchini Flower Omelet

This is a glorious omelet, fit for a banquet. The zucchini flowers are stuffed with mozzarella, fried in batter, then placed in the frittata. In this way, the flowers maintain their integrity and impart to the dish their unique flavor.   SERVES 4 TO 6

FOR THE BATTER:
1 extra-large egg, separated
1 tablespoon olive oil
1 tablespoon lemon juice
½ cup water

1¼ cups unbleached all-purpose
    flour
Pinch of salt

FOR THE FLOWERS:
6 tablespoons chopped mozzarella
6 large fresh zucchini flowers,
    pistils, stems, and calyx
    removed

2 anchovy fillets, packed in oil,
    drained (optional)
½ cup light seed oil

FOR THE FRITTATA:
6 extra-large eggs
½ cup freshly grated Parmesan
1 tablespoon chopped fresh
    parsley

Salt and freshly ground pepper to
    taste
3 tablespoons olive oil

To make the batter, place the egg yolk in a mixing bowl and beat with a whisk until pale yellow. Add the oil, lemon juice, and water and beat until thoroughly blended. Add the flour, a little at a time, beating with the whisk to form a smooth, homogeneous batter with the consistency of heavy cream. Beat in the salt and set aside to rest for 1 hour. When ready to use, beat the egg white until stiff and fold into the batter.

Insert 1 tablespoon of mozzarella in each of the flowers and, if you wish, add a small piece of anchovy. Heat the seed oil in a skillet, dip the flowers in the batter and fry, a few at a time, until golden on both sides. Drain on paper towels and set aside.

Combine the eggs, Parmesan, parsley, and salt and pepper in a mixing bowl. Beat lightly. Heat the olive oil in a skillet and add the egg mixture and the fried flowers. Cook over low heat until the bottom browns and the top is almost firm, about 10 minutes, then place a plate over the skillet, invert, and return the omelet to the skillet, uncooked side down, and cook another 2 to 3 minutes until browned. Transfer to a serving platter and serve hot.

TORTILLA DE GAMBAS
Shrimp Omelet

Spain

The Spanish are very fond of egg dishes, in particular omelets. Along the shores of the Mediterranean, fish and seafood are standard components in *tortillas*. One of the most popular and best is a simple *tortilla* made with shrimp. In small wedges, it can be served as an appetizer, but we prefer it as the main course for a light dinner.

SERVES 4

4 tablespoons olive oil
2 garlic cloves, thinly sliced
½ pound extra-large shrimp, shelled and deveined
1 teaspoon sweet paprika

2 tablespoons chopped fresh parsley
4 extra-large eggs, beaten
Salt and freshly ground pepper to taste

Heat 2 tablespoons of olive oil in a skillet, add the garlic, and sauté over medium heat for 1 minute. Add the shrimp, paprika, and parsley and continue to sauté until the shrimp are cooked, about 2 to 3 minutes. Remove the shrimp from the skillet and, when cool enough to handle, chop.

Place the eggs in a large mixing bowl, add salt and pepper and shrimp. Heat the remaining 2 tablespoons of olive oil in a large skillet, add the egg mixture, and cook over medium-low heat until lightly browned, about 10 minutes. Cover the skillet with a plate, invert so that the omelet drops onto the plate, then return to the skillet, uncooked side down, and cook another 2 minutes until lightly browned. This omelet is best if served hot.

TORTILLA DE PATATAS
Potato Omelet

Spain

This is *the* Spanish omelet. It is a simple dish, easy to prepare, and blessed with a classless quality that makes it equally suitable for an elegant buffet or a simple family dinner.

SERVES 2

1 pound new potatoes, washed
5 tablespoons olive oil

Salt and freshly ground pepper to
   taste
4 extra-large eggs, beaten

Slice the potatoes very thinly and pat dry with a clean dish towel or paper towels. Set aside.

Heat the olive oil in a large skillet, distribute the potatoes evenly in the pan in 2 or 3 layers, sprinkling each layer with salt and pepper, cover, and cook over low heat, turning the potatoes occasionally until all are tender and lightly browned, about 10 minutes. Drain excess oil from the skillet and reserve.

Place the potatoes in a large mixing bowl, taking care to keep them flat and unbroken. Pour the eggs over the top. Do not stir.

Heat 2 tablespoons of the remaining oil in a large skillet, add the egg-potato mixture, and cook over low heat until the bottom begins to brown and the top is almost firm, about 10 minutes. Cover the top of the skillet with a plate of equal size, invert so that the omelet drops onto the plate, return the omelet to the skillet, uncooked side down, and cook for another 2 or 3 minutes until browned. Serve at room temperature.

OMELETTE PROVENÇALE   *France*
Provençal Omelet

One bite of this spectacular omelet and you'll discover what they've known in Provence for a very long time—tomatoes, garlic, anchovies, olives, and capers are the perfect complements for eggs.   SERVES 2

1 tablespoon finely chopped capers
1 tablespoon black olives, pitted, rinsed, and finely chopped
3 anchovy fillets, packed in oil, drained and finely chopped
1 large garlic clove, finely chopped
2 tablespoons drained and finely chopped canned Italian plum tomatoes

1 tablespoon finely chopped fresh parsley
¼ teaspoon cayenne pepper
4 extra-large eggs, beaten
1 tablespoon olive oil
1 tablespoon butter

Combine capers, olives, anchovies, garlic, tomatoes, parsley, and cayenne pepper in a mixing bowl. Add the eggs and blend thoroughly.

Heat the oil and butter in a skillet over medium heat, add the egg mixture, reduce the heat, and cook until the bottom is browned and the top almost firm, about 10 minutes. Place a plate over the skillet, invert so that the omelet drops onto the plate, return to the skillet, uncooked side down, and cook for another 2 or 3 minutes, until brown.

Transfer to a serving platter and serve warm or at room temperature.

OMELETTES AVEC TAPENADE   *France*
Omelets with Tapenade

Tapenade, the pungent Provençal sauce made with olives, capers, anchovies, garlic, and olive oil, brings out the best in mildly flavored omelets and makes a terrific and relatively easy main course. The entire dish can be made and assembled ahead of time.

SERVES 4 TO 6

4 tablespoons chopped
combination of parsley,
thyme, dill, basil, and chives
½ cup freshly grated Parmesan
2 tablespoons tomato paste
Freshly ground pepper to taste
9 extra-large eggs

4½ tablespoons butter
4½ tablespoons olive oil
1 large ripe tomato, peeled,
seeded, minced, and drained
6 scallions, trimmed, cut in half
lengthwise
1 cup Tapenade (see recipe)

Place the herbs, Parmesan, and tomato paste in separate small bowls. Add freshly ground pepper to taste and set aside. Beat 3 eggs in a mixing bowl, add to the herbs, and set aside. Beat 3 more eggs and add to the Parmesan. Beat the final 3 eggs and add to the tomato paste.

Heat 1½ tablespoons of butter and 1½ tablespoons oil in a skillet, add the herbs and egg mixture and cook over medium heat until the top begins to solidify and the bottom to brown, about 7 minutes. Place a plate over the top of the skillet, invert so that the omelet drops onto the plate, return to the skillet, uncooked side down, and cook until lightly browned on bottom. Transfer to a plate and set aside. Repeat the same process with the remaining eggs, stacking the omelets as they cook. Set aside.

When ready to serve, cut the omelet stack into 6 or 12 wedges. Distribute equal portions on individual plates, arrange some of the raw tomato, a scallion, and 1 to 2 tablespoons of the *tapenade* on each plate, and serve at room temperature.

TORTINO DI MELANZANE   *Italy*
Eggplant Torte

Eggs and eggplant make a marvelous combination in this Sicilian variation of eggplant Parmesan. The eggplant is usually fried before baking with the eggs, tomato sauce, and cheese, but we prefer to broil it or cook it without oil on a prepared griddle. The taste is unimpaired and the eggplant more digestible.   SERVES 6

2 pounds eggplants

4 tablespoons bread crumbs

4 tablespoons olive oil

2 extra-large eggs, hard-boiled
   and thinly sliced

¼ pound mild Cacciocavallo or
   mild provolone, diced

½ cup freshly grated Romano

2 tablespoons chopped fresh basil
   or parsley or a combination

½ cup Tomato Sauce (see recipe)

3 extra-large eggs, beaten

Large pinch oregano

Salt and freshly ground pepper to
   taste

Peel strips of skin off the eggplants lengthwise, to create a striped pattern. Sprinkle with salt and place in a colander to drain for ½ hour. When ready, wipe off the salt with a paper towel, cut into ¼-inch-thick rounds, and broil or cook on an oiled cast-iron griddle until done on both sides, about 5 minutes per side. Set aside.

Preheat the oven to 400°F. and oil well a 7-by-11-inch baking dish or the equivalent.

On the bottom of the baking dish sprinkle 2 tablespoons of bread crumbs. Cover the bread crumbs with a layer of eggplant slices. Sprinkle 2 tablespoons of oil over the eggplant, cover with the sliced hard-boiled eggs, then distribute the diced cheese, ¼ cup of the Romano, the basil and/or parsley, and the tomato sauce. Cover with the remaining eggplant slices and sprinkle with the remaining oil and bread crumbs. Combine the beaten eggs and remaining Romano in a mixing bowl and pour evenly over the eggplant, making sure the egg penetrates to the lower layers. Bake until the eggs are set, about 10 to 15 minutes. Allow to cool to room temperature before serving.

CROQUE-CHÈVRE   *France*
Fried Goat Cheese Sandwiches

Croque-chèvre is nothing more than a Provençal version of a grilled cheese sandwich. On the other hand, that's like saying a chilled bottle of vintage Meursault is a Burgundian version of a cold drink. Fresh goat cheese blended with crushed peppercorns and fresh

chives makes an exquisite filling for grilled cheese sandwiches.
Serve as the main course for either a luncheon or a light dinner.

SERVES 4

½ pound fresh goat cheese
1 teaspoon peppercorns, roughly
    crushed in a mortar
1 teaspoon chopped fresh chives
8 slices hearty French or
    whole-wheat bread,
    approximately 3 inches
    square, crusts removed

4 tablespoons butter
2 tablespoons milk
4 tablespoons flour
2 extra-large eggs, beaten
Salt to taste
1 cup Provençal Tomato Sauce
    (see recipe)

Blend the goat cheese with the crushed peppercorns and
chives and set aside.

Butter 4 slices of bread with 1 tablespoon of butter, spread the
cheese mixture evenly over the buttered slices, and cover with the
remaining bread slices to make sandwiches. Sprinkle both sides of
the sandwiches with milk and dredge with flour. Combine the eggs
and salt in a mixing bowl, dip each sandwich in the eggs to coat
each one completely. Set aside.

Heat the remaining butter in a skillet, add the sandwiches, and
fry until golden on both sides. Serve hot with warm Provençal
Tomato Sauce on the side.

Vegetables

Mediterranean vegetable dishes rely on high-quality produce, simply cooked to enhance the natural flavor of the vegetable. The range is enormous. Some vegetables, such as artichoke, fennel, mushrooms, and turnips, are native to the area, while others, such as eggplant, tomatoes, and potatoes, are relative newcomers from Asia or the New World; but all, old or new, receive the same brilliant treatment in the hands of Mediterranean chefs.

Vegetables grow year-round in most areas of the Mediterranean and people there eat seasonally. No one looks for zucchini in January or fennel in July. We urge you to follow the same practice. Vegetables in season usually cost less and taste better than those grown out of season.

The quality of produce in Mediterranean markets is excellent, in large part because shoppers are demanding. If you are unsatisfied with the produce where you shop, complain or shop elsewhere. Good, fresh vegetables have more flavor than old, worn-out ones and there is some evidence that they have more nutritional value as well. You certainly get more for your money buying quality.

We include recipes for vegetables such as broccoli, spinach, and zucchini, which are commonplace in North America, and for many such as artichokes and fennel that are less common although available almost everywhere. If some of these are difficult to find in your normal grocery, try Italian, Greek, or Portuguese markets.

CARCIOFI ALLA PIZZAIOLA   *Italy*
Artichokes with Cheese and Tomato Sauce

The artichoke, a member of the thistle family and native to Southern Europe and North Africa, came into its own during the Renaissance. In North America, it is most often boiled and the leaves and heart eaten dipped in vinaigrette or butter. While good, this hardly exploits the culinary possibilities of artichokes. This recipe, in which artichokes are first simmered then baked with cheese and tomatoes, and others in the book will give you an inkling of the range of Mediterranean artichoke dishes.   SERVES 6

Juice of 1 lemon
6 medium artichokes
3 garlic cloves, finely chopped
3 tablespoons chopped fresh
   parsley

¼ cup Tomato Sauce (see recipe)
Salt and freshly ground pepper to
   taste
¼ pound mozzarella, thinly sliced

Combine the lemon juice with 6 cups of water in a large mixing bowl and set aside.

Cut off and discard the stems of the artichokes and remove all but the most tender inner leaves. Cut away any green that remains at the base of the artichokes, trim the tops, cut in half, remove the chokes, and place in the acidulated water until ready to use.

Preheat the oven to 375°F. and oil well an 8-by-8-inch baking dish.

Bring 4 cups of salted water to a boil in a saucepan, add the artichokes, cover, and simmer until the artichokes are tender, about 20 minutes. Drain and place the artichokes, hump side up, in the baking dish, sprinkle with the garlic and parsley, spread the tomato sauce evenly over the artichokes, season with salt and pepper, then top with cheese, and bake until lightly browned, about 10 minutes. Serve hot.

TIAN D'ARTICHAUX
Artichokes au Gratin

SERVES 6

Juice of 1 lemon
8 medium artichokes
8 anchovy fillets, packed in oil,
　　drained and coarsely chopped
1 tablespoon chopped fresh basil
1 teaspoon dried thyme

3 large ripe tomatoes, peeled,
　　seeded, chopped, or 1½ cups
　　drained canned Italian plum
　　tomatoes
3 tablespoons black olives, pitted,
　　rinsed, quartered
3 tablespoons olive oil
2 tablespoons bread crumbs

Combine the lemon juice with 6 cups of water in a large mixing bowl and set aside. Cut off and discard the stems of the artichokes and remove all but the most tender inner leaves. Cut away any green that remains at the base of the artichokes, trim the tops, cut in quarters, remove the chokes, and place in acidulated water until ready to use. Combine the anchovy fillets with the basil and thyme, and set aside.

Preheat the oven to 375°F. and oil an attractive 12-inch-diameter baking dish. Bring 4 cups salted water to a boil in an enamel or stainless steel saucepan, add the artichokes, and cook for 7 minutes, drain, and distribute them in the baking dish in a circular pattern. Distribute the anchovy mixture over the artichokes, then add the tomatoes and olives. Drizzle with the olive oil, sprinkle the top with bread crumbs, and bake for 45 minutes. Serve warm or at room temperature.

ALCACHOFAS CON SALSA DE LIMÓN
AL HUEVO
Artichokes with Egg-Lemon Sauce

A successful combination like tomatoes and eggplant or squash and rice has a way of turning up in a number of different cuisines. This is certainly the case with artichokes in an egg-lemon sauce, a dish found in Turkey, Greece, Italy, and Spain. The Spanish version, which we first sampled in Andalusia, is particularly satisfying. It can be prepared in advance, but combine the artichokes with the egg-lemon sauce at the last minute.   SERVES 4 TO 6

Juice of 1½ lemons
6 medium artichokes
2 tablespoons olive oil
1 garlic clove, finely chopped
1 tablespoon finely chopped fresh
*   parsley*
¼ cup dry white wine

¼ cup Vegetable Broth (see
*   recipe) or water*
Salt and freshly ground pepper to
*   taste*
2 egg yolks
1 teaspoon Dijon mustard

Combine the juice of 1 lemon with 6 cups of water in a large mixing bowl and set aside.

Cut off and discard the stems of the artichokes, remove all but the tender inner leaves, cut away any green that remains at the base of the artichokes, cut off the tops of the leaves, quarter, remove the chokes, and place the quarters in the acidulated water until ready to use.

Heat the oil in a stainless steel or enamel saucepan, add the garlic, and sauté 1 minute. Add the artichokes, parsley, wine, broth, and salt and pepper. Cover, and simmer until the artichokes are tender, about 20 minutes. Add water as necessary to prevent the artichokes from sticking. When cooked, some sauce should remain.

Combine the egg yolks, mustard, and juice of ½ lemon in a small mixing bowl. Remove the artichokes from the heat, add the egg sauce, mix well, and serve immediately.

CARCIOFI CON PATATE
Artichokes with Potatoes

Italy

SERVES 6

Juice of 1 lemon
6 medium artichokes
1 pound new potatoes
2 tablespoons olive oil
3 garlic cloves, finely chopped

2 tablespoons chopped fresh
* parsley*
1 cup Vegetable Broth (see recipe)
Salt and freshly ground pepper to
* taste*

Combine the lemon juice with 6 cups of water in a large mixing bowl.

Cut off and discard the stems of the artichokes, remove all but the tender inner leaves, cut away any green that remains at the base, and trim the tops of the leaves. Cut each artichoke into 6 wedges, remove the chokes, and place in the acidulated water.

Peel the potatoes and cut into wedges roughly the same size as the artichoke pieces. Heat the olive oil in a medium-sized stainless steel or enamel saucepan, add the garlic, and sauté for 1 minute. Add the artichokes, potatoes, parsley, and ½ cup vegetable broth. Season with salt and pepper, taking care not to oversalt in case the broth is salty. Cover and simmer over low heat until the vegetables are cooked but still firm, about 15 to 20 minutes. Add broth as needed to prevent sticking but avoid excess liquid. The vegetables should be moist when cooked but not drowning in broth.

When ready, transfer to a heated bowl and serve hot. This can be prepared in advance and reheated, but avoid overcooking.

AGINÁRES ME FAVA
Braised Artichokes and Fava Beans

Greece

This is another of those felicitous vegetable combinations popular throughout the Mediterranean, artichokes braised with fava beans in a wine, garlic, onion, and herb sauce. If using large fava beans, first shell, then blanch 30 seconds in boiling water, and peel. Fro-

zen fava beans are fine but do not use lima beans—they have the
wrong texture and flavor. In Tuscany, mint is used instead of dill,
in Provence, savory, while in Andalusia, they use parsley and saffron.   SERVES 4 TO 6

Juice of 1 lemon
6 medium artichokes
3 tablespoons olive oil
1 large onion, chopped
½ cup dry white wine
½ cup Vegetable Broth (see
   recipe)

2 cups shelled fava beans
3 garlic cloves, peeled
Salt and freshly ground pepper to
   taste
2 tablespoons chopped fresh dill

Combine the lemon juice with 6 cups of water in a large
mixing bowl and set aside.

Cut off and discard the stems of the artichokes, remove all
but the most tender inner leaves, cut away any green that remains
on the base of the artichokes, trim the tops of the leaves, quarter, remove the chokes, and place in the acidulated water. Set
aside.

Heat the oil in a stainless steel or enamel saucepan, add the
onion, and sauté over low heat until the onion is translucent, about
7 minutes. Add the artichokes and all the remaining ingredients,
cover, and simmer, stirring occasionally, for 40 minutes, until the
vegetables are very tender. Serve warm.

CARCIOFI SULLA BRACE   *Italy*
Grilled Artichokes

An artichoke roast in late May is an unforgettable feast. We were at a
friend's farm in the Roman countryside, where the artichokes were
the last of the season, huge, flavorful, tender, and fresh, perfect for
grilling. After sprinkling them with salt and olive oil, we cooked
them over coals until crisp on the outside, soft and juicy on the
inside. The same preparation, with minor variations, is found
throughout the Mediterranean. The best artichokes for grilling are
the large Italian violets with very little choke, but you can also use

the green variety. Although they are more tasty if cooked over charcoal, you can also broil them in an oven.   SERVES 6

Juice of 1 lemon   *Olive oil*
6 large, tender artichokes   *Coarse salt to taste*

Combine the lemon juice and 6 cups of water in a large mixing bowl and set aside.

Remove the tough outer leaves from the artichokes, cut off and discard all but ½ inch of the stem, cut top of leaves to remove sharp points, and trim the stem and base to expose the tender white flesh. Spread the center leaves and remove the choke with a sharp knife or serrated spoon, and place in the acidulated water until ready to cook.

When ready, drizzle 1 tablespoon olive oil over the top of each artichoke and sprinkle with salt. If cooking over coals, place them on the grill, stem facing the heat, about 2 inches away from the fire, and cook about 10 minutes. Reverse and continue cooking until the exterior is browned and crisp, about 15 to 20 minutes. Take care not to let the leaves burn. Serve hot. Follow the same procedure if broiling. Adjust times to the strength of the heat and the tenderness of the artichokes. Drizzle with additional olive oil before serving.

VARIATION Force slices of garlic between the leaves of the artichokes before cooking.

TOPINAMBOURI ALL' ERBETTE   *Italy*
Jerusalem Artichokes with Herbs

Jerusalem artichokes, the root of a variety of sunflower, are native to North America and were introduced in Europe, via France, in the seventeenth century. They look like knobby potatoes but have a nutty, sweet flavor, somewhat like the heart of a fresh artichoke. When cooked with herbs, garlic, and olive oil, as in this recipe, the modest, nutritious little tuber comes into its own as a first-class vegetable. They quickly lose their texture and flavor if overcooked, so be careful.   SERVES 4

3 tablespoons olive oil
1 tablespoon fresh rosemary
    leaves, chopped, or 1
    teaspoon dried rosemary
2 teaspoons fresh thyme leaves, or
    1 teaspoon dried thyme
2 garlic cloves, chopped
1 pound Jerusalem artichokes,
    scrubbed, cut into ½-inch
    cubes

½ cup Vegetable Broth (see
    recipe)
1 tablespoon chopped fresh basil
1 tablespoon chopped fresh
    parsley
1 tablespoon chopped fresh chives
Salt and freshly ground pepper to
    taste

Heat the olive oil in a large, low-sided saucepan, add the rosemary, thyme, and garlic, and sauté over medium heat for 1 minute. Add the Jerusalem artichokes and continue to cook for 2 minutes, stirring constantly. Add the broth, cover, and simmer over low heat until the vegetable is tender, about 10 to 15 minutes. Add water as necessary, a little at a time, during cooking. The dish, when cooked, should be moist and juicy but not soupy. When done, add the remaining herbs, correct for salt and pepper, blend well, and serve hot.

ZEYTINYAĞLI YER ELMASI   *Turkey*
Jerusalem Artichokes with Rice

When we first had this delectable creation, in a café in Bodrum, we couldn't believe the main ingredient was Jerusalem artichokes— the lemon juice and carrot draw out the root's natural sweetness, and rice complements its earthy taste. Do not overcook.

SERVES 4

4 tablespoons olive oil
1 small carrot, peeled, cut into
    thin slices
1 small onion, chopped
1 pound Jerusalem artichokes,
    scrubbed, cut into ½-inch
    cubes

Juice of 1 lemon
Pinch of sugar
Salt and freshly ground pepper to
    taste
2 tablespoons long-grain rice
½ cup water

Heat the oil in a large, low-sided saucepan, add the carrot and onion, and sauté for 5 minutes, until the vegetables begin to soften. Add the Jerusalem artichokes and cook another 2 minutes, stirring constantly. Add the lemon juice, sugar, salt and pepper, the rice, and water, and simmer, covered, until the artichokes are tender, about 15 minutes. Add water as necessary, a little at a time, during cooking. The dish, when cooked, should be moist but not soupy. Serve at room temperature.

HARICOTS VERTS AUX OEUFS DE SAUMON France
Green Beans with Salmon Caviar

Friends with a chateau near Montpellier first introduced us to this delicious and wonderfully extravagant way to prepare green beans. Asparagus can also be done with the same sauce.   SERVES 4

1 pound green beans, washed and trimmed	*Juice of ½ lemon*
¼ cup **Crème Fraîche** *(see recipe)*	*Salt and freshly ground pepper to taste*
Zest of 1 lemon	*5 tablespoons chopped fresh chives*
	4 tablespoons salmon caviar

Steam the green beans until cooked but still firm, about 10 to 15 minutes. While they cook, combine all the remaining ingredients except the caviar in a mixing bowl. When the beans are ready, place them on a serving platter, add the *crème fraîche* sauce, top with the caviar, and serve warm or at room temperature.

JUDIAS VERDES A LA ANDALUZA   *Spain*
Green Beans, Andalusian Style

In this simple but satisfying dish, green beans are simmered in a rich, flavorful sauce of tomatoes, onions, garlic, oil, vinegar, and hot pepper. The dish can be made in advance and reheated before serving.   SERVES 4 TO 6

4 tablespoons olive oil
¾ pound ripe tomatoes, peeled,
   seeded, and minced
½ pound onions, thinly sliced
3 garlic cloves, finely chopped

1 pound green beans, washed,
   trimmed, and cut into 2-inch
   segments
1 small dried hot pepper, crushed
2 tablespoons wine vinegar
Salt and freshly ground pepper to
   taste

Heat the oil in a saucepan, add all the ingredients, and simmer, covered, for 15 minutes. Remove the cover and continue to cook another 15 minutes, until most of the liquid evaporates and the beans are tender. Serve warm.

TAGINE BEL FOULE AU GUERÂ HAMRA   *Morocco*
Tagine of Green Beans and Squash

SERVES 4 TO 6

2 tablespoons olive oil
2 tablespoons peanut oil
4 garlic cloves, minced
½ pound green beans, trimmed,
   cut into 2-inch pieces
1 teaspoon ground ginger
1 teaspoon turmeric
½ teaspoon freshly ground black
   pepper
2 tablespoons chopped fresh
   coriander leaves

1 pound butternut squash, peeled,
   cut into 1½-inch cubes
Rind of 1 preserved lemon (p.
   15), rinsed, cut into 1-inch
   pieces
10 to 15 black olives, Moroccan
   if possible, pitted and rinsed
   well if salty
Juice of 1 lemon
2 tablespoons flour
Salt to taste

Place the two oils in a *tagine,* or an enamel or stainless steel saucepan, preferably a *tagine.* Distribute the garlic on the bottom, add the beans, then sprinkle with half the amount of ginger, turmeric, black pepper, and coriander leaves. Distribute the squash on top of the beans, then add the other half of the spices. Add hot water to cover, and simmer, covered, for 30 minutes. Remove the cover and simmer 20 minutes, until the liquid is reduced by half.

Do not stir, but you can occasionally poke the vegetables or shake the pan.

Distribute the lemon rind and the olives on top of the squash. Mix the lemon juice and flour in a small mixing bowl, add 2 tablespoons of cooking liquid, then pour over the vegetables. Allow to cook 5 minutes until the sauce thickens. Taste and adjust for seasoning and serve hot.

LOUBIA BE SALSA HARRA   *Morocco*
White Kidney Beans in Piquant Sauce

Beans were brought to the Mediterranean in the sixteenth century by explorers returning from South America and were rapidly integrated into local cuisines. In this intensely flavored dish, kidney beans are simmered in a sauce of cayenne pepper, coriander leaves, and tomato.   SERVES 4 TO 6

1 cup dried white kidney beans
1 tablespoon flour
2 tablespoons peanut oil
¼ teaspoon cayenne pepper
1 teaspoon turmeric
1 teaspoon ground ginger
*3 tablespoons chopped fresh
    coriander leaves*
*3 tablespoons chopped fresh
    parsley*

*1 large ripe tomato, peeled,
    seeded, and chopped, or ½
    cup drained canned Italian
    plum tomatoes*
5 garlic cloves, chopped
½ teaspoon salt
*¼ teaspoon freshly ground black
    pepper*
1 bay leaf
⅓ cup chopped celery leaves

Soak the beans in 4 cups of water with the flour 8 hours or overnight.

When the beans are ready to cook, drain, rinse, and place them in a saucepan with all the remaining ingredients and 4 cups of water. Bring to a boil, lower the heat, and simmer, covered, stirring occasionally, for 1 to 1½ hours, until the beans are tender. When the beans are cooked, some liquid should remain in the pan. Discard the bay leaf, and serve hot.

LOUBIA M'THOUNA HARRA   *Morocco*
Spicy White Kidney Bean Purée

With the addition of the right spices, a modest purée of kidney beans becomes a remarkable dish. Although in one form or another this dish is found throughout the Mediterranean, we are partial to the Moroccan version. It can be made in advance and reheated before serving.   SERVES 4 TO 6

1½ cups dried white kidney
* beans*
1 tablespoon flour
5 garlic cloves
½ onion, roughly chopped
¾ teaspoon salt
Juice of 1 lemon

3 tablespoons olive oil
1½ teaspoons sweet paprika
¼ teaspoon cayenne pepper
¼ teaspoon freshly ground black
* pepper*
1 teaspoon ground cumin

Soak the beans in 6 cups of water with the flour 8 hours or overnight.

When the beans are ready to cook, drain, rinse, and place them in a large saucepan with 2 garlic cloves, the onion, and salt. Add 7 cups of water, bring to a boil, lower the heat, and simmer, covered, for 1 to 1½ hours, until the beans are tender. As an alternative, cook in a pressure cooker for 25 minutes, reducing the amount of salt to ¼ teaspoon and the amount of water to 4 cups. When cooked, drain, and reserve 1 cup of cooking liquid.

Place the beans in a skillet and crush with a potato masher or the tines of a fork to make a purée. Do not use a food processor or blender. Add 3 garlic cloves, crushed, and the reserved liquid and simmer for 15 minutes, stirring occasionally. The water should evaporate and the beans have the consistency of porridge.

Place in a heated serving bowl, add the remaining ingredients, mix well, and serve hot.

BROCCOLI AL VINO ROSSO *Italy*
Broccoli Simmered in Red Wine

The robust flavor of broccoli is enhanced by the dry, mellow flavor of the red wine in this dish from southern Italy. The broccoli can be cooked ahead of time since it benefits from marinating in its cooking liquid. SERVES 4

2 tablespoons light olive oil
3 garlic cloves, finely chopped
1 large bunch broccoli cut into
*   flowerets, stems trimmed and*
*   cut into 1-inch segments*
1 cup dry red wine

3 tablespoons raisins or currants
2 tablespoons pine nuts
1 tablespoon red wine, cider, or
*   other fruit vinegar*
Salt and freshly ground pepper to
*   taste*

Heat oil in a large saucepan, add garlic, and sauté over medium heat for 1 minute. Add broccoli and continue to cook for a few minutes, stirring constantly to amalgamate ingredients. Add the remaining ingredients. Simmer, covered, over low heat, stirring occasionally, until tender, about 20 to 25 minutes. Add more wine as necessary during cooking to prevent broccoli from sticking to pan.

Serve hot or at room temperature.

CELERI À LA PROVENÇALE *France*
Braised Celery, Provençal Style

Celery in ancient Greece and Rome was worn, not eaten; in the former as a crown for athletes, in the latter as funeral wreaths. It is rich in vitamins, minerals, and iron, most of which are more easily assimilated when the celery is cooked. In this recipe, the mild anise flavor of the celery is perfectly complemented by the natural sweetness of pearl onions. It can be made in advance and reheated, but do not overcook. SERVES 4

3 tablespoons olive oil

4 small or 2 large celery hearts,
    outer leaves removed,
    trimmed, cut into 6-inch
    segments, cut in half
    lengthwise if large

1 cup peeled pearl onions

2 carrots, cut into 1-inch
    segments

1 bay leaf

2 teaspoons black peppercorns,
    crushed in a mortar

1 garlic clove, crushed

1 teaspoon dried thyme

1 cup dry white wine

Salt to taste

Heat the oil in a low-sided saucepan, place the celery in the center, and surround it with onions and carrots. Add the remaining ingredients, making sure that the pepper is distributed evenly over the celery. Cover with a tight-fitting lid and simmer for 20 to 30 minutes, until the vegetables are tender. Baste occasionally with the juices in the pan and serve hot.

ACELGAS A LA CATALUÑA   *Spain*
Swiss Chard, Catalonian Style

Similar combinations, Swiss chard or spinach cooked with anchovies, pine nuts, and raisins, are found throughout the Mediterranean, but nowhere is it more popular than in Catalonia. It can be made in advance and reheated before serving.   SERVES 6

3 pounds Swiss chard, washed,
    stems removed, and thinly
    sliced

3 tablespoons olive oil

3 garlic cloves, thinly sliced

4 anchovy fillets, packed in oil,
    drained

½ cup pine nuts

½ cup raisins or currants, soaked
    in warm water for 20
    minutes, drained

Salt and freshly ground pepper to
    taste

Bring 1 cup of water to boil in a large saucepan, add the Swiss chard, and simmer, uncovered, for 15 to 20 minutes, until tender. Drain well in a colander and set aside.

Heat the oil in a large skillet, add the garlic, and sauté 1 minute. Add the anchovies and cook until dissolved. Blend in the pine nuts and cook another minute, stirring constantly. Add the Swiss chard, raisins or currants, and salt and pepper, and cook another 5 to 10 minutes, stirring frequently, until all water evaporates and the ingredients are well blended. Serve warm.

PAZI KOTCHO   *Turkey*
Swiss Chard with Rice in Lemon Sauce

A wonderful Judeo-Spanish way to prepare Swiss chard, it also works well with spinach. The recipe is a modified version of one found in Esther Benbassa's delightful book, *Cuisine Judeo-Espagnole.*

SERVES 4 TO 6

2 pounds Swiss chard, washed
    well, stems removed
¼ cup Italian or Carolina
    long-grain rice
3 tablespoons olive oil

Juice of 1 lemon
½ teaspoon sugar
Salt and freshly ground pepper to
    taste

Chop the Swiss chard and set aside. Bring ½ cup of water to a boil in a large saucepan, add all the ingredients, combine well and cook, covered, until the rice and Swiss chard are done, about 30 minutes. Serve at room temperature.

TAGINE BEL HOMESS, LOUZ OU BESSLA   *Morocco*
Chick-pea, Onion, and Almond Tagine

Most tagines, including this one, are made with some meat, often very little, to add flavor to the vegetables. We omit the meat and add vegetable broth without compromising the taste. To achieve full flavor, the tagine must cook slowly for a long time.

SERVES 4

½ cup dried chick-peas
2 tablespoons flour
3 tablespoons butter
3 cups Vegetable Broth (see
    recipe)
2 medium onions, cut into
    1-inch-thick slices
1 teaspoon freshly ground black
    pepper

Pinch saffron, crushed in a
    mortar and soaked in ½ cup
    water
2 tablespoons chopped fresh
    parsley
2 tablespoons chopped fresh
    coriander leaves
Salt to taste
½ cup blanched almonds

Soak the chick-peas in 3 cups of water with 1 tablespoon of flour 8 hours or overnight. Drain, rinse, peel (see Note, p. 208), and set aside.

Heat the butter in a *tagine,* or an enamel or stainless steel saucepan, add the chick-peas and vegetable broth, cover, and simmer 30 minutes. Add the onions, pepper, saffron and water, parsley, coriander leaves, salt, and additional water to cover, and simmer, covered, for 30 minutes.

Add the almonds, mix well, add more water if necessary to just cover the vegetables, and simmer, covered, for 20 minutes.

Remove ½ cup of cooking liquid from the *tagine,* combine in a small mixing bowl with the remaining tablespoon of flour, return to the saucepan, stir, and simmer, covered, until the sauce thickens. Serve hot.

MUSAKA   *Turkey*
Cauliflower and Lentil Stew

In Turkey, one finds a number of dishes in which vegetables and ground meat are stewed together, all of which are referred to as *musaka.* We substitute lentils for ground meat and cook them together with cauliflower. The results are spectacular, the earthy, rich flavor of the lentils perfectly balancing the mild taste of the cauliflower. The entire dish can be prepared in advance and reheated before serving.   SERVES 4 TO 6

1½ *pounds cauliflower, in*
  flowerets

FOR THE LENTILS:

4 *tablespoons olive oil*
1 *cup finely chopped onions*
1 *carrot, peeled, finely chopped*
2 *garlic cloves, finely chopped*
2 *tablespoons finely chopped fresh*
  parsley
1 *cup green or brown lentils*

½ *cup undrained and chopped*
  canned Italian plum
  tomatoes, or 1 medium ripe
  tomato, peeled and chopped

Salt and freshly ground pepper to
  taste
¼ *teaspoon cayenne pepper*
½ *teaspoon ground allspice*
4 *cups Vegetable Broth (see*
  recipe) or water

1 *red bell pepper, thinly sliced*
2 *tablespoons chopped fresh dill*

Steam the cauliflower flowerets in a vegetable steamer or the equivalent until barely tender, about 7 minutes. Drain and set aside.

Heat the oil in a saucepan, add the onions, carrot, garlic, and parsley, and sauté over medium heat for 5 minutes. Add the lentils and the spices, the vegetable broth or water, and simmer, covered, stirring occasionally, until the lentils are just tender, about 30 minutes. Set aside.

Place the tomatoes in a large saucepan, add the cauliflower, the lentils with their cooking liquid, the bell pepper, and simmer, covered, over very low heat, without stirring, for 30 minutes. Add water or broth during the cooking as necessary but do not stir the vegetables. Serve hot with the dill sprinkled on top.

BOHÉMIENNE   *France*
Baked Eggplant with Anchovy Sauce

Eggplant, most probably native to tropical India, made its way, via Africa, to the shores of the Mediterranean by the fourteenth century, took root, and flourished. It is now as much a part of the diet as another relative newcomer, the tomato, and figures in almost as many dishes. In this exquisite recipe from Western Provence, egg-plant is cooked together with a pungent anchovy and tomato sauce. It can be assembled in advance but it is best to brown just before serving. SERVES 4

1½ pounds small eggplants, peeled and cut into ½-inch-thick slices
6 tablespoons olive oil
3 garlic cloves, roughly chopped

½ cup Tomato Sauce (see recipe)
1 cup Anchoïade (see recipe)
¼ cup bread crumbs, lightly toasted

Sprinkle the eggplant slices with salt and place in a colander to drain for 30 minutes. Drain, rinse, and pat dry with paper tow-els. Heat 4 tablespoons olive oil in a skillet. Add the garlic and eggplant and sauté over medium heat for 3 minutes, until the eggplant just begins to soften. Add the tomato sauce, stir, cover, and simmer until the eggplant is cooked but still firm, about 15 minutes.

When the eggplant is done, add the *anchoïade* and mix well. The dish can be prepared in advance to this point.

Preheat the oven to 400°F. and oil a 10-by-6-inch baking dish.

Place the eggplant mixture in the baking dish, sprinkle the top with bread crumbs, then drizzle with the remaining olive oil. Bake for 10 minutes, until the top is lightly browned. Serve hot.

AUBERGINES À LA CRÈME FRAÎCHE France
Grilled Eggplant with Crème Fraîche and Green Peppercorns

A delicious way to dress up grilled eggplant. We occasionally serve this dish as a main course for a luncheon or light dinner. The eggplant slices can be broiled, grilled over charcoal, or baked on an oiled cast-iron griddle. SERVES 6

2 large eggplants, about 2
  pounds
2 tablespoons olive oil
1 cup Crème Fraîche (see
  recipe)

¼ cup green peppercorns, lightly
  crushed
1 teaspoon tomato paste
Salt to taste

Wash but do not peel the eggplants. Cut lengthwise into pieces about ½-inch thick, sprinkle with salt, and place in a colander to drain for 30 minutes.

When ready, rinse and pat dry. Coat the slices with olive oil and grill, broil, or bake on an oiled cast-iron griddle until browned on both sides and tender. Do not overcook. Place the eggplant on a serving platter.

Combine the remaining ingredients, spread over the eggplant, and serve hot.

YOĞURT PATLICAN   *Turkey*
Eggplant with Yogurt

We discovered this fiery combination many years ago in a small family restaurant in İzmir and it has been a favorite of ours ever since.   SERVES 4

1½ pounds eggplant
6 tablespoons olive oil
3 garlic cloves, chopped
2 tablespoons chopped fresh
  parsley or basil

Salt and freshly ground pepper to
  taste
4 hot Italian frying peppers,
  stems removed
1 to 1½ cups yogurt

Remove the stems from the eggplant, cut lengthwise into ¼-inch-thick pieces without peeling, sprinkle with salt, and drain in a colander for 30 minutes. When ready, rinse and pat dry.

Heat 4 tablespoons of oil in a skillet, add the eggplant slices, and fry until tender and browned on both sides, about 10 to 15 minutes. Remove from the skillet, drain on paper towels, then place on a serving platter. Sprinkle with the garlic and parsley or basil, season with salt and pepper, and set aside.

Heat the remaining oil in a skillet, add the peppers, and fry until tender, about 10 minutes. Remove from the skillet, drain on paper towels, then place the peppers on the serving platter on top of or next to the eggplant. Serve warm or at room temperature, passing the yogurt in a bowl.

MELITZANES ME DOMATA   *Greece*
Braised Eggplant and Tomatoes

This was another of the specialties Maria would make in the tiny kitchen of her little taverna near our summer house in Samos. It is a marvelous dish, a scrumptious blend of fried eggplant cooked slowly with tomatoes and whole garlic cloves. It is traditional to brown the eggplant first by frying but we prefer to bake it on a griddle or to broil it. The dish loses a little in flavor but gains in lightness and digestibility. It can be made ahead of time and reheated or served at room temperature.   SERVES 4

1½ pounds eggplant
4 tablespoons olive oil
1 large onion, chopped
1½ pounds ripe tomatoes, peeled
    and quartered, or 1¾ cups
    canned Italian plum
    tomatoes with juice

6 garlic cloves
Salt and freshly ground pepper to
    taste

Peel the eggplant, cut into lengthwise pieces about ½-inch thick, place in a colander, sprinkle with salt, and allow to drain for 30 minutes. When ready, rinse to remove the salt, pat dry with paper towels, and cook on an oiled cast-iron griddle or in a broiler until browned on both sides. Cut into ½-inch cubes and set aside.

Heat the oil in a large saucepan, add the onion, and sauté until golden, about 5 minutes. Add the tomatoes, garlic cloves, the eggplant, and salt and pepper, cover, and simmer over low heat, stirring occasionally, for 30 minutes. Uncover and cook another 20 minutes, until the vegetables are very tender and the cooking juices are thick.

BERENJENAS A LA CATALUÑA
Spain

Eggplant, Catalonian Style

SERVES 6

4 medium eggplants, about 2
    pounds
6 shelled walnuts
2 tablespoons olive oil
1 medium onion, chopped
2 garlic cloves, sliced

Pinch of sugar
Salt to taste
2 tablespoons chopped fresh
    parsley
3 tablespoons Vegetable Broth (see
    recipe) or water

Peel the eggplants, cut into slices about ¼-inch thick, sprinkle with salt, and place in a colander to drain for 30 minutes. When ready, wipe with a paper towel to remove juice and salt (do not wash) and broil or bake on an oiled cast-iron griddle until just tender. Set aside.

Crush the walnuts in a mortar and set aside.

In a saucepan, heat the oil, add the onion, and cook until soft and transparent, about 7 minutes. Add the garlic, sugar, salt, parsley, and walnuts. Cook another 2 minutes. Add the eggplants and enough broth or water to just cover the bottom of the saucepan. Simmer over low heat for 5 to 10 minutes, until tender. Serve warm or at room temperature.

TAGINE BE L'BISBAS
Morocco

Fennel Tagine

Fennel was known in ancient Greece and Rome but was used almost exclusively for its medicinal properties. It was only in the sixteenth century that it began to be cultivated in Europe as a vegetable. The herbs and spices with which it is cooked in this tagine, instead of overwhelming its delicate anise flavor, actually enhance it. It can be made in advance and reheated before serving.

SERVES 6

3 tablespoons olive oil
3 tablespoons peanut oil
2 tablespoons ground ginger
1½ teaspoons turmeric
1½ teaspoons freshly ground
    black pepper
1 cup chopped onions
3 medium fennel bulbs, trimmed
    and cut into 1-inch-thick
    wedges

3 medium carrots, peeled,
    trimmed, and cut into 1-inch
    slices
2 medium ripe tomatoes, peeled,
    seeded, and chopped, or ⅔
    cup drained canned Italian
    plum tomatoes
Salt to taste
2 cups fresh or frozen fava beans

Heat the oils in a *tagine,* or an enamel or stainless steel sauce-pan, add the ginger, turmeric, and black pepper, stir to combine, then add the onions. Stir and heat through. Place the fennel wedges in a single layer in the pan, add the carrots and tomatoes, sprinkle with salt, and cover with water. Simmer, covered, for 1 hour. Do not stir.

If the fava beans are large and tough, peel them before adding to the pan. Squeeze the beans among the fennel wedges, add more water if necessary to cover the vegetables halfway, cover, and sim-mer another 20 to 30 minutes, until the beans are cooked. Again, do not stir the vegetables. You can, however, shake the pan occa-sionally to prevent the fennel from sticking. Serve hot.

FINOCCHI AL VINO BIANCO   *Italy*
Fennel Simmered in White Wine

SERVES 4

3 large fennel bulbs
2 tablespoons olive oil
2 garlic cloves, finely chopped
1 medium onion, finely chopped
½ cup Vegetable Broth (see
    recipe)

½ cup dry white wine
2 tablespoons Tomato Sauce (see
    recipe)
Salt and freshly ground white
    pepper to taste

Trim fennel, cut into medium-size wedges, and set aside.

Heat the oil in a large saucepan, add the garlic and onion, and sauté over medium heat until they begin to color, about 5 minutes. Add fennel, ¼ cup broth, wine, tomato sauce, and salt and pepper. Combine, cover, and cook over low heat, stirring occasionally, until the fennel is tender, about 20 minutes. Add broth as necessary to prevent fennel from sticking. The vegetable should be moist when cooked but not inundated with broth. Serve hot.

PUERROS CON PATATAS Y AZAFRÁN   **Spain**
Leeks and Potatoes with Saffron

SERVES 4 TO 6

3 tablespoons olive oil
6 scallions, washed, trimmed, with some green, and cut into 3-inch-long thin strips
2 garlic cloves, sliced
3 large leeks, trimmed, with some green, washed and cut into 3-inch-long thin strips
½ cup Tomato Sauce (see recipe)

Pinch of saffron, crushed in a mortar and soaked in ½ cup water
1 teaspoon paprika
Salt and freshly ground pepper to taste
1 pound new potatoes, peeled and thickly sliced

Heat the oil in a large, low-sided saucepan, add the scallions and garlic, and sauté for 2 minutes. Add the leeks, tomato sauce, saffron and water, paprika, salt and pepper, and enough water to cover the vegetables, and simmer, covered, 10 minutes.

Add the potatoes, mix well, cover, and simmer until the potatoes are tender, 10 to 15 minutes. When cooked, the water should be absorbed. Serve hot.

KEROMBE M'THOUN
Stewed Kale

Morocco

Once a week in Tangier, farm women come in from the country-side, decked out in red-and-white striped skirts, long white shawls, and broad-brimmed straw hats, to sell their wares, squatting along curbs and in dusty vacant lots. Among many other things, the women bring huge bundles of wild plants, mostly thistles, that, with a little patience, can be turned into a marvelous vegetable. Thistles and other wild greens are not readily available in North America but kale or chicory make a good substitute. The dish can be cooked in advance and reheated before serving. SERVES 4

1 pound kale or chicory
2 tablespoons olive oil
2 tablespoons peanut oil
5 garlic cloves
2 tablespoons chopped fresh
 coriander leaves
2 tablespoons chopped fresh
 parsley

1 medium tomato, peeled, seeded,
 and chopped, or ½ cup
 drained canned Italian plum
 tomatoes
1 tablespoon tomato paste
 (optional)
1 teaspoon ground cumin
1 tablespoon sweet paprika
2 cups water

To prepare the kale or chicory, wash well, removing the leaves from the stems. Chop the leaves roughly and set aside.

Heat the oils in a large skillet, add the garlic, and sauté for 30 seconds. Add the coriander, parsley, tomato, and tomato paste. Cook over low heat, stirring occasionally, for 3 to 4 minutes. Add the cumin and paprika, combine, then add the kale or chicory and water. Mix well, cover, and simmer for 1 hour. Uncover and stir a few times. Add more water if necessary. The vegetable should be dry when cooked. Serve hot.

AIL FRAÎCHE AU FOUR   *France*
Baked Whole Garlic

When we first tasted this dish at a friend's house in Antibes, we were astounded. The exterior, brown and shriveled like old shoe leather, was prosaic enough but the interior was soft and creamy with a delicious nutty flavor. The dish is best made with fresh-picked garlic but any good juicy heads will do. The garlic is eaten by separating the cloves and squeezing the flesh onto your plate. Consume it straight or spread on bread.   SERVES 4

4 large garlic heads   *2 tablespoons olive oil*
2 teaspoons salt

Preheat the oven to 400°F.

Remove the outer papery skins of the garlic cloves, leaving only the last skin, which holds the cloves together. The heads should remain intact. Place the heads in a saucepan with cold water to cover and add the salt. Bring to a boil and simmer for 1 minute. Remove with a slotted spoon, drain, and place in an oiled baking dish. Reserve ¼ cup of cooking liquid. Sprinkle garlic with the oil and bake for 30 to 40 minutes, until browned. Baste occasionally with the reserved cooking liquid. Spoon the liquid from the pan over the garlic just before serving. Serve hot.

FUNGHI AL PARMIGIANO IN FORNO   *Italy*
Baked Mushrooms with Parmesan

Uno Rosso, a restaurant in Florence, makes the best baked mushrooms we've ever eaten. Like many truly inspired culinary creations, the dish is very simple—just Parmesan, fresh porcini mushrooms, and butter, but together they are superb. You can use cultivated mushrooms, enhanced with dried porcini, but one note of warning. Cultivated mushrooms are watery and shrink when cooked, so pack the individual ramekins tightly if using cultivated mushrooms. If you have access to porcini, use sliced caps for this dish. You can also use shiitake, chanterelles, or oyster mushrooms. The stems are generally tougher than the caps and should be finely chopped. Although we consider this a vegetable dish, it can also be served as a main course for a light dinner or luncheon.

SERVES 6

2 ounces dried porcini (Boletus
　edulis)
1½ pounds mushrooms, washed,
　trimmed, and sliced

2 cups freshly grated Parmesan
6 tablespoons unsalted butter
Salt and freshly ground pepper to
　taste

Soak the dried mushrooms in 2 cups of warm water for 20 minutes, remove from the water, taking care not to stir up grit and sand that may have fallen to the bottom of the bowl, drain, and chop. If using fresh porcini or other wild mushrooms, omit the dried ones.

Preheat the oven to 425°F. and butter well 6 individual ramekins.

Distribute a layer of mushrooms in each ramekin, sprinkle with the dried mushrooms and 2 tablespoons of Parmesan. Repeat until all the ingredients are used. Dot with butter, season with salt and pepper, and bake for 20 minutes. Serve hot directly from the oven.

FUNGHI AL CARTOCCIO　　　　　　　　　　　*Italy*
Mushrooms Baked in Parchment

The preferred mushrooms for this dish as for the previous one are fresh porcini. If unavailable, use chanterelles, shiitake, oyster mushrooms, or, in a pinch, cultivated mushrooms. If using a wild variety, keep the caps intact, unless very large, and chop the stems. To cook, use either parchment paper or aluminum foil. You can cook them in one big packet or 4 individual ones.　　　SERVES 4

1 pound mushrooms, washed, trimmed, and thinly sliced

2 small onions, thinly sliced

2 tablespoons unsalted butter

⅓ cup dry white wine

Salt and freshly ground pepper to taste

2 tablespoons chopped fresh basil or parsley

Preheat the oven to 350°F.

Place the mushrooms in 1 large piece or 4 individual small pieces of parchment paper or foil. Spread the onions on top, distribute the butter over the onions, drizzle with the wine, and season with salt and pepper. Seal the packets with another piece of parchment or foil or by folding in half. Place on a cookie sheet and bake for 40 minutes. Remove from the oven, cut open, sprinkle with basil or parsley, and serve immediately.

BÁMIES ME SALTSA DOMATA   *Greece*
Okra with Tomato Sauce

We rented a house one summer in Corfu, right on the water in a little cove called Kalami Bay, the same bay on which Lawrence Durrell lived when he wrote *Prospero's Cell.* Andreas, a burly ex-fisherman, ran the local general store in the nearby village. One day fresh okra arrived in his store and he put aside a few pounds for us. When he heard we didn't like it—too slimy, we explained—he said we just didn't know how to cook it. He prepared it for us that night and proved his point. The secret, he later told us, was to dry the okra before cooking it. He sprinkled it with vinegar and left it for a few hours in the hot Greek sunshine. A warm oven works almost as well as natural heat.   SERVES 4

1 pound small fresh okra
¼ cup vinegar
3 tablespoons olive oil
1 cup minced onions
1 cup drained canned Italian
    plum tomatoes, or 1 cup ripe
    tomatoes, peeled, seeded, and
    chopped

Juice of 1 lemon plus 2
    tablespoons
Salt and freshly ground pepper to
    taste

Preheat the oven to 150°F. or warm. It should be warm enough to dry the okra but not so hot that the okra cooks.

Trim the stem end of the okra into a conical shape. Place on a cookie sheet, drizzle with vinegar, and dry in the oven for 1 hour, turning occasionally.

Heat the olive oil in a skillet, add the onions, and sauté over medium heat until golden, about 7 minutes. Add the okra to the onions, mix well, and sauté for 3 minutes. Add the tomatoes, juice of 1 lemon, and salt and pepper. Cover, and simmer, stirring occasionally, for 20 minutes, until the okra is tender. Add the remaining lemon juice and serve hot or cold. We like okra still firm. If you prefer it softer, cook it longer.

TAGINE DE MLOUKHIA OU CHEFARJEL   **Morocco**
Okra and Quince Tagine

Quince is a wonderful fruit, firm-fleshed and tart, a bit like an unripe pear. Most probably native to Iran, it is used almost exclusively in North America in jams and tarts, an unfortunate restriction, as you will discover when you try this tagine. Normally made with meat, as are most tagines, our friends in Asilah worked out this excellent meatless version for us.   SERVES 4 TO 6

1 pound okra
¼ cup fruit vinegar
3 tablespoons olive oil
1 pound ripe quinces, cored,
    unpeeled, and cut into
    1½-inch pieces
Pinch of saffron, ground in a
    mortar and soaked in 1 cup
    water

2 teaspoons ground ginger
¼ teaspoon cayenne pepper
2 cups Vegetable Broth (see
    recipe)
Rind of ½ preserved lemon (p.
    15), cut into ½-inch pieces
3 tablespoons flour
Salt and freshly ground black
    pepper to taste

Preheat the oven to 150°F. or warm. It should be warm enough to dry the okra but not so hot that the okra cooks.

Trim the stem end of the okra into a conical shape. Place on a cookie sheet, sprinkle with vinegar, and put in the oven for 1 hour, turning occasionally.

While the okra dries, heat the oil in a *tagine* or an enamel or stainless steel saucepan, add the quince pieces, saffron and water, ginger, cayenne pepper, vegetable broth, and, if necessary, enough water to cover the quince with liquid. Simmer, covered, for 30 to 40 minutes, until the tines of a fork pierce the flesh of the quince with some resistance.

Remove the okra from the oven, rinse, cut into 1½-inch pieces, and add to the quince. Continue cooking for another 15 to 20 minutes, until the okra is tender. Add more water if necessary. When cooked, the sauce should half cover the vegetables. Do not stir.

Five minutes before the tagine is cooked, add the preserved lemon rind.

Blend the flour with ½ cup of the cooking liquid in a small mixing bowl and add to the vegetables. Stir gently over low heat until the sauce begins to thicken. Taste and adjust for salt and black pepper and serve hot.

CIPOLLINE AGRO-DOLCE   *Italy*
Pearl Onions in Sweet and Sour Sauce

This dish can be made in advance and reheated just before serving. Take care, however, not to overcook the onions.   SERVES 4

1½ pounds pearl onions	*1 teaspoon flour*
2 tablespoons butter	*2 teaspoons sugar*
3 bay leaves	*Salt to taste*
1 teaspoon black peppercorns	*⅓ cup white wine vinegar*

Bring 3 cups of water to boil in a saucepan, add the onions, blanch for 20 seconds, drain, and set aside. When cool enough to handle, peel the onions.

Combine all the ingredients except the vinegar in a saucepan, add ¾ cup of water, cover, and cook over low heat for 20 minutes, stirring occasionally. Add the vinegar and simmer, covered, for 10 to 15 minutes, until the tines of a fork easily pierce the onions. When cooked, a creamy sauce should remain in the pan. Remove the bay leaves and serve hot.

PEPERONI IMBOTTITI   *Italy*
Peppers with Olives and Capers

There are certain vegetables, peppers among them, that are as much a part of the Mediterranean as the sea itself. And yet, peppers were completely unknown in the region until the explorers brought them back from the New World in the early sixteenth century. In this preparation, typical of southern Italy, peppers are dressed with a rich sauce of tomatoes, olives, and capers and baked.   SERVES 4 TO 6

1 pound ripe tomatoes, peeled,
    seeded, and finely chopped
½ cup Italian black olives,
    pitted, rinsed well if salty,
    and chopped
3 tablespoons chopped capers
½ cup freshly grated Parmesan
2 tablespoons each chopped fresh
    parsley and basil

6 tablespoons olive oil
Freshly ground pepper to taste
4 large red or green bell peppers,
    cored, seeded, and cut in
    half lengthwise
4 tablespoons bread crumbs,
    lightly toasted

Preheat the oven to 375°F.

Combine the tomatoes, olives, capers, Parmesan, herbs, 4 tablespoons of oil, and pepper in a mixing bowl. Use this mixture to fill the pepper halves. Cover the top of each with bread crumbs, drizzle with 2 tablespoons of oil, place in a baking dish, cover the dish with foil, and bake for 30 minutes. Remove the foil and bake another 20 minutes. Transfer the peppers to a serving dish and serve warm or at room temperature.

PIMIENTOS CON CEBOLLAS Y COMINO   **Spain**
Peppers and Onions with Cumin

We first sampled this delicious summer vegetable, a blend of roasted peppers, onions, and garlic seasoned with cumin, oil, and vinegar, in a modest restaurant in Murcia. The recipe is a modified version of one included in a book by Luis Bettonica, *Cocina Regiónal Española*.   SERVES 4

1 pound Spanish onions, unpeeled
3 garlic cloves
3 large red bell peppers, peeled
    (p. 13); cored, seeded, and
    cut into thin strips
1 teaspoon cumin

Salt and freshly ground pepper to
    taste
3 tablespoons olive oil
2 tablespoons wine vinegar
2 tablespoons finely chopped fresh
    parsley

Heat the oven to 350°F. and place the onions on a cookie sheet with the garlic. Bake for 10 minutes, remove garlic and reserve. Bake another 5 minutes, remove onions, and let cool.

When ready, peel the onions, cut in half and slice thinly. Place in a large serving bowl. Add the pepper strips to the onions. Peel the garlic, slice finely, and add to the onions and peppers. Add the remaining ingredients, combine thoroughly, and serve at room temperature.

PIMIENTOS Y TOMATES A LA ANDALUZA   *Spain*
Peppers and Tomatoes, Andalusian Style

Many of the best Andalusian dishes show a pronounced Arabic influence and this one, in which peppers and tomatoes are simmered slowly in their own juices, is no exception. The peppers are tastier if peeled but the dish works even with peels intact. It should be spicy, but adjust the quantity of hot peppers to suit your own palate.   SERVES 6

4 tablespoons olive oil
4 large green bell peppers (about 2 pounds), peeled (p. 13), cored, and cut into quarters
3 garlic cloves, sliced
2 tablespoons chopped fresh parsley

2 or 3 red or green hot peppers, seeded and chopped
1½ pounds ripe tomatoes, peeled, seeded, and sliced
Salt and freshly ground pepper to taste

Place the olive oil in a large, low-sided saucepan, distribute the bell peppers on the bottom of the pan, sprinkle with the garlic, parsley, and hot peppers, then top with the tomatoes. Season with salt and pepper, cover, and simmer for 20 minutes. Uncover and cook another 20 to 25 minutes, until the liquid is absorbed. Do not stir as the vegetables cook. Serve hot.

PATATE ALL'ANDREA *Italy*
Potatoes, Andrea Style

Great culinary innovations, like scientific breakthroughs, are often serendipitous. Our cousin Andrea, a concert pianist, invited us to dinner one night and, when we arrived, he was busy in his garden, collecting rosemary and whistling a Schumann sonata. Still whistling, and clearly more preoccupied with the sonata than the food, he returned to the kitchen, dropped the rosemary into a roasting pan filled with potatoes, added an enormous quantity of olive oil, and placed the pan in the oven. About 15 minutes later, his whistling stopped. Silence, then an exclamation—Too much oil and rosemary! "Too late," he said. "Let's see what happens," and returned to his sonata. The rest, as they say, is history. The potatoes were superb. You can, if you wish, cut the quantities of oil and rosemary, but the dish won't be the same.   SERVES 6

2 pounds new potatoes, unpeeled,
*   cut into 1- to 1½-inch cubes*
3 tablespoons dried rosemary, or
*   3 or 4 large sprigs fresh*
*   rosemary*

6 garlic cloves, peeled
½ cup extra-virgin olive oil,
*   preferably from Tuscany*
Salt to taste

Preheat the oven to 425°F. Place the potatoes, rosemary, and garlic in a roasting pan, drizzle with the olive oil, sprinkle with the salt and bake, stirring the potatoes occasionally, until browned and crisp on the outside, tender on the inside, about 30 to 40 minutes. Serve hot.

ESTOFADO DE PATATAS *Spain*
Braised Potatoes with Garlic and Saffron

This is a spectacular dish, potatoes braised in wine with whole garlic cloves, flavored with saffron. It makes a wonderful vegetable dish for an elegant dinner party.   SERVES 6

6 tablespoons olive oil
1 pound onions, minced
2 pounds new potatoes, peeled,
    cut into ½-inch cubes
Large pinch saffron
1½ cups dry white wine

¼ cup water
2 bay leaves
14 to 16 large garlic cloves,
    peeled
Salt and freshly ground white
    pepper to taste

Heat the oil in a large, low-sided saucepan, add the onions, and sauté over medium heat until golden, about 5 to 7 minutes. Add the potatoes and sauté 1 or 2 minutes, stirring constantly, to combine the ingredients.

Grind the saffron threads in a mortar, mix with some of the wine, and add to the potatoes. Add the rest of the wine, the water, and the remaining ingredients. Combine, then cover the saucepan well and simmer over very low heat, stirring occasionally, until the potatoes are tender, about 40 to 45 minutes. When cooked, the potatoes should be moist but not swimming in sauce. Add water if necessary, a little at a time, as the potatoes cook to prevent them from sticking. Serve warm.

FOGLIE DI SALVIA FRITTE   *Italy*
Fried Sage Leaves

When Paola's brother Alberto heard that we had a sage plant in our garden, he urged us to try fried sage leaves. You coat large leaves with batter and fry them in a light seed oil. The only constraint is that you must use fresh leaves. We calculate about 6 leaves per person.   SERVES 4

1 extra-large egg, separated
1 tablespoon olive oil
1 tablespoon lemon juice
Pinch of salt
1 cup water

1¼ cups unbleached all-purpose
    flour
½ cup light seed oil
24 large fresh sage leaves
Salt

Place the egg yolk in a large mixing bowl and beat with a whisk until pale yellow. Add the oil, lemon juice, and salt, and combine.

Blend in water, then add the flour, a little at a time, beating constantly with a whisk until the mixture is smooth and the consistency of pancake batter. Set aside to rest for 1 hour.

When ready, beat the egg white until it forms stiff peaks, then fold into the batter.

Heat the oil in a large skillet, coat the leaves a few at a time in the batter, and fry until golden on both sides. Drain on paper towels, sprinkle lightly with salt, and continue until all the leaves are fried. Serve immediately.

ESPINACAS CON GARBANZOS Y HUEVOS   **Spain**
Spinach with Chick-peas and Eggs

In this interesting combination of ingredients, spinach and chick-peas are sautéed together and garnished with hard-boiled eggs. It makes a delicately flavored, substantial vegetable dish.

SERVES 4

1 pound spinach
2 tablespoons butter
1 medium onion, finely chopped
1 tablespoon flour
1 tablespoon chopped fresh
    parsley

½ cup dry white wine or
    Vegetable Broth (see recipe)
1 cup cooked chick-peas
Salt and freshly ground pepper to
    taste
2 hard-boiled eggs, chopped

Wash the spinach well and place in a saucepan without adding water, bring to a boil, lower heat, and simmer, covered, until tender, about 5 minutes. Drain well, chop, and set aside.

Heat the butter in a large saucepan, add the onion, and sauté over low heat until transparent. Add the flour and cook another 2 to 3 minutes, until the flour begins to color. Add the parsley, wine or broth, and stir until the mixture begins to thicken. Add the chick-peas and spinach and salt and pepper, combine thoroughly and heat through. Transfer to a serving dish, sprinkle the eggs on top, and serve warm or at room temperature.

SPINACHAS OU SILK
Spinach and Swiss Chard

Morocco

SERVES 4

1 pound spinach, washed well,
   tough stems removed
1 pound Swiss chard, washed
   well, stems removed, roughly
   chopped
4 tablespoons olive oil
2 garlic cloves, chopped
1 tablespoon sweet paprika

2 teaspoons turmeric
¼ teaspoon freshly ground pepper
6 large green or black olives,
   pitted, rinsed, and roughly
   chopped
1 preserved lemon (p. 15), rinsed
   and cut into thin wedges

Place the spinach in a saucepan without adding water, bring to a boil, lower heat, and simmer, covered, until tender, about 5 minutes. Drain well, purée in a blender or food processor, and set aside.

Place ½ cup of water in a saucepan, bring to a boil, add the Swiss chard, reduce heat, and simmer, covered, until tender, about 10 minutes. Drain and set aside.

Heat the oil in a low-sided saucepan, add the garlic, and sauté over medium heat for 1 minute. Add the spices, mix well, then blend in the spinach, Swiss chard, and olives. Continue cooking, stirring constantly, for 3 or 4 minutes. Add the preserved lemon, cook another 2 minutes, and serve hot.

EL GUERÂ HAMRA M'THOUNA   *Morocco*
Squash Purée

SERVES 4 TO 6

2 tablespoons olive oil
1½ pounds butternut squash,
    peeled, seeds removed, and
    cut into 1-inch cubes
3 garlic cloves, chopped
½ cup water
1 tablespoon chopped fresh
    parsley
1 tablespoon chopped fresh
    coriander leaves

Pinch of saffron, crumbled in ¼
    cup warm water
1 teaspoon ground ginger
¼ cup lemon juice
1 tablespoon sugar
¼ teaspoon cayenne pepper
    (optional)
Salt and freshly ground pepper to
    taste
1 tablespoon ground cumin

Place the olive oil in a large, low-sided saucepan. Add the squash, garlic, and water. Cover and cook, stirring frequently, for 15 to 20 minutes, until the squash is tender.

Combine the rest of the ingredients except for the cumin. Pour over the squash and simmer another 10 minutes. Add a little water if necessary to prevent sticking. The squash will start to disintegrate.

Bring to the table warm, sprinkled with cumin.

RAPE CON ACCIUGHE   *Italy*
Turnips with Anchovies

SERVES 4 TO 6

3 tablespoons olive oil
4 garlic cloves, thinly sliced
4 anchovy fillets, packed in oil,
    drained and cut into small
    pieces
1 tablespoon dried rosemary, or 2
    tablespoons fresh rosemary

2 pounds small fresh turnips,
    peeled and thinly sliced
Salt and freshly ground pepper to
    taste
2 tablespoons minced fresh parsley

Heat the oil in a saucepan, add the garlic, anchovy fillets, and rosemary, and sauté over medium heat for 1 minute. Add the turnips, season with salt and pepper, and continue cooking until the turnips are tender, about 10 minutes. Sprinkle with parsley and serve hot.

COURGETTES AU FOUR AVEC CRÈME FRAÎCHE   *France*
Baked Zucchini with Crème Fraîche

SERVES 6

1½ pounds zucchini
1 tablespoon butter
2 ounces Gruyère, grated
2 ounces Parmesan, freshly grated
1 cup Crème Fraîche (see recipe)

1 tablespoon chopped fresh parsley
1 teaspoon dried thyme, or 1 sprig fresh thyme
Salt and freshly ground pepper to taste

Heat the oven to 425°F. and butter a 6-cup gratin pan or the equivalent.

Scrub the zucchini, trim, and cut into julienne strips. Heat the butter in a large skillet, add the zucchini, and sauté over medium heat until the zucchini are tender and all the liquid has evaporated, about 10 to 15 minutes. Remove from the heat and combine with the remaining ingredients.

Place the mixture in the gratin pan and bake until the top browns, 20 to 25 minutes. Allow to cool for 10 minutes, then serve.

ZUCCHINI ALLA PARMIGIANA   *Italy*
Zucchini, Parmesan Style

This is an excellent dish, as good as the better-known eggplant Parmesan.   SERVES 4 TO 6

½ cup light seed oil for frying
2 pounds zucchini, cut lengthwise
    into ¼-inch-thick strips,
    dried with paper towels
1 cup Tomato Sauce (see recipe)
4 garlic cloves, finely chopped

4 tablespoons finely chopped fresh
    parsley
¼ cup mozzarella or sharp
    Provolone, thinly sliced
½ cup freshly grated Parmesan

Heat the oil in a skillet, add the zucchini strips, a few at a time, and fry until golden on both sides. Drain on paper towels and set aside.

Preheat the oven to 375°F. and oil lightly an 8-by-8-inch baking dish.

Spread one-third of the tomato sauce on the bottom of the baking dish. Cover with half the zucchini, sprinkle with half the garlic and parsley, spread on another third of the tomato sauce, add half the mozzarella or provolone and half the Parmesan. Repeat, beginning with zucchini and ending with the Parmesan. Bake until browned, about 15 minutes. Serve hot.

CALABACINES RELLENOS   *Spain*
Zucchini Stuffed with Tomato and Pepper

SERVES 4

4 medium to large zucchini
    (about 2 pounds), cut in
    half lengthwise
1 large ripe tomato, peeled,
    seeded, and minced
1 green bell pepper cored, seeded,
    and finely chopped
3 garlic cloves, finely chopped

2 tablespoons finely chopped fresh
    parsley
Salt and abundant freshly ground
    pepper
1 extra-large egg, beaten
2 tablespoons bread crumbs
2 tablespoons olive oil

Preheat the oven to 375°F. and oil well a baking dish large enough to hold 8 zucchini halves.

Scoop the pulp out of the zucchini halves, reserving the shells and the pulp of 2 halves. Steam the shells until barely tender, about 5 minutes, drain, and place in the baking dish.

Finely chop the reserved zucchini pulp and combine with the tomato, bell pepper, garlic, parsley, salt and pepper, and egg, and use to stuff the zucchini shells. Sprinkle the surface of the stuffed zucchini with bread crumbs, drizzle with olive oil, then bake until golden, about 30 minutes. Serve warm.

COURGETTES AU GRATIN   *France*
Gratin of Zucchini

SERVES 4

*1 pound small zucchini, scrubbed,
    cut into ¼-inch-thick slices
2 tablespoons unsalted butter
1 medium onion, minced
2 tablespoons flour
1¼ cups whipping cream*

*Salt and freshly ground pepper to
    taste
Pinch of nutmeg
6 tablespoons freshly grated
    Parmesan*

Steam the zucchini until tender, about 10 minutes. Set aside.
Preheat the oven to 400°F. and butter well a 10-by-6-inch baking dish.

Heat the butter in a saucepan, add the onion, and sauté over medium heat until golden, about 5 minutes. Add the flour and cook another 2 minutes, stirring constantly. Add the cream, a little at a time, stirring constantly, then blend in the salt and pepper and nutmeg. Cook, stirring, for 5 minutes. Add 4 tablespoons of Parmesan and the zucchini, and mix well.

Place the zucchini mixture in the baking dish, sprinkle with the remaining Parmesan, and bake until lightly browned, about 10 to 15 minutes. Serve hot.

KALAVASA KON PRICHIL   *Turkey*
Baked Zucchini with Parsley and Onion

If Jon had to be stuck on a desert island with one vegetable dish, this would be it. He's been partial to this way of preparing squash for as long as he can remember, way back to his childhood in Alabama. He always thought this was a typically Southern dish, something like black-eyed peas or grits, only a hundred times better. Doing the research for the book, however, he was surprised to find an almost identical dish in Esther Benbassa's book, *Cuisine Judeo-Espagnole.* What, he wondered, was his good old Southern dish doing in a book like that? It turns out that his mother got the dish from a Sephardic Jewish friend, taught it to the cook, and thereby domesticated it.   SERVES 4 TO 6

1 pound zucchini, scrubbed,
  trimmed, and chopped
1 medium onion, grated
4 tablespoons bread crumbs,
  lightly toasted

2 extra-large eggs, beaten
Salt and abundant freshly ground
  pepper to taste

Preheat the oven to 375°F. and butter well a 9-inch pie plate or the equivalent.

Bring 3 cups of salted water to a boil, add the zucchini, and cook for about 5 minutes, until just tender. Drain, squeezing out excess water by pressing the squash against the sides of a colander with a wooden spoon, and transfer to a mixing bowl.

Add the remaining ingredients, mix well, place in the baking dish, and bake 25 minutes, until firm. Serve warm.

VARIATIONS Substitute matzo meal for bread crumbs. Use yellow summer squash instead of zucchini.

LAHANIKA YIAHNI   *Greece*
Vegetable Stew

A dish found, in one guise or another, throughout the Mediterranean, it's similar to the French *ratatouille,* to a Sicilian baked vegetable dish, and to *menestra* from Spain. It can be made in advance and reheated before serving.   SERVES 6 TO 8

*1 pound eggplant, preferably
    small, peeled and cut into
    ¼-inch-thick slices*
*¾ pound potatoes, peeled and
    thinly sliced*
1 pound onions, sliced
*1 pound zucchini, scrubbed and
    cut into ¼-inch-thick slices*

3 garlic cloves, chopped
*1 pound tomatoes, peeled and
    thinly sliced, or 1½ cups
    canned Italian plum
    tomatoes, with juice*
*Salt and freshly ground pepper to
    taste*
4 tablespoons olive oil

Place the eggplant in a colander, sprinkle with salt, and set aside to drain for 30 minutes. When ready, rinse, pat dry, and set aside.

Preheat the oven to 400°F., and oil well a large earthenware baking dish. You can also use Pyrex, porcelain, or metal, but clay works best.

Place half the potatoes on the bottom of the dish, layer with half the onions, half the zucchini, sprinkle with half the garlic, then cover with half the tomatoes. Sprinkle with salt and pepper and repeat, using the remaining ingredients, beginning with the potatoes and ending with the tomatoes. Add the olive oil, cover, and bake, basting occasionally with the juices that accumulate in the dish, for 1 hour, until all the ingredients are very tender. Serve warm.

TIMBALES DE LÉGUMES D'ÉTÉ   *France*
Summer Vegetable Timbales

Three separate timbales—one of peppers, one of eggplant, and one of green or yellow beans—are served together with tomatoes and cucumbers to make an outstanding summer dish for a buffet or elegant dinner. The timbales take time to prepare but can be made in advance.   SERVES 6

2 pounds red bell peppers, peeled (p. 13), cored, seeded, and chopped
1¼ pounds eggplant
1¼ pounds green or yellow beans, trimmed
3 tablespoons olive oil
6 large basil leaves, torn
1 garlic clove, minced
Pinch of cayenne pepper
Salt and freshly ground pepper to taste

3 tablespoons Tapenade (see recipe)
4 tablespoons whipping cream
3 tablespoons chopped fresh chives
6 medium eggs
Sprigs of parsley
1 large ripe tomato, peeled, seeded, and finely chopped
1 medium cucumber, peeled and thinly sliced

Preheat the oven to 400°F.

Purée the peppers in a blender or food processor and set aside.

Place the eggplant on a cookie sheet, prick with the tines of a fork, and bake until tender, about 30 minutes. Remove and, when cool enough to handle, peel, purée in a blender or food processor, and set aside.

Steam the beans until tender, about 15 minutes, purée in a blender or food processor, and set aside.

Heat 1 tablespoon of oil in a skillet, add the pepper purée, and sauté for a minute or two to evaporate excess liquid. Remove and set aside. Repeat with the two other vegetable purées.

Combine the peppers with the basil, garlic, cayenne pepper, and salt and pepper, and set aside. Combine the eggplant with the *tapenade* and 2 tablespoons of cream, blend, and set aside. Combine the beans with the chives, season with salt and pepper, add 2 tablespoons of cream, blend, and set aside.

Reduce oven heat to 375°F. and butter well 3 molds or small flan dishes. Bring 4 cups of water to a boil.

Beat two eggs, add to the pepper purée, mix well, and pour into a mold. Repeat with the other two vegetable purées. Place the molds in a large baking dish, pour enough boiling water into the dish to come halfway up the sides of the molds, then bake until the vegetables are firm, about 30 minutes. Remove from the water bath and set aside to cool. When ready, unmold onto an attractive serving platter. Serve garnished with parsley sprigs, the tomato, and cucumber. If made in advance, store in the refrigerator, but remove at least 30 minutes before serving. You can also prepare individual plates with wedges of the vegetable timbales, tomato, cucumber, and parsley.

Desserts

Before sugar, there was honey. The Greeks, including those who settled in Magna Grecia, Greek colonies in southern Italy, were reputed to produce some of the best in the ancient world. One summer many years ago, we were driving along a secondary road in the interior of Sicily when Alberto, Paola's brother, called our attention to the fact that we were in the Iblei mountains. This meant nothing to us but he recalled that Virgil had singled out the area as one where exceptional honey was produced. We detoured, arrived in a small village, and asked about local honey. A number of villagers were still in the business and, as we discovered, still stored their honey, as their ancestors did, in large earthenware amphorae. The honey was superb, light, fragrant, and subtle.

Honey was, of course, the principal sweetener in antiquity and many Mediterranean desserts, especially those from southern Italy and Greece, continue to reflect their ancient heritage. We give recipes for a few delightful honey-sweetened ones.

Fruit, another source of natural sweetness, has been produced in abundance and variety in the Mediterranean since ancient times. Our favorite dessert is a bowl of fresh fruit, especially after a substantial meal, and we are partial to fruit-based sweets. Aside from a number of desserts in which fruit dominates, we also include a rice pudding with apples, a couple of citrus-flavored custards, and a fruit ice.

We have tried to balance the traditional with the modern, the elaborate with the simple. We have, however, made no effort to achieve regional representation. We happen to like French and Italian desserts and these, inevitably, predominate.

PASTA FROLLA   *Italy*
Short Sweet Dough I

A rich, flaky pastry dough, this is delicious but more difficult to handle than ordinary doughs. Use for tart shells and pie crusts.

MAKES ONE 10-INCH TART SHELL

2 cups unbleached all-purpose
    flour
½ cup sugar
⅜ pound unsalted butter, at
    room temperature

Grated zest of ½ lemon
3 extra-large egg yolks
Pinch of salt
1 tablespoon lemon juice

Combine the flour and sugar in a mixing bowl, add the butter cut into small cubes, and mix with a pastry knife or your fingers until the butter is the size of small peas. Add the remaining ingredients and mix briefly, until dough forms a rough ball. Turn dough onto a lightly floured work surface and knead with the heel of your hand about ten times, then shape into a ball, wrap in wax paper, and set aside until ready to use.

If using a food processor, attach the metal blade, place the flour, sugar, and butter in the work bowl, and run until the dough has the texture of coarse oatmeal. Add the remaining ingredients and process until the dough just begins to clear the sides of the work bowl. If too dry, add a little more lemon juice, a few drops at a time, until the dough begins to clear the sides of the bowl. From this point, proceed as above.

Butter well a 10-inch tart pan. Roll the dough out on a lightly floured work surface until large enough to cover the bottom and sides of the pan. The dough should be approximately ⅛- to ¼-inch thick. Place the dough carefully in the pan, fitting it snugly along the bottom and sides, and proceed according to instructions in the specific recipe.

Since the dough may be difficult to handle because of the sugar, you can roll it out between pieces of wax paper and transfer it from the paper to the tart pan. When rolling the dough, remember to roll from the center to the edge and give the dough a quarter turn after each roll.

PÂTE BRISÉE SUCRÉE   *France*
Short Sweet Dough II

This dough is more tractable than *Pasta Frolla* but also less rich and flavorful. It is used for tart shells and pie crusts.

MAKES ONE 10-INCH TART SHELL

2 cups unbleached all-purpose
    flour
2 tablespoons sugar
¼ pound chilled butter

2 extra-large eggs
Pinch of salt
1 tablespoon cold water

Combine the flour and sugar in a mixing bowl, add the butter cut into small cubes, and mix with your fingers or a pastry knife until the butter is the size of small peas. Add the remaining ingredients and mix thoroughly. Turn onto a lightly floured work surface and knead with the heel of your hand until the butter is incorporated with the flour. Do not overwork dough. Roll into a ball, wrap with wax paper, and place in the refrigerator for at least 1 hour.

If using a food processor, attach the metal blade, place the flour, sugar, and butter in the work bowl, and run the machine until the dough has the texture of coarse oatmeal. Add the remaining ingredients and process until the dough just clears the sides of the work bowl. If too dry, add a little more water, a few drops at a time, until the dough clears the sides. From this point, proceed as above.

Butter well a 10-inch tart pan. Roll out the dough on a lightly floured work surface until large enough to cover the bottom and sides of the pan. Remember to roll from the center to the edges and to give the dough a quarter turn after each roll. Transfer the dough to the pan and fit it snugly along the bottom and sides. Proceed according to instructions in the specific recipe.

COULIS DE FRAMBOISES
France
Raspberry Purée

MAKES 1 ½ CUPS

2 cups fresh or frozen raspberries   ¼ cup sugar

Wash and dry the berries. Combine with the sugar, then pass through a sieve fine enough to trap the seeds. In France, the berries are crushed with a wooden spoon in a *chinoise* (a fine sieve). You may wish to add more sugar, depending on the sweetness of the berries. The purée will keep for a week in the refrigerator. Serve as a sauce for ice cream or as directed in the recipes.

VARIATIONS Substitute blueberries, strawberries, or peaches for raspberries.

A small amount mixed with champagne or sparkling wine makes a wonderful cocktail.

POIRES AU FRANGIPANE ET COULIS
France
DE FRAMBOISES
Pears with Almond Cream and Raspberry Purée

Restaurants in France occasionally serve special warm desserts such as soufflés that must be ordered at the beginning of a meal in order to be ready at the end. The problem is that the waiter launches into his mouth-watering description of these delicacies before you've even had a chance to nibble on a piece of bread, so choosing is practically impossible—you want at least two of everything. So it was when we arrived, ravenous, at La Tamasserie, a delightful and excellent little restaurant at the mouth of the Hérault River, in Languedoc, on a lovely spring day in early April. The one we finally chose, pears with almond cream and raspberry purée, was a spectacular combination. It's relatively easy to prepare. All steps, aside from the browning of the pears, can be done in advance, and it looks as good as it tastes.   SERVES 6

6 large ripe Bartlett or similar
    pears
Juice of 1 lemon
2½ cups dry white wine

FOR THE ALMOND CREAM:
2 eggs plus 2 egg yolks
⅔ cup sugar
⅓ cup unbleached pastry or
    all-purpose flour
2 cups milk, scalded

1 cup Raspberry Purée (see
    recipe)

1-inch stick of cinnamon
2 whole cloves
½ cup sugar plus 3 tablespoons

2 tablespoons butter
½ cup blanched almonds, lightly
    toasted and ground finely
1 tablespoon kirsch

12 fresh raspberries or
    strawberries and fresh mint
    leaves for garnish

Peel the pears, cut in half, core, and then place in a large mixing bowl filled with water and lemon juice. Set aside.

Combine the white wine, cinnamon, cloves, and ½ cup of sugar in a large saucepan, bring to a boil, and cook 5 minutes. Add the pears and simmer, covered, until the pears are just tender, about 5 minutes. Remove the pears, drain, and set aside.

To make the almond cream, combine the eggs and yolks in a mixing bowl, blend in 2/3 cup sugar, and beat until light, 2 to 3 minutes. Beat in the flour, then add the hot milk, a little at a time, beating constantly. Place in a saucepan and cook over medium-low heat, beating constantly with a wire whisk, for 7 to 10 minutes, until the cream thickens and the flour cooks. Do not allow the cream to boil. Remove from the heat, blend in the butter, almonds, and kirsch. Set aside. If not using immediately, coat the top lightly with butter to prevent a skin from forming.

When ready to serve, spread approximately 2 to 3 tablespoons of the almond cream on 6 individual ovenproof dishes. Slice pear halves with a sharp knife on a cutting board, taking care to keep the sliced halves together. Carefully transfer 2 pear halves to each dish. Sprinkle 3 tablespoons of sugar over the pears and broil until the sugar begins to brown. Spread the raspberry purée around the pears, garnish with the whole raspberries or strawberries and mint leaves, and serve hot.

PERE RIPIENE   *Italy*
Pears with Zabaione

In this scrumptious dessert, the pears are first poached, then filled
with zabaione.   SERVES 6

6 large, ripe Bosc pears   ¾ cup Marsala
1 cup sugar   Grated zest of 1 lemon
Juice of ½ lemon   Few drops vanilla
2 cups water   ½ cup whipping cream
6 egg yolks

Remove the core from the top of the pears with an apple corer
or a similar instrument, taking care not to cut through the bottom.
Scoop out some of the pulp to make an enlarged space for the
zabaione. Combine ½ cup of sugar and lemon juice with the water
in a saucepan suitable for poaching the pears and boil for 5 minutes. Add the pears, cover, and simmer gently until the pears are
tender, about 20 minutes. When cooked, transfer the pears from
the saucepan to a serving platter and set aside. Return the syrup
to the heat and continue cooking until it becomes viscous and
begins to color.

While the syrup boils, make the zabaione. Combine the egg
yolks with 1/2 cup sugar in the top half of a double boiler and cook,
stirring constantly with a wire whisk until the sugar-and-yolk mixture thickens and becomes pale yellow, about 5 minutes. Add the
Marsala, a little at a time, beating continuously with the whisk. Add
the lemon zest and vanilla and continue cooking the zabaione,
beating constantly until thick and doubled in bulk, about 10 to 15
minutes. Remove from the heat and let cool.

When ready, fill the cavities in the pears with the zabaione,
allowing some to spill over the sides. Reserve extra zabaione to
serve separately for those who want it.

When the syrup is ready, allow it to cool slightly, then pour
over the pears and the zabaione. Whip the cream until stiff and
place a dollop on the top of each pear. Serve at room temperature.

GRATIN DE FRUITS FRAIS　　　　　*France*
Gratin of Fresh Fruit with Cream

A wonderfully delicate and extremely easy dessert, it is best with the red fruits and berries of late spring and early summer, but is delicious with almost any combination of fresh fruit.　　SERVES 6

4 egg yolks
⅓ cup sugar
1½ cups **Crème Fraîche** *(see recipe)*
1 tablespoon Cognac or fruit-flavored liqueur
2 tablespoons lemon juice

18 strawberries, washed, dried, and halved
18 cherries, washed, dried, and pitted
1½ cups raspberries, washed and dried
1 kiwi, peeled and sliced (optional)

Place the yolks in a heavy saucepan, add the sugar, and beat with a whisk until pale yellow and light, about 3 minutes. Add the *crème fraîche* and Cognac, place over low heat, and cook, beating constantly, until the sauce begins to thicken. Do not boil. This will take 10 to 15 minutes. Remove from the heat and blend in the lemon juice.

Distribute the fruit in 6 small baking dishes or ramekins. Pour the sauce over and around the fruit, then broil close to the heat for 2 or 3 minutes, until the sauce begins to form a light golden crust. Serve immediately.

FICHI FRESCHI AL FORNO　　　　　*Italy*
Baked Fresh Figs with Cointreau

It's difficult to imagine a simpler, more delightful dessert than fresh figs rolled in sugar, seasoned with Cointreau, and baked. The dish is particularly suited for figs that have not been tree ripened and thus need a little help to develop their full flavor. You can substitute honey for sugar if you wish. This recipe is adapted from

one appearing in *The Complete Book of Fruits and Vegetables* by Francesco Bianchini, Francesco Corbetta, and Marilena Pistoia.

SERVES 4

8 fresh figs   *2 tablespoons Cointreau*
¼ cup confectioner's sugar

Preheat the oven to 350°F.

Wash the figs and, while still wet, roll in the sugar. Place in a
baking dish large enough to hold the figs in a single layer. They
should, however, fit snugly in the dish. Add ½ inch of water to the
pan and drizzle with Cointreau. Bake for 15 minutes, until the
sugar is lightly browned. Serve warm with the juice.

MELON AUX CITRONS   *France*
Chilled Cantaloupe with Lemon Sauce

Guy Sagmoellen and Patrick Lucas have their share of rich traditional desserts at La Mirabelle, but they also serve some delectable
fruit combinations, such as this confection of melon with a lemon-
flavored cream sauce. It's the perfect end to an elegant dinner.

SERVES 4

2 lemons   *½ vanilla bean*
⅓ cup sugar plus ¼ cup   *1 ripe cantaloupe, cut in half,*
3 egg yolks   *   seeds removed*
1½ cups milk   *4 mint sprigs*

Peel the zest from the lemons and julienne. Squeeze the juice
from 1 of these lemons and set aside. Blanch the peel for 1 minute
in 1 cup boiling water, drain, rinse in cold water, and place in a
saucepan with ⅓ cup of sugar and 1 cup of water. Bring to a boil
and simmer 45 minutes, until a thick syrup is formed. Retain the
peel and 2 tablespoons of syrup. Set aside to cool.

Place the egg yolks in a mixing bowl and beat together with
¼ cup sugar until pale yellow. Place the milk in a small saucepan
with the vanilla bean, bring to a boil, and add to the yolks a little

at a time, beating the yolks constantly with a whisk. Transfer the mixture to a saucepan, place over very low heat, and cook, stirring constantly with a whisk or wooden spoon, until the sauce begins to thicken. Do not boil. If too hot, place the pan in cold water to cool rapidly and stop it from cooking. While still warm, remove and discard the vanilla bean and add the lemon peel and syrup. Set aside to cool.

With a melon-ball cutter or the equivalent, scoop balls out of the melon and place in a mixing bowl. Squeeze any remaining juice out of the melon and mix it with the reserved lemon juice. Mix the juices with the custard and pour over the melon balls. Cover the mixing bowl and place in the refrigerator for 3 hours.

When ready to serve, place the melon balls and custard on individual dessert plates or in shallow bowls, garnish with mint, and serve cold.

ORANGES ET POIRES AU CITRON VERT   *France*
Oranges and Pears with Hot Lime Sauce

Pears and oranges are sautéed briefly in butter with lime and orange juice, then served warm. Tart apples such as Wealthy or Winesap can be used instead of pears and oranges can be replaced with tangerines. The dessert should be made just before serving but the ingredients can be assembled in advance.   SERVES 4

1 lime
⅓ cup sugar
4 navel oranges

2 ripe Bartlett or Bosc pears,
  peeled, cored, cut into ½-
  inch wedges
4 tablespoons unsalted butter
4 mint sprigs

Remove the green peel from the lime, reserving the lime. Julienne the peel, blanch for 1 minute in 1 cup of boiling water, drain, rinse in cold water, and place in a small saucepan with 1 cup of water and the sugar. Simmer for 45 minutes until ¼ cup of thick syrup remains. Remove from the heat.

Peel 2 oranges, remove and discard all the white membrane

and cut the oranges into ½-inch segments. Squeeze the other 2 oranges and the lime and combine the juices.

Heat the butter in a skillet and add the pears and oranges. Sauté over high heat until the pears are slightly browned, turning frequently with a spatula.

Add the lime peel, syrup, and the juices. Heat through. Serve the fruit in individual bowls or deep plates. Garnish with mint.

TMAR MEÂMMAR BEL ÂGINA DE LOUZ   Morocco
Dates Stuffed with Almond Paste

The dates can be prepared a day or two in advance and stored in a well-sealed container.   MAKES ABOUT 35 DATES

1 cup blanched almonds, lightly   4 teaspoons orange blossom water
    toasted   ½ pound pitted dates
6 tablespoons confectioner's sugar

Grind the almonds in a mortar, food processor, or blender until finely ground. Place in a mixing bowl, add 4 tablespoons confectioner's sugar and the orange blossom water, and mix well.

Insert ½ teaspoon of the stuffing into each pitted date, leaving it slightly open so that the stuffing shows. Repeat until all the dates are stuffed.

Spread the remaining confectioner's sugar on a plate and roll the dates in it to coat. Arrange the dates on a small serving plate in the shape of a pyramid and serve.

CREMA DI LIMÓN Y NARANJA   Spain
Lemon and Orange Custard

Custard desserts, like their close relations, flans, are very popular in Spain, especially those made with citrus fruit. The basic principle is simple: eggs cooked slowly with flavoring, then chilled. Lemon and orange together provide the perfect combination of

tart and sweet for a delicious, refreshing dessert. The dish is un-
complicated, although it does require 20 minutes of nonstop stirring. SERVES 6

6 extra-large eggs
⅔ cup sugar
Grated zest of 1 lemon

Juice of 3 oranges
Juice of 2 lemons

Combine the eggs and sugar in a mixing bowl and beat with
a wire whisk or electric beater until light and fluffy. Add the remaining ingredients and mix well. You should have 1½ cups of
fruit juice. Transfer to a large saucepan and cook over medium-low
heat, stirring constantly, for about 20 minutes, until the mixture
has thickened. It should have the consistency of dense pancake
batter. Transfer to 6 small dessert bowls and chill for 2 hours
before serving.

RISOGALO   *Greece*
Rice with Milk

Rice pudding is not everyone's idea of a great dessert, but in our
family it ranks close to the top. It seems suited for every season,
and for most occasions. The pudding can be made in advance and
kept in the refrigerator. SERVES 4 TO 6

1 cup Italian or Carolina
    short-grain rice
5¼ cups of milk
Grated zest of ½ lemon

½ cup sugar
1 cup water
3 tablespoons cornstarch
1 teaspoon ground cinnamon

Place the rice, 5 cups of milk, lemon zest, and sugar in a
saucepan, add the water, bring to a boil, stirring occasionally, then
lower heat and simmer, partly covered, for 40 minutes.

Combine the cornstarch with the remaining ¼ cup of milk and
blend, stirring into the rice mixture 3 minutes before it is cooked.
When ready, pour into individual bowls and let cool. Sprinkle with
cinnamon and store in the refrigerator until ready to serve. If

making the pudding in advance, cover the top of each with wax paper to prevent drying.

ARROZ CON LECHE Y MANZANAS   *Spain*
Rice Flan with Apples

SERVES 4 TO 6

2¼ cups milk
¾ cup Arborio rice
¼ cup sugar plus 1 tablespoon
Grated zest of ½ lemon

2 tablespoons raisins, soaked in
     water for 20 minutes,
     drained
1 extra-large egg, beaten
2 large cooking apples
½ teaspoon ground cinnamon

Preheat the oven to 375°F. and butter well a 6-by-6-inch baking dish.

Place the milk in a saucepan, bring to a simmer, add the rice, and cook until tender, stirring frequently, about 20 minutes. When cooked, the rice should be moist. Remove from the heat, add ¼ cup of sugar, the lemon zest, the raisins, and, when slightly cooled, the egg. Mix well, pour into the baking dish, and set aside.

Peel, core, and quarter the apples, then cut into thin slices. Distribute the apples over the surface of the pudding, overlapping so that the pieces fit in a single layer. Sprinkle with the cinnamon and the remaining tablespoon of sugar and bake until the flan is firm and the apples tender, about 20 minutes. Serve at room temperature.

ZABAIONE ALL'ARANCIO   *Italy*
Orange Zabaione

The addition of orange juice and zest gives the traditional zabaione a fresh, lively twist. It's easy to make and suitable for any occasion. It can also be used instead of regular zabaione in Pears with Zabaione.   SERVES 6

4 medium navel oranges
½ cup sugar
6 egg yolks
1 tablespoon lemon juice

2 tablespoons Marsala
1 cup whipping cream
3 thin slices orange, cut in half,
    for garnish

Remove the rind from 3 of the oranges, taking care not to include any white. Cut the rinds into very fine slivers. Squeeze the juice from all 4 oranges and place in a small saucepan with the sugar and rinds. Simmer, uncovered, for 15 minutes. Remove from the heat and allow to cool to room temperature.

Place the egg yolks in a heavy saucepan or in the top half of a double boiler. Add the lemon juice and cook over low heat, stirring constantly with a whisk or wooden spoon, until the eggs begin to thicken. This can take from 10 to 20 minutes. Add the orange juice and slivered peel, a little at a time, stirring constantly. Blend in the Marsala and continue cooking, stirring constantly, until the mixture achieves the consistency of custard. Remove from the heat, continue to stir for another minute, then set aside to cool.

When ready, whip the cream until firm and combine thoroughly with the zabaione. Spoon into individual glass dessert bowls and chill before serving. Garnish with orange slices.

CREMA CIOCCOLATA AL MASCARPONE   *Italy*
Mascarpone with Chocolate and Marsala

Mascarpone, similar in taste to a delicately flavored whipped cream cheese, is now available in most well-stocked cheese shops. It is less readily available in summer than in other seasons. In this dessert, Mascarpone is blended with chocolate and Marsala to create a rich, scrumptious dish.   SERVES 4

4 egg yolks
½ cup sugar
Few drops vanilla extract
¼ cup unsweetened cocoa
¾ cup Marsala

½ pound fresh Mascarpone
½ cup whipping cream, whipped
    until firm (optional)
5 walnuts, shelled, crushed in a
    mortar

Beat the yolks and sugar together in a mixing bowl until the mixture begins to form ribbons. Then add the vanilla and cocoa, a little at a time, beating constantly.

Place the mixture in the top half of a double boiler and add the Marsala a little at a time, stirring constantly with a wooden spoon or whisk. Cook for 10 minutes. Remove from the heat and set aside to cool.

When cool, blend in the Mascarpone and mix until thoroughly incorporated. Place in 4 individual dessert bowls and chill. As an alternative, place the mixture in a pastry bag, and squeeze into the bowls in a spiral shape.

When ready to serve, add a dollop of whipped cream and sprinkle with the nuts.

BUDINO DI RICOTTA   *Italy*
Ricotta Pudding

With a few simple ingredients—fresh ricotta, eggs, sugar, perhaps some currants and almonds—you can make a delicious, nourishing dessert in almost no time. It's a favorite of ours, one that we serve frequently in our country house near Fiesole and in Toronto. It can be made ahead of time.   SERVES 4 TO 6

1¼ pounds fresh ricotta, drained
  if very moist
4 extra-large eggs, beaten
½ cup sugar
2 tablespoons currants, soaked in
  rum to cover for 20 minutes,
  drained

2 tablespoons slivered almonds,
  lightly toasted
Grated zest of 1 lemon
1 to 2 tablespoons bread crumbs

Preheat the oven to 350°F. and butter well a 6-cup pudding mold or the equivalent.

Combine the ricotta, eggs, and sugar, and beat until a smooth, homogeneous mixture is obtained. You can use a food processor or electric beater if you wish. Add the remaining ingredients, except the bread crumbs, and combine thoroughly.

Sprinkle the bread crumbs over the entire buttered surface of the mold, eliminating excess crumbs. Pour in the ricotta mixture and bake until a skewer inserted into the center of the pudding comes out clean, about 35 to 40 minutes. Remove from the oven and allow to cool before unmolding. Serve warm or at room temperature.

SFINGI   *Italy*
Fried Ricotta with Honey

A specialty of the south, *sfingi,* basically fried ricotta, are perfect as an afternoon snack or at the end of a light meal.

SERVES 4 TO 6

1 pound fresh ricotta
2 extra-large eggs, beaten
1 teaspoon vanilla extract
2 teaspoons ground cinnamon
1 tablespoon baking powder

4 to 6 tablespoons unbleached
  all-purpose flour
½ cup light seed oil
2 tablespoons honey

Combine all the ingredients except the oil and the honey, adding the flour 1 tablespoon at a time until the ricotta mixture has the consistency of fairly stiff cookie dough.

Heat the oil in a pan suitable for deep frying and, when hot, add the ricotta mixture by the tablespoonful, a few at a time, to the oil. When the dumplings are browned on all sides, remove with a slotted spoon, drain on paper towels, and serve coated with honey.

GLACE AUX CLEMENTINES   *France*
Clementine Sherbet

Clementines from Morocco or Spain are now widely available in North America. They are smaller and sweeter than tangerines and have no seeds. They make an excellent ice. If you cannot find clementines, substitute tangerines or mandarin oranges.

SERVES 6

12 *clementines*   *3 tablespoons* Crème Fraîche
½ *cup sugar*   *(see recipe)*
2 tablespoons lemon juice

Cut a circle about 1 inch in diameter in the top (stem side) of
6 of the clementines. Remove the caps and reserve. Carefully remove the fruit from the skins, keeping the skins intact. The skins
will eventually be used as containers for the sherbet.

Peel the remaining 6 clementines and combine all the fruit
sections with the lemon juice and sugar in a blender or food
processor and blend or process until smooth. Strain the juice into
a mixing bowl, combine with the *crème fraîche,* place in a glass or
plastic container, and freeze until almost solid, about 2 hours.
Remove from the freezer, blend or process to break up the ice
crystals. Transfer the sherbet to the 6 clementine skins, cover with
the caps, return to the freezer, and freeze until ready to serve.
Remove 10 minutes before serving to allow the ice to mellow.

KREMLI KURU   *Turkey*
Apricot Mousse

In this rich, delicately flavored dessert, dried apricots are cooked,
puréed, combined with whipped cream, and chilled.   SERVES 6

1 pound dried apricots, soaked in   *Juice of ½ lemon*
    water to cover for 2 hours   *1 cup whipping cream*
    and drained   ½ *cup blanched almonds, toasted*
1-inch stick of cinnamon   *and chopped*
¼ *cup sugar plus 1 tablespoon*

Combine in a saucepan the apricots, cinnamon stick, ¼ cup
sugar, lemon juice, and 2 cups of water. Simmer, covered, over low
heat until the apricots are very tender, about 2 hours. Add water,
a little at a time, if necessary.

When the apricots are cooked, remove and discard the cinnamon stick. Purée the apricot mixture in a blender or food processor, pass through a sieve or strainer to remove tough fibers, and

set aside to cool completely. All this can be done a day ahead of time.

About 2 hours before serving, whip the cream, adding the remaining tablespoon of sugar halfway through the process. Combine the whipped cream with the apricot purée and place in individual serving bowls. Chill in the refrigerator until ready to serve. Just before serving, sprinkle with the almonds.

BERLINGOZZO   *Italy*
Anise-Flavored Coffee Cake

SERVES 8

1 extra-large egg plus 3 yolks
1¼ cups sugar
1 tablespoon aniseed or fennel
    seed, soaked in 2 tablespoons
    water for 20 minutes,
    drained, roughly crushed

¼ pound unsalted butter, at
    room temperature
Pinch of salt
3 tablespoons milk
3 cups cake flour
2 teaspoons baking powder

Preheat the oven to 350°F. and butter well a 6-cup ring mold.

Beat the egg and yolks and sugar together until pale yellow and light. Add the aniseed or fennel seed, the butter, salt, and milk, and blend thoroughly. Sift the flour together with the baking powder, then add to the egg mixture a little at a time, beating well after each addition. The dough should be homogeneous, dense, and sticky.

Transfer to the ring mold and bake until a skewer inserted into the cake comes out dry, about 40 minutes. Allow to cool 20 minutes before unmolding. Serve at room temperature.

SCHIACCIATA ALLA FIORENTINA   *Italy*
Florentine Flat Coffee Cake

This is the single most popular winter dessert in Florence. It is found in the window of every *pasticceria* and is the kind of cake one brings as a matter of course when visiting friends. It has all the characteristics that Florentines value in food—simplicity, inexpensive ingredients, subtle flavors. It is traditionally made with lard but vegetable shortening is a perfect substitute.   SERVES 8

FOR THE SPONGE:

1 teaspoon active dry yeast
½ cup warm water

1 cup unbleached all-purpose flour

FOR THE DOUGH:

¾ teaspoon active dry yeast
½ cup warm water
1 cup cake flour
1½ cups unbleached all-purpose flour
6 tablespoons sugar
Pinch of salt

1 extra-large egg plus 1 egg yolk
½ cup vegetable shortening
Grated zest of 1 lemon or orange
¼ teaspoon vanilla
Pinch of saffron
1½ tablespoons confectioner's sugar

To make the sponge, dissolve the yeast in the water and set aside for 10 minutes. Place the flour in a mixing bowl, add the yeast and water and combine with a wooden spoon until homogeneous. Coat the inside of another mixing bowl with a little vegetable shortening, add the sponge, cover tightly with a plastic wrap, and set aside for 1 to 1½ hours until doubled in bulk and bubbly.

To make the dough, dissolve the yeast in the water and set aside for 10 minutes. Combine the flours, sugar, and salt in a mixing bowl, add the water and yeast, the egg and yolk, shortening, grated zest, vanilla, saffron, and the sponge and mix well with a wooden spoon. Turn onto a lightly floured board and knead until smooth and homogeneous, about 5 minutes. The dough will be very soft and slightly sticky.

Coat lightly the inside of a large mixing bowl with vegetable shortening, add the dough, roll to coat with the shortening, cover tightly with a plastic wrap, and set aside to rise for 2½ hours, until doubled in bulk.

Coat the inside of a 7-by-12-inch baking dish with vegetable shortening. Place the dough on a board and knead briefly to remove air pockets. Spread evenly in the baking dish. The dough will be about ½-inch high. Cover with a clean dish towel and set aside to rise in a warm place for 2 to 2½ hours, until doubled in bulk.

About 15 minutes before baking, preheat the oven to 350°F. When ready, bake the *schiacciata* for 25 to 30 minutes, until browned on top and a skewer inserted into the center comes out clean. Remove from the oven and set aside for 30 minutes. Unmold and transfer to a serving platter and, when cooled, cover the top completely with confectioner's sugar passed through a fine sieve. Serve at room temperature.

‖ GATEAU AU FROMAGE BLANC   *France*
‖ Provençal Cheesecake

If you like a light, delicately flavored cheesecake, you will love this one. The recipe is a modified version of one given to us by Guy Sagmoellen and Patrick Lucas. It takes time and care to prepare but once you have the knack, it's not difficult. Ricotta is much easier to find in North America than *fromage blanc* and is a good substitute for the French cheese.   SERVES 6 TO 8

1 pound fresh ricotta or *fromage blanc*	*¾ cup sugar plus 1 tablespoon*
1½ cups milk	*1¼ cups corn or potato starch*
1 vanilla bean	*3 tablespoons butter*

4 extra-large eggs, separated, plus
   2 egg whites
	¾ cup Crème Fraîche *(see*
	   recipe)

	1 tablespoon confectioner's sugar

If the ricotta or *fromage blanc* is runny, place in a fine sieve to drain for 30 minutes.

Meanwhile, bring the milk to a boil in a small saucepan, add the vanilla bean, remove from the heat, and set aside to steep until ready to use.

Place 3 of the egg yolks in a mixing bowl, add ¾ cup of sugar, and mix with a wooden spoon a couple of minutes, until the mixture turns pale yellow. Add the starch and mix until thoroughly combined. Remove and discard the vanilla bean from the milk, beat in the remaining yolk, and slowly add the milk mixture to the yolk mixture, stirring constantly with a wooden spoon. Transfer the mixture to the top half of a double boiler and cook. Stir constantly, covering the entire bottom of the pan, until the mixture begins to thicken. It will take about 20 to 25 minutes. Remove from the heat, blend in the butter, *crème fraîche,* and ricotta, mix thoroughly, set aside, and keep warm.

Preheat the oven to 450°F. and butter well a 12-inch springform pan.

In a mixing bowl, beat the 6 egg whites until they form soft peaks, add the remaining tablespoon of sugar, then beat until they form stiff peaks. Add one-quarter of the egg whites to the ricotta mixture and blend. Then add the mixture to the egg whites and fold in quickly, using a plastic spatula. Do not work too long. It is more important to maintain the loft of the whites than to achieve a perfectly homogeneous mixture.

Pour mixture into prepared springform pan. Bake in the oven for 12 minutes, reduce the heat to 400°F., and bake for about 20 minutes, until the cake has risen and the top is well browned. If the cake begins to burn, reduce the oven temperature slightly.

Remove from the oven and place on a wire rack to cool. After 20 minutes, unmold, and invert onto a large platter. The cake will have lost its loft but, as you will see, none of its lightness. Allow the cake to cool completely, at least 1½ hours, then turn right side up on a serving platter. Sprinkle the top with confectioner's sugar, rubbing it through a fine sieve.

YOĞURT TALISI   *Turkey*
Yogurt Cake

In this unusual but popular Turkish dessert, yogurt is combined with eggs and flour to make a substantial cake that is then sweetened with lemon-flavored syrup. The cake should be made a few hours in advance to give it time to marinate in the syrup.

SERVES 8 TO 10

FOR THE CAKE:

1½ cups plain yogurt
6 extra-large eggs, beaten
1 teaspoon baking soda

½ cup sugar
3 cups unbleached all-purpose
 flour

FOR THE SYRUP:

Juice of 1 lemon
1-inch stick of cinnamon

1¼ cups sugar
2 cups water

Preheat the oven to 400°F. Butter well a 12-inch springform cake pan.

Place the yogurt in a large mixing bowl, add the eggs, and combine well. Stir in the baking soda, sugar, and then the flour. Beat until smooth and homogeneous. Pour into the cake pan and bake until done, about 45 minutes. The cake is cooked when a wooden skewer or toothpick inserted into the middle comes out dry. Remove from the oven and, when cooled slightly, transfer from the pan to a relatively deep serving platter.

While the cake is cooking, make the syrup. Combine all the ingredients in a saucepan, boil for 2 minutes, remove and discard the cinnamon stick, and set the syrup aside.

Pour the syrup over the cake, a little at a time, while the cake is still warm. Allow to sit for a few hours before serving.

KARIDOPITA
Greece
Spiced Walnut Cake

This recipe was provided by Gianoula Vasilopoulos and her daughter Voula. Voula stood in the kitchen armed with measuring instruments while her mother went about preparing the dessert in her normal way, by touch, taste, and aroma. It is exquisite—the best Greek dessert we've ever had.   MAKES 48 3-INCH SQUARES

FOR THE SYRUP:

2 *cups sugar*   6 *cups water*

FOR THE CAKE:

3 *cups light seed oil*   3 *cups walnuts, chopped*
3 *cups sugar*   4 *tablespoons baking powder*
12 *extra-large eggs*   2 *teaspoons baking soda*
2 *teaspoons ground cinnamon*   6 *cups unbleached all-purpose*
2 *teaspoons ground cloves*   *flour*

To make the syrup, combine the sugar and water in a saucepan, bring to a boil, lower heat, and simmer, uncovered, for 15 minutes. Set aside.

Mix the oil with your hands in a large mixing bowl for 2 minutes to warm. As an alternative, warm to tepid in a saucepan, then transfer to the mixing bowl. Add the sugar, eggs, cinnamon, cloves, and walnuts. Combine and set aside.

Preheat oven to 400°F. and oil lightly an 18-by-13-inch baking dish.

Sift together the baking powder, baking soda, and flour and combine with the other ingredients in the mixing bowl. Pour into the baking dish, spread evenly, and bake for 45 minutes.

To serve, place the cake on a large serving platter, pour on the syrup, cut into 3-inch squares, and serve. If the cake is eaten hot, the syrup should be cold; if eaten cold, the syrup should be hot.

FOCACCIA DI PERE   *Italy*
Pear Pizza

In this unusual but excellent dessert, pears together with raisins and nuts are baked on a rich, flavorful bread dough. It's ideal for a large dinner party or buffet.   SERVES 8 TO 10

FOR THE DOUGH:

4 tablespoons milk
1 tablespoon whipping cream
1 teaspoon active dry yeast
2½ cups unbleached all-purpose
*   flour*

1 extra-large egg
½ cup sugar
¼ pound unsalted butter

FOR THE FILLING:

½ cup raisins
Juice of 1 orange
4 tablespoons Cointreau
1 pound ripe Bartlett or Bosc
*   pears*

⅓ cup pine nuts
½ cup slivered almonds, lightly
*   toasted*

To make the dough, scald together the milk and cream in a small saucepan and when cooled to tepid (110°F. to 115°F.), add the yeast and set aside for 10 minutes. When ready, combine with the remaining ingredients and knead for a few minutes on a lightly floured board to obtain a smooth, homogeneous dough. It will be more flexible than ordinary bread dough but should not be sticky. Place in a large mixing bowl, cover well with a plastic wrap, and set aside in a warm, draft-free place for 2 hours, until double in bulk.

Meanwhile, place the raisins in a small mixing bowl, add 3 tablespoons of orange juice, 1 tablespoon of Cointreau, and set aside.

Peel and core the pears and cut them into wedges ¼ inch thick. Place in a mixing bowl, add the remaining orange juice and Cointreau, mix, and set aside to marinate for 1 hour.

Preheat the oven to 375°F. and lightly butter an 8-by-12-inch baking dish.

Punch down the dough and shape into a ball. Roll it out on a lightly floured board until roughly the size of the baking dish. Place in the dish and spread it with your fingers to cover the entire bottom. Drain the pears and distribute over the dough, overlapping the wedges, in symmetrical columns. Drain the raisins and sprinkle them along with the pine nuts and almonds over the pears and between the rows. Bake 30 to 45 minutes until the crust is cooked and the pears golden brown. Serve at room temperature.

TARTE AUX PIGNONS   *France*
Pine Nut Tart with Prunes and Dried Apricots

This very traditional Provençal dessert is one that can be made any time because it relies on ingredients that are available all year round.   SERVES 6 TO 8

Short Sweet Dough II (see recipe)
    made with:
    2½ cups unbleached
      all-purpose flour
    ¼ cup sugar
    ⅜ pound chilled unsalted
      butter
    2 extra-large eggs
    1 tablespoon lemon juice
    Pinch of salt

15 jumbo prunes, soaked in water
    to cover for 6 hours
25 dried apricots, soaked in water
    to cover for 6 hours
3 tablespoons butter
Grated zest of 1 lemon
5 tablespoons apricot jam
1¼ cups pine nuts
1 egg yolk diluted with 1
    tablespoon water

Make the dough, roll into a ball, wrap with wax paper, and refrigerate for at least 1 hour.

Meanwhile, drain the prunes and apricots and squeeze out excess water. Pit the prunes, chop finely, and combine with the apricots. Blend the butter together with the lemon zest and set aside.

Preheat the oven to 350°F. and butter well a 10-inch tart pan.

Reserve a small piece of dough (about one-fifth of the total) and roll out the rest about ⅛ inch thick in a circle large enough to cover the bottom and sides of the pan. Line the bottom and sides of the pan snugly with the dough, allowing extra to drape over the sides. Poke holes in the dough with the tines of a fork, then spread the jam evenly over the surface. If the jam is very dense, dilute with a tablespoon of water. Distribute the chopped dried fruit over the jam, then dot the surface with the butter-zest combination. Sprinkle the pine nuts evenly over the surface. Roll out the remaining dough ⅛ inch thick, cut into strips ½ inch wide, and use it to make a lattice over the surface of the tart. Seal the strips to the borders of the dough lining the pan, using a little water to bind them together. Roll the rolling pin along the edge of the pan to remove excess dough. Brush the surface of the dough with the diluted egg yolk and bake until the nuts are brown and the dough cooked, about 40 minutes. Serve at room temperature.

TARTE AU CITRON   *France*
Lemon Tart

Although popular throughout France, we associate lemon tarts with the south, especially with Menton, the lemon capital of the country, where each year a festival is held to celebrate the fruit. You may wish to add more sugar than we suggest. Simply taste the filling before baking and adjust.   SERVES 6

Short Sweet Dough I (see recipe)   *3 tablespoons unsalted butter,*
2 extra-large eggs plus 2 yolks   *melted*
½ cup confectioner's sugar   *Grated zest of 1 lemon*
                                         Juice of 3 lemons

Preheat the oven to 350°F. Lightly butter and flour a 10-inch tart pan.

Make dough, roll into a ball, wrap with wax paper, and set aside until ready to use. Roll out the dough ⅛ to ¼ inch thick and fit it snugly in the tart pan, Prick the dough in several places with the tines of a fork, cover the bottom and sides with buttered aluminum foil, cover the foil with dried beans or baking weights, and bake for 10 minutes. Remove from the oven, remove the beans or weights, remove and discard the foil, and set the partially baked shell aside.

Combine the remaining ingredients in a mixing bowl, beating with a wire whisk. At this point, taste and adjust for sugar. Transfer the mixture to the tart shell and bake for 40 minutes. Check occasionally to see if the edges of the dough are scorching. If so, cover with a strip of aluminum foil. Remove from the oven, let cool, and serve.

VARIATION Beat 3 egg whites with 3 tablespoons confectioner's sugar until they form stiff peaks. Place on top of the tart when it has cooled. Broil for 2 minutes to brown.

PASTEL CABELLO D'ANGEL   *Spain*
Squash Tart

The squash, when cooked, takes on a deep, golden hue, similar in color, so the Spanish figure, to the hair of an angel—thus the metaphorical name, "Angel Hair Tart." It makes an excellent tart, elegant and impressive with a sweet, rich, slightly earthy flavor.

SERVES 6 TO 8

FOR THE DOUGH:

3 cups cake or unbleached
*   all-purpose flour*
½ cup sugar
⅓ cup chilled unsalted butter

1 tablespoon lemon juice
2 extra-large eggs plus 2 yolks
Pinch of salt

FOR THE FILLING:

1½ pounds golden Hubbard
*   squash*
1 tablespoon butter
1 cup sugar
2-inch stick of cinnamon

Peel of 1 lemon, cut into large
*   pieces*
1 egg yolk diluted with 1
*   tablespoon of water*

To make the dough, place the flour in a large mixing bowl, add the sugar, and combine well. Add the butter, and cut into the flour with a pastry knife until you have a granular dough with the texture of coarse oatmeal. Form a well in the center and add the lemon juice, eggs, and salt. Mix to combine, then turn onto a floured work surface and knead briefly with the heel of your hand, just enough to ensure that the butter blends with the flour. Wrap in wax paper and place in the refrigerator for at least 1 hour.

If using a food processor, insert the metal blade, add the flour and sugar to the work bowl, and process for a few seconds. Add the butter and process until the dough has the texture of coarse oatmeal. With the machine running, add the remaining ingredients, and process until the dough forms a ball and pulls away from the sides of the work bowl. Then proceed as above.

While the dough rests, make the filling. Peel the squash, remove and discard the seeds, and cut into small cubes. Melt the butter in a skillet, add the squash and 3 tablespoons of water, cover, and simmer, stirring occasionally, until tender, about 10 minutes.

Place ¾ cup of water in a saucepan, add the sugar, cinnamon, and lemon peel, and simmer for 5 minutes. When ready, add the squash, crush it with a wooden spoon or the tines of a fork, then simmer, uncovered, for 15 to 20 minutes, until a thick purée is formed. Remove and discard the cinnamon stick and set the filling aside.

Preheat the oven to 375°F. and butter well a 10-inch flan pan.

Divide the dough into 2 unequal parts, the larger roughly two-thirds of the total. Roll out the larger piece in the shape of a circle about ⅛ inch thick between sheets of wax paper, and use it to line snugly the bottom and sides of the flan pan. Allow excess to drape over sides.

Spread the filling over the dough. Roll out the remaining dough as before and use it to cover the flan. Pinch the edges to make a good seal, then roll the rolling pin along the border to cut off excess dough.

Poke the top with the tines of a fork to allow steam to escape during baking, paint the top with the diluted egg yolk, then bake for 40 minutes, until the top is golden. Remove and let cool on a wire rack for 20 minutes before removing the rim of the pan. Serve at room temperature.

TARTE DE BLETTES SUCRÉE   *France*
Sweet Swiss Chard Tart

Swiss chard is to the folks who live along the Côte d'Azur as the potato is to the Irish, with the distinction that the French have shown incredible culinary skill in transforming this basic green into a gourmet's delight. No dish demonstrates this talent more

than Tarte de Blettes Sucrée, in which Swiss chard appears as the
star attraction in a dessert tart. We like to serve this as a midafter-
noon snack or with tea—it's almost too rich to come at the end of
a meal.   SERVES 6 TO 8

Short Sweet Dough II (see
   recipe), made with:
   3 cups unbleached all-purpose
   flour

½ pound butter
2 extra-large eggs
½ cup sugar
2 tablespoons lemon juice

FOR THE FILLING:
1½ cups Swiss chard, well
   washed, roughly chopped
2 tablespoons currants or raisins,
   soaked in 3 tablespoons dark
   rum for 20 minutes
2 extra-large eggs, beaten
⅓ cup pine nuts, lightly toasted

½ cup sugar
¼ cup freshly grated Parmesan
Pinch of freshly ground black
   pepper
4 cooking apples, peeled, cored,
   thinly sliced

Preheat the oven to 375°F. and butter well a 10-inch flan
pan.

Make the dough, roll into 2 unequal balls, one about two-
thirds of the dough, the other one-third, wrap them separately in
wax paper, and place in the refrigerator for at least 1 hour.

To make the filling, bring 1 cup of water to a boil in a saucepan, add the Swiss chard, and cook, covered, over medium heat for
10 minutes. Drain and squeeze out excess water. This step is important—the chard must be dry. Set aside to cool.

Combine all the remaining ingredients except the apples in a
large mixing bowl, then blend in the chard.

When ready, roll out the larger ball into a circle roughly ⅛
inch thick and use it to line the bottom and sides of the flan pan.

Distribute the Swiss chard mixture evenly in the flan pan,
cover with the sliced apples, and set aside. Roll out thinly the
remaining dough and use it to cover the flan pan. Remove excess
dough by passing the rolling pin over the border of the pan. Prick
holes in the top with the tines of a fork, then bake for 50 minutes
to 1 hour, until the dough is browned and the filling firm. If the

dough begins to burn while baking, cover with aluminium foil. Remove and let cool for 20 minutes. Serve warm or at room temperature.

VARIATIONS Although not traditional, the tart can also be made without a top. Pears can be substituted for apples.

TORTA AL CIOCCOLATO CON MANDORLE *Italy*
Chocolate Cake with Almonds

When Mimi Serani overheard us one day complaining that we hadn't found a rich chocolate cake that we liked enough to include in the book, she proposed one. It is indeed rich and has the added advantage that it is very easy to prepare, at least relative to others in its class.   SERVES 8 TO 10

8 extra-large eggs, separated
1 cup sugar
½ cup butter, softened
½ cup blanched almonds, lightly
    toasted, and pulverized

Grated zest of 1 orange
8 ounces good-quality bittersweet
    chocolate
1 cup whipping cream

Preheat the oven to 350°F. and butter well a 10-inch spring-form pan.

Combine the egg yolks and sugar in a mixing bowl and beat with a wire whisk or electric beater until pale yellow and light. The mixture should form ribbons when the beater is raised from the batter. Blend in the butter, almonds, and orange zest. Melt the chocolate in the top half of the double boiler, and beat it into the egg mixture. Set aside.

Beat the egg whites until they form stiff peaks. Mix one-fourth of the egg whites into the batter to lighten it, then fold the batter into the remaining whites. This operation should be accomplished quickly. Transfer to the springform pan and bake for 45 to 50 minutes, until a skewer inserted into the center of the cake comes out clean. Allow cake to cool for 30 minutes before removing the sides of the springform pan. In cooling, the cake will lose some of its loft but none of its lightness. Whip the cream lightly and serve with the cake.

GÂTEAU À LA MENTHE   *France*
Chocolate Mint Cake

We first sampled this cake, a delectable blend of mint, *crème fraîche*, and bittersweet chocolate, in Digne, a charming village high in the Provençal Alps. The cake is light, fresh, easy to prepare, and impressive, perfect for an elegant dinner party or buffet.

SERVES 6 TO 8

FOR THE CAKE:

4 extra-large eggs, separated   *1 cup cake flour*
½ cup sugar

FOR THE FILLING AND ICING:

½ cup Crème Fraîche *(see*   *½ cup peppermint syrup*
recipe)   *½ cup water plus 2 teaspoons*
10 ounces high-quality bittersweet *2 tablespoons butter*
chocolate

2 to 3 kiwis, peeled and sliced,
for garnish

Preheat the oven to 325°F. and butter lightly and flour a 12-by-8-inch baking dish.

First make the cake. Combine the egg yolks and sugar in a mixing bowl and beat together until pale yellow. The mixture is ready when it forms a ribbon. Beat the egg whites separately until very firm. Combine one-fourth of the whites with the yolks to lighten the yolk mixture. Carefully but swiftly fold in the remaining whites. Place the flour in a sifter and sift into the egg mixture, adding a little flour at a time and folding in quickly. Spread the batter in the baking dish and bake for 30 minutes, until the cake is done. You can test for doneness by inserting a toothpick into the cake. If it comes out dry, the cake is done. Remove from the oven and set aside to cool completely.

When ready to assemble the cake, bring the *crème fraîche* to a boil, remove from the heat, and add 5 ounces of the chocolate cut into small pieces. Combine well and set aside.

Dilute the peppermint syrup with ½ cup water. Cut the cake in half to form two layers. Place bottom layer on a platter from which cake will be served. Place strips of wax paper under all sides of the bottom layer to catch chocolate during preparation. Paint the top surfaces of the two layers with the mint syrup, using all of it. Allow the pieces to soak up the mint syrup for a minute or two, then spread the *crème fraîche*–chocolate mixture over the top of the bottom layer.

Place the top layer over the bottom one, mint-soaked side up. Combine the remaining chocolate, cut into small pieces, with 2 teaspoons of water in the top half of a double boiler and heat until completely melted. Remove from the heat, add the butter, and combine thoroughly. If it begins to harden, return to the heat for a few seconds. When tepid, spread the chocolate mixture evenly over the cake and place sliced kiwis on top. The chocolate will begin to harden at once. Remove pieces of wax paper once coating has hardened.

Chill in the refrigerator until ready to serve.

SAFFA
Sweet Couscous

Morocco

Although Moroccans serve sweet couscous between the savory dishes and the real sweets, we like to serve it as a dessert. The three steamings make the grains so light that they almost melt in the mouth. It is generally served very sweet, but we have modified it to suit our taste.

SERVES 4 TO 6

1½ cups couscous
1 tablespoon peanut oil
8 tablespoons butter
½ teaspoon salt
½ cup blanched almonds, toasted
   and roughly chopped

1 cup prunes and/or dates, pitted
   and chopped
⅓ cup confectioner's sugar
4 tablespoons ground cinnamon
2 cups cold milk

Place 4 cups of water in the bottom half of a *couscousière* and bring to a boil. Meanwhile, wash and dry the couscous (see instructions, p. 205, Step 1), and sprinkle with the oil. Place the couscous in the top half of the *couscousière* and steam 30 minutes.

Transfer couscous to a large platter, add 3 tablespoons of butter, and sprinkle with 2 cups of water. Set aside to absorb the water (see instructions, p. 205, Step 2).

Steam the couscous a second time for 15 minutes. Remove, blend in 3 tablespoons of butter, and up to 2 cups of cold water. Add the water as long as the grains absorb it.

Steam the couscous a third time for 20 minutes. Transfer to a large platter and blend in the remaining 2 tablespoons of butter. Mix in the almonds and prunes or dates, shape into a cone, sprinkle with the confectioner's sugar, and decorate with the cinnamon.

Place the cold milk in a pitcher and serve with the hot couscous for those who wish to moisten the grains. Serve extra confectioner's sugar to add sweetness.

CRISPELLE DI RISO   *Italy*
Rice Fritters

There is, as this dish demonstrates, a strong Arabic influence on Sicilian cooking. We like to serve these fritters for snacks or with tea.   **MAKES ABOUT 25 FRITTERS**

2¼ cups milk
1 cup Arborio rice
2 tablespoons sugar
Grated zest of 1 lemon
¼ teaspoon vanilla extract
2 extra-large eggs

7 tablespoons flour
1 teaspoon baking powder
½ cup light seed oil for frying
⅔ cup clover or wildflower honey
3 tablespoons water

Place the milk in a saucepan, add the rice, sugar, lemon zest, and vanilla extract, and simmer, stirring frequently, until the rice is well cooked, about 20 minutes. Add water as necessary during cooking. The rice should be dense and moist, but not liquid, when cooked.

Remove from the heat, let cool slightly, then blend in the eggs, 3 tablespoons of flour, and the baking powder.

Spread the remaining flour on a work surface, place a teaspoon of the rice batter on the flour, and roll into a cylinder about 2 inches long and the thickness of an index finger. Continue until the batter is consumed. Heat the oil in a skillet and, when hot, fry the fritters, a few at a time, until golden on all sides. Drain on paper towels, then transfer to a serving platter and set aside.

Combine the honey with water, heat slightly, then pour over the fritters. Serve at room temperature.

CASTAGNACCIO   *Italy*
Chestnut Flour Cake

This ancient Tuscan specialty is one of our favorite desserts, a simple, rustic cake made with chestnut flour, olive oil, pine nuts, and rosemary. In Italy it is eaten as a snack or after a meal with a glass of Vin Santo, the Tuscan dessert wine. *Castagnaccio* is a winter dish, made after the chestnuts have been harvested, dried, and ground into flour. Chestnut flour is not always easy to find, even in Italy, but most Italian specialty food stores should be able to order it even if they don't have it in stock.   SERVES 8

2½ cups sifted chestnut flour   2 cups water
4 tablespoons olive oil   3 tablespoons pine nuts
Pinch of salt   1 tablespoon fresh or dried
1 tablespoon sugar   rosemary leaves

Preheat the oven to 375°F. and oil a 9-by-15-inch baking dish.

Combine in a large mixing bowl the chestnut flour, 2 table-spoons of oil, salt, sugar, and approximately 2 cups of water. Mix well to eliminate lumps, then pour into the baking dish. The batter should resemble pancake batter. Sprinkle the pine nuts and rosemary on the surface of the cake, drizzle the remaining oil on top, and bake until browned and the surface cracked, about 30 minutes. Serve when cooled.

NECCI   *Italy*
Chestnut Flour Pancakes with Ricotta

We like to make *necci* in fall and winter, when chestnut flour is fresh. Serve when a substantial dessert is desired. In Italy, a special utensil is used for cooking, but a griddle or heavy skillet, preferably of cast iron, is fine.   SERVES 6

2 cups chestnut flour   2 tablespoons sugar
2¼ cups water   2 ounces bittersweet chocolate,
3 tablespoons butter   grated
1½ cups fresh ricotta

Combine the flour with water to form a batter roughly the same consistency as pancake batter. Set aside for 20 minutes.

When ready, heat ½ tablespoon of butter in a large skillet, add enough batter to form a pancake roughly 8 inches in diameter and ⅛ inch thick. Cook over medium heat until the top of the pancake is full of holes, about 2 minutes, carefully loosen the pancake from the pan with a large spatula, then flip, and cook another 2 minutes, until the bottom is brown. Transfer the *necci* to a plate and repeat until you have 6 pancakes. Set aside.

Combine the ricotta with the sugar and chocolate. You can

either serve the pancakes and ricotta separately and let guests roll their own or you can place 2 or 3 tablespoons of the ricotta mixture on each pancake, roll, and serve at room temperature on a serving platter.

MELOMAKÁRONA   ***Greece***
Spiced Walnut Cookies

Gianoula Vasiloupolos, the mother of a friend in Toronto, makes an enormous quantity of these and the following cookies because they keep for months if stored in a cool, dry place. You can, of course, reduce quantities to suit your needs.

MAKES ABOUT 120 COOKIES

FOR THE SYRUP:

1 cup honey

1 cup sugar

4 cups water

FOR THE COOKIE DOUGH:

2½ cups light seed oil

2½ cups vegetable shortening, melted

2 cups sugar

3 egg yolks, beaten

4 tablespoons baking powder

1½ cups freshly squeezed orange juice, strained

2 tablespoons grated orange zest

2 tablespoons grated lemon zest

⅓ cup Cognac

3 tablespoons honey

1½ tablespoons ground cinnamon

1½ tablespoons ground cloves

1½ cups coarsely ground walnuts

16 cups cake flour

Combine the ingredients for the syrup in a saucepan, bring to a boil, reduce heat, simmer 15 minutes, remove from the heat, and set aside.

Place the oil and shortening in a large mixing bowl and mix with your hands for 2 minutes to warm. As an alternative, heat to tepid in a saucepan, then transfer to the mixing bowl. Add the sugar and yolks and blend. Dissolve the baking powder in the orange juice and add to the large mixing bowl. Place the orange and lemon zest in the Cognac and allow to marinate for a few minutes, then add to the mixing bowl. Mix in all the remaining ingredients except ½ cup ground walnuts and the flour.

Blend thoroughly, then add the flour, a little at a time, mixing well with your hands after each addition. The dough should be fairly stiff but flexible. Allow the dough to rest 15 minutes.

Preheat the oven to 350°F. and oil lightly 2 or 3 large cookie sheets.

Take some dough about the size of a golf ball and shape into a cylinder about 3 inches long and ¾ inch in diameter, place the edge of a teaspoon against the bottom to form a slight indentation, and place on a cookie sheet. The indentation helps the syrup to be absorbed evenly. This is a test cookie. Put on a cookie sheet and place in the oven for 15 minutes. The cookie should rise, not spread. If it spreads, add more flour to the dough. After this test, shape the remaining dough into cookies and bake 40 minutes.

If you wish to store the cookies, stop at this point. To serve, soak with the syrup, and sprinkle with the ½ cup of ground walnuts.

KOURABIÉDES   *Greece*
Sugar Cookies with Almonds
                                    MAKES ABOUT 100 COOKIES

1 pound unsalted butter, at room temperature
1 pound vegetable shortening, at room temperature
3 cups confectioner's sugar plus ½ cup
3 egg yolks
2 teaspoons baking powder
⅓ cup ouzo
2 teaspoons baking soda
2 cups blanched almonds, lightly toasted and coarsely chopped
7 cups unbleached all-purpose flour

Place the butter and shortening in a large mixing bowl and mix with your hands for 2 minutes. As an alternative, heat to tepid in a saucepan, then transfer to a mixing bowl. Sift in 3 cups of confectioner's sugar, then beat in the yolks. Dissolve the baking powder in the ouzo, add to the mixing bowl, then blend in the baking soda, almonds, and flour. Turn onto a lightly floured board or marble slab and knead vigorously with the heel of your hand for about 10 minutes. Cover the dough with a clean dish towel and set aside to rest for 15 minutes.

Preheat the oven to 350°F. and butter lightly 2 or 3 large cookie sheets.

When ready, take a piece of dough roughly the size of a golf ball, shape into a cylinder 3 inches long by ¾ inch in diameter, and place on a cookie sheet in the shape of an **S**. Make another cookie or two and place on the cookie sheet. This is a test batch. Bake for 20 or 30 minutes. The cookies should not spread. If they do, add flour to the remaining dough to make it stiffer. Once the test is completed, make the remaining cookies, and bake 40 minutes.

Place the remaining confectioner's sugar in a fine sieve and sprinkle it on the cookies. Serve at room temperature or store.

BECHKETTO DEL KAOKAO   *Morocco*
Peanut Cookies

These cookies are a specialty of Mrs. Melehi, the mother of our friends Abdillah and Dries. They are terrific—light, delicate, not too sweet. To make them the traditional way, once the peanuts are roasted, shelled, and peeled, they are ground finely in a mortar, then mixed with the other ingredients in a huge earthenware bowl where the dough is kneaded for 30 minutes or so. The cookies, when ready, are baked in one of the town's bread ovens. We have made very satisfactory imitations of the real thing using a food processor and our kitchen oven.   MAKES 18 TO 20 COOKIES

1 cup freshly roasted, shelled and peeled peanuts
1¼ cup unbleached all-purpose flour
1 teaspoon baking powder
⅓ cup sugar

¼ pound unsalted butter
1 extra-large egg
¼ teaspoon cinnamon
1 heaping tablespoon confectioner's sugar

Grind the peanuts in a mortar or food processor until very fine.

Sift the flour together with the baking powder, then blend with the ground peanuts. Add all the remaining ingredients except the confectioner's sugar, combine thoroughly, then knead until smooth and homogeneous, about 10 minutes. If using a food processor, the kneading can be done by the machine. Roll into a ball and set aside for 30 minutes.

Preheat the oven to 350°F. and lightly butter a cookie sheet.

When ready, break off a piece of dough the size of a walnut, shape into a circle about 1½ inches in diameter, and place on the cookie sheet. Continue until all the dough is used. Do not crowd —the cookies will expand as they cook. Bake 20 minutes, remove, and when cooled, sprinkle with the confectioner's sugar.

Sample Menus

The menus included here are suggestions, not hard and fast rules, of how dishes can be combined to create exciting meals. We encourage you to alter the menus as you wish or to design your own. To help in this, here are some tips. Mix textures, flavors, and colors to achieve meals that delight the eye as well as the palate. Do not hesitate to combine across countries, but avoid serving a subtly flavored dish after a highly spiced one. We also urge you to avoid combining dishes that require last-minute or elaborate preparation. You should enjoy your dinner party as much as your guests.

The dishes should be served in the order in which they are listed in the menus, with the exception, of course, that vegetable dishes are usually served with the main course. We recommend that you serve pasta and soups Italian style, after the appetizers and before the main dishes. You can vary this to suit your tastes, but we would discourage you from including both soup and pasta in the same meal. Menus with five or six courses are fairly elaborate and thus suited for dinner parties, while those with four courses are, by and large, more appropriate for luncheons or dinners with family or close friends.

When we say green salad, we have in mind a combination of lettuces such as Romaine or Cos with curly endive, escarole, radicchio, or arugula, dressed with a vinaigrette of extra-virgin olive oil from Tuscany, wine vinegar, salt, and pepper. Vary the greens

according to availability, but don't settle for tasteless salads. Our
idea of a tomato salad is one made with fresh, ripe, flavorful
tomatoes cut into wedges or thin slices and served with a few thinly
sliced onion rings, chopped fresh basil or parsley, dried oregano,
and a vinaigrette dressing. To make a cucumber salad, peel and
slice a firm cucumber, season with salt, pepper, fresh chopped mint
or dill, and dress with a combination of minced garlic, a little
yogurt, olive oil, and lemon juice or wine vinegar.

Fresh fruit is wonderful at the end of a meal and certainly the
most common dessert in the Mediterranean. If you want to vary the
theme a little try one of the following:

Peel and slice an orange (one for each diner), sprinkle with
confectioner's sugar and a few drops of Cointreau, and serve.

Peel and pit ripe, fresh peaches. Slice into thin wedges, then
marinate for an hour in a dry red wine sweetened with a little sugar.
Serve in bowls with the marinade. A similar dish can be made with
ripe Bosc or Bartlett pears. In this case, add a couple of cloves and
a stick of cinnamon to the marinade.

Wash, trim, and quarter fresh, ripe strawberries. Season with
lemon juice and sugar and serve.

•

Spaghetti with Sharp Pecorino and Pepper (p. 100)
Stuffed Sardines, Antibes Style (p. 185)
Braised Eggplant and Tomatoes (p. 256)
Green Salad
Lemon and Orange Custard (p. 292)

•

Stuffed Mussels on the Half Shell (p. 83)
Octopus, Provençal Style (p. 198) or
Braised Spicy Octopus (p. 80)
Rice with Herbs and Wine (p. 119)
Artichokes au Gratin (p. 239) or Baked Eggplant
with Anchovy Sauce (p. 253)
Green Salad
Fresh Fruit

•

Shrimp with Mixed Salad and Warm Vinaigrette (p. 89)
Sole with Marsala (p. 170)
Braised Potatoes with Garlic and Saffron (p. 269)
Endive Salad with Fresh Coriander (p. 46)
Provençal Cheesecake (p. 301)

•

Sweet and Sour Vegetable Soup (p. 128)
Tagine of Fish Balls in Pungent Sauce (p. 173) or Tagine with
Stuffed Sardines (p. 183)
Swiss Chard with Rice in Lemon Sauce (p. 251)
Tomato Salad
Fresh Fruit

•

SERVE SALADS TOGETHER:
Lemon Salad with Olives (p. 44)
Endive Salad with Fresh Coriander (p. 46)
Grated Carrots with Orange Juice (p. 46)
Eggplant Salad (p. 59)

Onion Couscous with Raisins (p. 208) or Couscous with
Vegetables (p. 210)
Dates Stuffed with Almond Paste (p. 292)
Fresh Fruit

•

Roasted Peppers on Toast (p. 52)
Squash Risotto (p. 115)
Shrimp with Spinach (p. 193)
Tomato Salad
Fresh Fruit

•

Valencian Chick-pea and Spinach Soup (p. 132) or Bulgur and
Bean Soup (p. 133)
Cuttlefish with Spinach (p. 196) or Bell Pepper Tart (p. 212)
Cucumber Salad
Rice with Milk (p. 293)

•

Provençal Squash Soup (p. 138)
Lentil Salad with Herb Vinaigrette (p. 68)
Baked Rice with Vegetables (p. 223)
Green Salad
Oranges and Pears with Hot Lime Sauce (p. 291)

•

Salmon Tartare with Assorted Sauces (p. 76) or Warm Scallop
Salad with Peppers (p. 90)
Provençal Fish Soup with Aïoli (p. 202)
Salad of Fresh Peppers and Tomatoes (p. 54)
Pears with Zabaione (p. 288)

•

Shells with Bell Pepper Sauce (p. 104)
Fresh Tuna Brochettes with Provençal Tomato Sauce (p. 166)
Baked Zucchini with Crème Fraîche (p. 274) or Grilled
Artichokes (p. 242)
Green Salad or Tomato Salad
Pears with Almond Cream and Raspberry Purée (p. 286)

•

Vegetable Paella (p. 121)
Cheese and Herb Pie (p. 216)
Jerusalem Artichokes with Herbs (p. 243)
Spicy Pepper Salad with Tomatoes and Pine Nuts (p. 44)
Fresh Fruit

•

Fried Artichokes Marinated in Garlic Vinaigrette (p. 58) or
Zucchini-Yogurt Salad (p. 53)
Fish Couscous (p. 206)
Green Salad
Spiced Walnut Cake (p. 303)

•

Fried Dumplings (p. 151) or Baked Dumplings (p. 152)
Cream of Asparagus with Mascarpone (p. 137)
Potato Omelet (p. 229)
Green Beans, Andalusian Style (p. 245)
Green Salad or Tomato Salad
Gratin of Fresh Fruit with Cream (p. 289)

•

Shrimp Pancakes (p. 88)
Sweet and Sour Vegetable Soup (p. 128)
Gratin of Salt Cod with Spinach (p. 190)
Cucumber Salad
Fresh Fruit

•

Vegetable Soup (p. 133)
Fried Dumpling with Egg (p. 153) or Sicilian Pizza with Onion,
Cheese, and Anchovies (p. 154)
Broccoli Simmered in Red Wine (p. 249)
Radicchio with Gorgonzola Vinaigrette (p. 42)
Fresh Fruit

•

Eggs Poached in Pungent Sauce (p. 226)
Stewed Kale (p. 260)
Green Salad or Tomato Salad
Fresh Fruit

•

Fresh Pasta with Goat Cheese and Basil (p. 99)
Monkfish with Clams and Shrimp (p. 172)
Zucchini Stuffed with Tomato and Pepper (p. 275)
Green Salad
Baked Fresh Figs with Cointreau (p. 289) or Orange Zabaione
(p. 294)

•

Cream of Fennel Soup (p. 139)
Fried Polenta with Eggs (p. 226)
Steamed Broccoli with Aïoli
Fresh Fruit

•

Chick-pea Flour Crêpe (p. 65) or Niçoise Onion Pizza (p. 157)
Shrimp Tagine (p. 192)
Squash Purée (p. 273)
Shredded Lettuce and Orange Salad (p. 45)
Peanut Cookies (p. 319)

•

Mixed Salad with Warm Goat Cheese (p. 41)
Fish Soup, Leghorn Style (p. 201)
Pepper and Tomato Salad (p. 43)
Clementine Sherbert (p. 297)

•

Spaghetti with Oregano (p. 104)
Eggplant Torte (p. 232) or Zucchini Flower Omelet (p. 227)
Green Salad
Chilled Cantaloupe with Lemon Sauce (p. 290)

•

Garlic Soup (p. 124)
Peppers Stuffed with Fish (p. 148)
Green Salad or Tomato Salad
Fresh Fruit

•

Lentil Soup (p. 135)
Fried Goat Cheese Sandwiches (p. 233)
Tomato Salad or Cucumber Salad
Fresh Fruit

•

Peppers Stuffed with Goat Cheese (p. 40)
Leek and Potato Tart (p. 146)
Vegetable Stew (p. 277) or Okra with Tomato Sauce (p. 263)
Fresh Fruit

•

Mussels with Parsley and Garlic (p. 84)
Scallops with Saffron and Vegetables (p. 195)
Green Salad
Lemon Tart (p. 307) or Squash Tart (p. 308)

•

Saffron Risotto with Peppers and Marsala (p. 116) or Risotto
with Pomegranate (p. 114)
Omelets with Tapenade (p. 231)
Fennel Tagine (p. 257)
Mascarpone with Chocolate and Marsala (p. 295)

•

Yogurt Soup (p. 126)
Fish Fillets Baked in Parchment with Wild Mushrooms (p. 178)
Pearl Onions in Sweet and Sour Sauce (p. 266)
Green Salad
Sweet Swiss Chard Tart (p. 309) or
Chestnut Flour Cake (p. 315)

•

Rice with Fish Broth, Shrimp, and Mussels (p. 123)
Provençal Omelet (p. 230)
Tagine of Green Beans and Squash (p. 246)
Green Salad or Tomato Salad
Fresh Fruit

•

Fatima's Mussels (p. 86)
Spicy Marinated Baked Fish (p. 168)
Okra and Quince Tagine (p. 264)
Sweet Couscous (p. 313)
Fresh Fruit

•

Provençal Sage Soup (p. 130)
Eggplant Moussaka with Lentils (p. 217)
Braised Artichokes and Fava Beans (p. 241)
Green Salad
Fried Ricotta with Honey (p. 297) or Chestnut Flour Pancakes
with Ricotta (p. 316)

Suggestions for Cold Buffets

Cold Tomato Soup (p. 127)
Carrot and Celery Root Salad (p. 47)
Potatoes with Puréed Pepper Dressing (p. 63)
Fava Bean Salad with Yogurt (p. 69)
Tuna and Potato Loaf (p. 222) or Cold Poached Salmon with
Mustard Sauce (p. 176)
Green Beans with Salmon Caviar (p. 245)
Eggplant with Yogurt (p. 255)
Florentine Flat Coffee Cake (p. 299) or Pear Pizza (p. 304)

•

Mussel Salad (p. 82)
Chilled Squid Salad with Peppers (p. 78)
Purée of Roasted Vegetables (p. 62)
Vegetable Pizza (p. 158)
Cold Swordfish Steaks with Vegetable Sauce (p. 188)
Jerusalem Artichokes with Rice (p. 244)
Steamed Zucchini with Aïoli
Apricot Mousse (p. 298)
Sugar Cookies with Almonds (p. 318)

Bibliography

BENBASSA, ESTHER. *Cuisine Judeo-Espagnole.* Paris: Éditions du Scribe, 1984.

BENNANI-SMIRES, LATIFA. *Moroccan Cooking.* Casablanca: Al Madariss, n.d.

BETTONICA, LUIS, ed. *Cocina Regiónal Española.* Barcelona: Hymsa, 1981.

BIANCHINI, FRANCESCO, FRANCESCO CORBETTA, and MARILENA PISTOIA. *The Complete Book of Fruits and Vegetables.* New York: Crown, 1976.

COLERA, ANA MARIA. *Cocina Valenciana.* León, Spain: Everest, 1983.

DAVID, ELIZABETH. *Mediterranean Food.* London: John Lehmann, 1950.

DAVIDSON, ALAN. *Mediterranean Seafood.* Harmondsworth: Penguin, 1981.

HIERRO, MIGUEL SALCEDO. *La Cocina Andaluza.* León, Spain: Nebrija, 1984.

KARSENTY, IRENE, and LUCIENNE KARSENTY. *Cuisine Pied-Noir.* Paris: Denoël, 1974.

MORAND, MARIUS. *Manuel Complet de la Cuisinière Provençale.* Marseilles: Laffitte Reprints, 1984.

POMAR, ANNA. *Antichi Sapori di Sicilia.* Napoli: Edizioni del Mezzogiorno, n.d.

RAYES, GEORGES N. *L'Art Culinaire Libanais.* 1960.

RODEN, CLAUDIA. *A Book of Middle Eastern Food.* London: Thomas
  Nelson, 1968.

THIBAUD COMELADE, ELAINE. *La Cuisine Catalane.* Malakoff, France:
  Éditions J. Lanore, 1982.

WOLFERT, PAULA. *Couscous and Other Good Food from Morocco.* New
  York: Harper and Row, 1973.

——. *Mediterranean Cooking.* New York: Times Books, 1977.

Index

331